THE JOURNEY OF THE BEAN

THE JOURNEY OF THE BEAN

Samuel Mutter

PROSPECT BOOKS

2016

First published in 2016 in Great Britain and the United States by Prospect Books, 26 Parke Road, London, SW13 9NG

BRITISH LIBRARY CATALOGUING IN PUBLICATION DATA:
A catalogue entry of this book is available from the British Library.

Typeset and designed by Rebecca Gillieron and Catheryn Kilgarriff in Adobe Garamond Pro

Cover design by Prospect Books
All photographs © 2016 Samuel Mutter

ISBN 978-1-909248-42-7

Printed and bound by the Gutenberg Press, Malta.

CONTENTS

ACKNOWLEDGEMENTS

First thanks must go to Catheryn Kilgarriff, for allowing me the opportunity to write under the proud name of Prospect Books, and for her limitless encouragement, imagination and hard work. Also to Rebecca Gillieron, who worked with Cathy to unite this book's disparate parts into a coherent and attractive whole.

To Tessa, who approached me for this project in the first place, and whose quiet devotion to knowledge has been an inspiration in itself.

To my parents, Ruth and Andrew Mutter, who bravely tasted every experiment – even when it meant fishing it out of the bin – and, without even a mumbled complaint, put up with their kitchen being converted into a culinary scrapheap, and much of the rest of their home into a makeshift photography studio.

To my siblings, Joe, Rachel and Andy, with whom many of my most amazing food experiences so far have been shared, and to my niece and nephews, Alice, Jamie and Jack, with whom I hope to share many more in the future.

And to every one of my brilliant and talented friends, who have had to hear me hesitantly utter the phrase 'I'm writing a book about chocolate' hundreds of times over the past months, and still their enthusiasm has not wavered. Special mention should go to Hussein and Alex for their resolute belief in my ideas and my writing; to Chris and Evan, for the joy they've taken in introducing me to strangers as a 'published author' and then watching me squirm; to Georgie – a more skilled cake-maker than I could ever hope to be – for lending me her beautiful paraphernalia; and to Naomi, for being the most impressive hostess (not to mention one of the most impressive individuals) I know.

And to everybody I have not mentioned by name, friend or family, that has shared a meal, a cup of tea, a pint, or something a little stronger with me during the past few years – yours was as important a contribution as any.

INTRODUCTION

Eat your chocolates, little girl,
Eat your chocolates!
Believe me, there's no metaphysics on earth like chocolates,
And all religions put together teach no more than the candy shop.
Eat, dirty little girl, eat!
If only I could eat chocolates with the same truth as you!

Fernando Pessoa, *The Tobacco Shop*, 1928

If religious faith was, for Karl Marx, the opium of the masses, then chocolate has been nothing less than the substance in the midst of his metaphor, with the sanctity of the former, the profanity of the latter, and the addictiveness of both. Chocolate has, for the duration of its existence, verged on the metaphysical. Like religion, it possesses the ability to stagger and dumbfound, and its sumptuous tastes and textures – the lacquer of its tempered surface; the proficiency with which it melts, in little gleaming puddles, at the slightest hint of warmth; the ease with which it slides between our lips – beg us to be entranced. Yet, for anyone on the verge of falling under hypnosis, it must be remembered that chocolate's graceful exterior covers the traces of its complexity.

Its escapism is one element of its appeal, and yet to view chocolate as a mystical object, a pure hedonism that transcends reality, also has its pitfalls. Chocolate's impartation of joy to those who buy it, unwrap it, and devour it, is just one of many roles. This book is ultimately about that role; about how the pleasures of eating chocolate might be heightened, but its means to that end is to lay out how all aspects of the performance have, together, moulded chocolate into what it is, and to posit from this a sketch for what chocolate *might be* given a little more thought and invention.

We can learn from the hidden difficulties, the roughness beneath chocolate's voluptuous surface; a roughness that reveals itself in many guises throughout the object's long history – its religious and cultural symbolism for the ancient Maya and Aztec civilizations (chapter one), its value as a commodity cultivated first for colonial and now neoliberal capitalist trade (chapters two and three), and its controversial place in the hotly contested issues of public health (chapter five) on the one hand, and international development (chapter four) on the other.

By tracing the path taken by chocolate's fundamental ingredient, cacao, from its origins as a dark and savoury drink, toward the heavily processed substance which is now so dear to us, this book does not wish to suggest that the original product was untainted and call for a historical regression; for the return of something pure or true. Invoking a thing's cultural roots in order to condemn its current corruptions is, as an argument, not only reductive but also slippery, for when informed by nostalgia, one always leans dangerously close to the precipice of exoticism. In any case, if it was a 'pure' chocolate we were searching for, then we would be disappointed to find that the densely-spiced varieties of the ancient civilizations were in many ways more heavily adulterated than ours. Rather, what is hoped for is a colourful illustration of the relationship we keep with chocolate, and how that relationship has changed, sometimes for better; sometimes for worse, over time.

Nor then, will this book adhere to the self-congratulatory optimism of steady and inevitable progress through history. Even where modern methods are 'better', more efficient, more ethical, than past approaches – and this is certainly not always the case – to hold this view has no purpose for the task of the present moment. Because there was more at a certain point in the past – more exploitation, more slavery – it does not mean that there will be less in the future.

Cacao holds no smooth historical narrative. Things change their forms. They melt only to solidify, and in congealing the particles arrange themselves differently each time. Sometimes things crumble, dissolve completely into the earth, only to erupt, without warning, from their own detritus, spritely in their youth, and then shortly to be cut down again. In the absence of any linear unity, of one event following neatly after another, the 'journey' from cacao to chocolate refers instead to the way in which those substances are handled; to their *mediation*. Our relationships with both cacao and chocolate have always been intensely mediated, and it is this idea which, more than chronology, ties together what follows.

The concept of mediation will remain central throughout, and will be applied in three senses. Most obviously, there is the mediation of the supply chain. From the moment the cacao fruit blooms from trees in the tropics, its seeds are a 'raw material', destined to be thrown forwards along the path of the commodity's flow chart, with arrows which point from growing, to harvesting, fermenting, marketing, roasting, grinding, and finally to consumption. The ethical problems of the modern cocoa industry, chief among them the poverty, insecurity and exploitation of its agricultural workforce, will not be resolved without considerable changes to the way in which this journey is structured and regulated.

This is a problem of production; the production of a cash crop, cacao, and we, the consumers of one of its end products, chocolate, must nonetheless ask what we can do to resolve it. This task relies upon a different mode of thinking about consumer power. Not only how to demand more – more for less (the Walmart model) – but how to demand *as such*; how to make demands on what exactly is produced and how it is produced. Here mediation is important in a second way, this time concerning the relationship between the modes by which cacao and chocolate are produced and consumed. It is a point upon which Marx is again helpful:

> the object is not an object in general, but a specific object which must be consumed in a specific manner, to be mediated in its turn by production itself. Hunger is hunger, but the hunger gratified by cooked meat eaten with a knife and fork is a different hunger from that which bolts down raw meat with aid of hand, nail and tooth.

> Karl Marx, *Grundisse*, 1857

What Marx was referring to is the mutual constitution; the *co-mediation*, of the characters of production and consumption. This is a vital property of exchange, shaping not only what is produced and what is consumed but also how. Most often, chocolate is purchased as a finished product, ready to be eaten straight from the wrapper. The simplicity of this specific way of consuming chocolate contrasts with its consideration as an ingredient, where it is reputed to be devilishly tricky. It is associated with elegant desserts, and with skills-based cookery: pastry and 'chocolate-work'. In this sense it is tied to a form of what the Ancient Greek philosophers called *techne*, translated variously as an embodied skill, craft or art: a practical talent that requires honing.

Most of us do not have the time to devote to the learning of, the tuning of our body to, such complex arts, but as the popularity of cooking and baking undergoes a dramatic resurgence, there is a growing trend towards the notion that anyone can overcome the trickiness of chocolate without the dedication of those who depend upon it for their whole livelihoods. There are two ways in which it is proposed that this can be achieved: first, by disembodying the art, the *techne* of chocolate; by relocating it outside the body, in *technology*. It is the market which makes this proposal, promising to overcome the trickiness of chocolate with a deluge of new products. It provides the remedies, flashing in front of our eyes a plethora of gleaming gadgets each of which pledge to make the arduous simple, even enjoyable. Our kitchens are beginning to overflow with these highly logical solutions; a nonsensical inundation of rationality and invention.

Since how we eat chocolate both shapes and is shaped by how it is produced, eating chocolate as an elegant ingredient in tricky desserts both encourages and is encouraged by the production of ever more ingenious gadgetry and paraphernalia. The second approach, which this book tends to favour, is to use chocolate more simply. But, since simplicity always requires the greatest innovation, we need to be more adventurous in our use of the ingredient, and less reliant on technology to do so. This can be accomplished first of all by recovering the simplicity in chocolate desserts; reminding ourselves that chocolate's most famous uses as an ingredient in baking – in cakes, brownies and cookies – came first from the recipes of the home cook (see chapter six).

Additionally, altering the way we consume chocolate cannot be considered separately to how we would like to alter the structure of the industry that produces it. What would a better cocoa industry look like? The stock answer is that it would be Fairtrade and 'bean-to-bar', but this does not go deep enough. It is over-reliant on terms whose meanings tend to slip away as soon as they are uttered. It is necessary to look back beyond these thin terms to the fundamentals of the commodity itself. Why and how did it become as it is? Envisioning the supply chain as a value chain is essential to this investigation, for it suggests a certain distribution of value among different agents, and poses the question of where a thing's value resides. Today we seem almost exclusively to locate cacao's value in various forms of solid chocolate, and it is easy to assume that this is where it has always been. But this assumption is unsettled by reflecting upon the reverence granted to cacao, predominantly in the form of a hot or cold beverage, by cultures of the past.

In communicating cacao and chocolate, there is a third and final mediation: that of the forms of knowledge that govern the consumer's interpretations of objects and their values. As Marx goes on to say:

[t]he need which consumption feels for the object is created by the perception of it. The object of art – like every other object – creates a public which is sensitive to art and enjoys beauty.

This idea of mediation by perception belongs principally to a realm of knowledge traditionally opposed to *techne*. In contrast to embodied skill, *episteme* is broadly defined as the knowledge evidenced by the proclamation of fact and classification.[1]

Certain notable eras of history can be characterized by their measures. At the heart of the French revolution, for example, was the metric system – one application of which (to weights and distances) lasts to this day; the other (Gilbert Romme's measure of time, which argued for ten day weeks, and months named after the seasons) only a few years.[2] And in the same way, each era of chocolate's history can be identified by the emergence of an expert or set of experts whom stood at the forefront of its valuation, dictating the frameworks through which the object was perceived. In order to deconstruct the value of chocolate, therefore, I will attempt to bring to light – comparing and contrasting – the processes by which it has been promoted; the expert knowledge which has informed the public why and how to consume it. The relevance of such processes are evidenced by the fact that chocolate is not something which has been 'naturally', universally loved (chapter seven).

The recipes in this book are themselves meant as mediators, intended to hint at the same link between producer and consumer – the journey from cacao to chocolate – to which the text refers, and have therefore been dreamt up from the cuisines of the many regions which have grown cacao over the centuries, from Central and South America, to the Caribbean, West Africa and South-East Asia. As well as aiming for the simplicity of chocolate in desserts, I have also attempted to rethink cacao and chocolate as savoury ingredients, akin to spices or seasoning that marry with and accentuate other flavours, rather than necessarily being the dominant protagonist of the dish.

END NOTES

1. For discussions of techne in relation to food and drink, see 'In Focus: the Techne and Technoscience of Food & Drink', edited by Heath, Deborah & Meneley, Anne, *The American Anthropologist,* Vol. 109, Iss. 4, May 2008.
2. Crosland, Maurice, 'The Officiers de Santé of the French Revolution: A Case Study in the Changing Language of Medicine', *Medical History,* Vol. 48, Iss. 1, 2004: 231.

CHAPTER ONE

ORIGINS OF THE BEAN

THEOBROMA CACAO AND CHOCOLATE

IN PRE-HISPANIC MESOAMERICA

hocolate is the still-youthful generation of an ancestry that stretches back over millennia. To examine this family tree, we must look first to a family of trees, *Sterculiaceae*, to the genus *Theobroma*, and then to one species in particular, *Theobroma cacao*, from which chocolate's origins protrude.

Theobroma cacao stems from the rainforests of Central and South America. It is thought that the species originated at the headwaters of the Amazon basin, and was first cultivated in Ecuador over 5,000 years ago, albeit most likely for the flesh of the *cacao* fruit, rather than for its bitter seeds.[1]

The man who in 1753 charted the genus, comprising of 21 species besides our *cacao*, was the Swedish botanist Carl von Linné. It seems that he was also afflicted by, or else employed intentionally, chocolate's transcendent aura in electing the name '*Theobroma*', from the Greek meaning 'food of the gods'. Putting to one side this title, it becomes apparent, from just a few simple observations of *Theobroma cacao*, that chocolate's difficulty is hereditary. To say that the tree is fastidious would be an understatement. Due to a non-negotiable demand for warmth and moisture, the geography of its growth is restricted to an area of the Tropics, between 18° North and 15° South of the Equator, and even then only in those lands that neighbour a body of water from which the air and soil can continually quench its thirst. It does not tolerate temperatures below 16°C, or any altitude over 300 metres. Even once these demands have been met, the tree seems to resist, in two fundamental ways, the harvesting of its fruit.

First of all, for its pollination (and thus fertilization and fruiting), *Theobroma cacao* relies almost entirely upon the action of midges. The omnipresence of these flitting bugs is a vital characteristic of the humid environment in which *T. cacao* flourishes, and it is not one which can be artificially reproduced with ease. Midges thrive only in wild surroundings, craving the litter of the forest floor. After this had been realised, *cacao* farmers could simulate the conditions with mulch, but, as Sophie and Michael Coe observe in their seminal work, *The True History of Chocolate* (2013), the *cacao* tree's need for a messy environment stumped the first owners of modern, tidy and striated plantations for a considerable time.[2] The *cacao* tree grows to between three and ten metres dependant on the variety. If fertilization is successful, the fruit blooms in clusters from the trunk, or hangs heavy from the larger interior branches. This is a common strategy of tropical species that keeps its fruit sheltered from the elements and low off the ground, accessible to animals which, when humans are not present to harvest them, are lured by the sweet innards of the fruit to eat and disperse what are at this stage astringent and indigestible seeds.

A few preliminary processes are required to make the seeds palatable. Once ripe, the pods are cleaved from the tree and left for around 10 days before being split open and their contents, around 30 to 50 seeds together with their glutinous flesh, removed. In order to facilitate the growth of micro-organisms (including yeast) on the wet pulp, and the brief germination of the seeds themselves, the fruit is fermented: piled into a sealed container and kept at a temperature of 40-45°C for 48 hours, before the heat is lowered and maintained for a further 1 to 3 days.

It is at this point however that *T. Cacao* throws a second spanner in the works: the moist conditions required for the crop to grow and ferment are in complete opposition to the intensely dry heat needed for the seeds to be dried and roasted. Drying is a gradual procedure that, in temperatures not exceeding 65°C (to avoid compromising the flavour), reduces the moisture content of the *cacao* seeds from 60% to approximately 7.5%, a loss of over half their weight.[3] This is often accomplished by spreading the beans sparsely across a flat surface (often a reed tray) and leaving them in the sun. Roasting, meanwhile, is more intensive, requiring a temperature of around 100°C for 1-2 hours. Both of these stages, alongside fermentation, are vital for removing some of the initial bitterness and developing the unique gravity of taste that we associate with chocolate. Finally, the roasted beans are 'winnowed': their husks are removed, leaving us, at last, with the cacao nibs, the true 'ingredient' of cocoa, chocolate and all its associated products.

Today these remain the fundamental preliminary stages of a set of lengthy industrial processes, but they were developed first by the ancient Mesoamericans in making their own chocolate: the beverage known to the Maya as ka'kau' (*kakaw*), and to the Aztecs as *cacahuatl*. It is thought that the word cacao came directly from the Mayan. According to the Mexican anthropologist cited by Michael Coe, Ignacio Davila Garibi, 'chocolate' on the other hand was coined by the Spanish, who intermixed the Maya noun for 'hot water', *chocol' haa*, with the verb *chokola'j* (meaning 'to drink chocolate together'), and then replaced its ending with the Aztec word for water, *atl* (pronounced até), to give us *chocolatl*. All very unscientific, really, but this is an explanation which continues to be believed and used in Mexico today.

CEREMONIAL CULTURES OF CACAO CONSUMPTION

The French gastronome Jean Anthelme Brillat-Savarin, writing in 1825, just prior to that period of the nineteenth century which marks the industrialization of chocolate, alludes to a distinction between two separate classes of chocolate. When deciding upon one's recipe for making the beverage, he cautions us that:

> other considerations must govern the choice and amount of flavouring, which cannot be the same for chocolates meant to be *used as food* and those meant to be *eaten as delicacies*.[4]

The impact here of verbs of consumption – 'using' versus 'eating' – upon the object produced – 'food' versus 'delicacies' – cannot help but remind us of Marx's identification of different hungers.

In this case it is the purpose of consumption which moulds the nature of the chocolate's production. But Brillat-Savarin, appearing to us as a sommelier distinguishing between the types of wine which should be drunk alongside certain meals, at certain times, and from certain glasses, also emphasizes the ceremonial aspect of modes of production and consumption: the connotations between etiquette and ritual. Etiquette in general can always be thought of as a sort of ceremony; a social institution made up from given (spoken or unspoken) rules and repetitions specifying acts, participants, times and places. Such an honour is reserved only for things which are widely considered important, and it is the objective of the ritual to represent and reproduce the object's prestige. Cacao and chocolate historically have been substances of great worth for a number of societies, and each has chosen to represent this in very different ways: a range of ceremonies both particular to the substance in question, and at the same time imbued in wider cultures of consumption.

CACAO IN MAYAN CULTURE

Recent archaeological research supports the idea that civilizations preceding the Maya, such as the Olmec of the Mexican Gulf Coast (1500-400 BC) and even before them the Barra (1800-1400 BC), were imbibers of a cacao-based drink.[5] It is likely that this was initially a variety of *chicha*, an alcoholic beverage made by fermenting the flesh of the cacao fruit, but recent evidence from the Ulúa Valley in Northern Honduras suggests that a non-alcoholic version made instead from the seeds came about as a by-product by 1100 BC.[6]

The evidence unearthed so far does not give us a precise picture of how these societies produced and consumed cacao, nor of its broader cultural status. However, we can be reasonably sure that alcoholic drinks including cacao-based *chicha* served a public function, often being offered to foreign guests. More so, it has been argued convincingly by Henderson *et al.* that this social function had a notably ceremonial air. From the design of the vases used to serve cacao uncovered in the Ulúa Valley, they assert that a shift from long narrow vessels to those with a convex body and a flared neck indicate the desire to transition from alcoholic to non-alcoholic cacao drinks whilst maintaining the ceremonial element. The vase design would have been intended in this case to allow the drink to be beaten, possibly at the table, creating a thick froth inside its spout without the liquid itself escaping.[7]

This theatrical method of preparation presents a notable continuity in the serving of chocolate up until it became a predominantly solid product in the nineteenth century. For the Maya, the ceremonial quality of the drink attains greater complexity in view of their religious belief system, and it is this knowledge of the position of cacao in society that means they remain for us the earliest perceivable culture of its consumption.

The Maya were not a singular civilization but rather a number of separate societies that nonetheless shared certain cultural elements. The geography of influence exerted by these societies, taken together, stretched from Mexico's Yucatán peninsula in the north, jutting out between the Gulf of Mexico and the Caribbean Sea, through what is now Belize, to modern Gautemala, El Salvador and Honduras to the south and east. The Classic era in which the Maya thrived is usually divided into three periods: the Early Classic (AD 200-600), the Late Classic (AD 600-900) and the Terminal Classic (AD 900-1000), much of our evidence for chocolate consumption coming from the written and archaeological relics of the latter two, and from ethnological studies into the systems of the few remaining Maya tribes.

As we search the cavities of buried objects for our answers to the origins of cacao, the Maya needed only to delve into their own minds, into the religious ideology that held the truth of their existence. According to the Quiché Mayan story of divine creation, narrated in the text of *Popol Vuh*, humanity was formed when the Maize God, incarcerated since defeat and decapitation at the hands of the Underworld Lords, was liberated at 'sustenance mountain' by his two sons, known as the Hero Twins. Maize was thus to the Maya what clay or dust is to Christianity: the founding essence of the human body. But there was another crop that was on occasion depicted as sprouting from the person of the Maize God in holy scripture: cacao.[8] From the very beginning then, chocolate really was a – if not *the* – food of the gods. But fundamentally it was also a symbol of vitality, of life transferred between the gods and man.

The polytheistic system of the Maya functioned via the coexistence of opposing forces. Despite their numerous gods, all were ultimately united in a single hegemonic figure: the Lord and Lady of Duality. The story of the Maize God is striking to us in particular because it demonstrates an attitude which has largely departed from our western scientific ways of thinking: a recognition of the duality of death and birth. It was a common trait of agrarian societies to treat human life according to the same rules they observed in their crops: dead matter, returned to the soil, brought new life. Thus in the Maize God's story, often shown as a sequential set of illustrations, the God's gradually deteriorating skeletal structure gives rise, in the following image, to a sapling which carries the God's head as one of the knots in its trunk.[9]

Cacao's frequent participation in the various versions of Maya creationism alludes to its own duality. It was at the same time creative and destructive; it was sustenance, a bringer and maintainer of life, and yet it was also carried to the tomb by certain individuals at the time of death, encased in pottery vases from which archaeologists now excavate their proof. This was concomitant with the religious belief in an afterlife, but, as Gabrielle Vail notes, it was also more specifically part of a culture of reciprocity between humanity and its gods.[10] By taking cacao to their graves alongside their own bodies, these individuals were returning materials to the realm of the gods from which it had come, and from which it could be reborn.

By looking at the recipes of the remaining Lacandón Maya of Chiapas in Mexico, we may guess that this was a culture of consumption with a ceremonial element that, like Brillat-Savarin some 800 years later, divided chocolate into superior and inferior kinds according to its preparations. Unlike the French gourmet's divide however, this border was drawn along a religious boundary, between the sacred and the secular; that is, between one chocolate fit for offering to the gods, and another fit only for mundane, earthly consumption. The differences in the preparation of the two types were accordingly symbolic ones: the sacred chocolate was ground and mixed, just as the secular would have been, with water, but in a dedicated hut beside the 'god house'. It was beaten, just as the secular would have been, in order to bring forth the froth that was the most desirable element of the drink, but only after the addition of a particular grass, 'aak'. And it was served, just like the secular, with maize or mead, but not before the maize or mead had been blessed.[11]

Cacao in Aztec Culture: Blood and Reciprocity

The Maya of the Terminal Classic, including the Lacandón, were largely extinguished by the Toltecs. This was a race that, over the following two centuries, extended the Mesoamerican trade of cacao – introducing it to the Anasazi people of what now constitutes New Mexico, for example – and established the rich culture that was a strong influence on their own eventual successors, the Aztecs.

The Aztec world was no less fractious than that of its predecessors, but was held together at the peak of its powers by a Triple Alliance formed in 1428 between three city-states: Mexico-Tenochtitlan,

Texcoco and Tlacopan, of which the first (and its Tenochtitlan borough in particular) quickly became the dominant partner. Aztec culture lent as much, if not more, religious significance to cacao as the Maya. Life was similarly based upon the idea of reciprocity, but in particular upon a set of rituals involving the exchange of blood. This originated in the fact that the Aztecs understood their existence to be owed to a gift of sacred blood, let from the pierced penises of the male gods to fertilise the maize for humanity's growth.[12] It was believed that from this moment onwards, the human race was locked into an exchange of vital energy with the gods, bound by eternal debt to their divine creditors. Reciprocity pervaded all walks of Aztec life, but by far its most infamous manifestation was the exercise of human sacrifice. These violent ceremonies were quite literally at the centre of the capital Tenochtitlan, a borough whose intricate middle district comprised almost 80 religious buildings.[13] Their significance was such that the mendicant friar Fray Bernardino de Sahagún, one of the first Europeans to study Aztec society, dedicated an entire book of his *General History of the Things of New Spain* (commonly known as the Florentine Codex) to *The Ceremonies*, in which he gives vivid interpretations of the many sacrificial rituals of their calendar.

Caroline Pennock, in her work on the broad cultural meaning of Aztec sacrifice, explains that the bond of reciprocity governed not only the relations between the divine and earthly spheres, but also those formed among men and women; humanity and their environment. The relationship of the emperor and his subjects was similarly one of close interdependence. The city-state (*Altepetl*) was divided into community plots known as *calpulli*, to which each family held right of membership. There was thus no principle of private ownership. Rather individuals were held fast to society at large by this tacit tenancy agreement. Two things were expected in return: Firstly, every individual must contribute, according to one's means, to the system of tribute which transferred goods of many kinds to the emperor's court. Secondly, all male citizens were expected to undertake the duty of military service. Beyond being simply a conscript army, this was a warrior culture. As well as being a tool of defence against external foes, the creation of warriors also provided the main source of sacrificial subjects. Conflicts hence served not only as a means to defeat adversaries but also to supply captives for the various ceremonies.[14] Crucially, these warriors were not left on the battlefield or locked away in sealed rooms at the periphery but were brought back in to the very centre of the empire.

Considering the intrinsic place of blood in such a society, the fact that cacao tended to symbolize the vital fluid is an indication of its significance. One of the most prevalent stories about the *cacao* tree's creation claimed that it sprouted from a pool of blood which had wept from the body of a *Mexica* princess, murdered for her heroic refusal to betray the hiding place of the royal treasure to a group of bandits.[15] In keeping with these sinister beginnings, *cacao* pods were often used as a metaphorical representation of the heart extracted from the sacrificial victim. Cacao was linguistically connected in this way to what was perhaps the most shocking act of the rite: the heart had to be torn from the dark cavity of the torso and presented to the sun whilst the blood was still fresh and hot and the heart still pulsing. In addition to this figurative role of the *cacao* pod though, a chocolate drink was physically present in the ceremonies. It served the purpose of a drug, intended to lull the one destined for the knife into a state of hypnotic calm, or even happiness, at their imminent fate. In this particular process, the components of the above metaphor – cacao and blood – were literally mixed. To create the medicine, the blood-encrusted obsidian blades used for past sacrifices were washed in a cup of chocolate, before being administered to the misbehaving subject. Though it is not immediately apparent, this cacao-based drug was also proscribed in the interests of a reciprocal bond. The sacrificial victim, often a captive apprehended from one of the many Aztec wars, was held in an intimate spiritual bind with his own captor. In the highly personal identity politics of Aztec warrior culture, the affiliation between the prisoner and his guard was far too common to be deemed a pathological irregularity. It could not be explained away, for instance, as an early manifestation of 'Stockholm Syndrome'. Rather, it has to do with the complex Aztec perspective on death.

Humans were formed of a composite of soul-essences, with the type of afterlife that beckoned for each one dependent on the life that it had led. Usually, this was a tragic existence, a torrid half-life in *Mictlan*, the lowest realm of the Underworld. However, the warrior's death – whether on the field of battle or the temple steps – offered a rare exception to this unfortunate fate. By dying in this way, the warrior soul was offered a 'flowery death', going east to the privileged realm of the rising sun. Flowers being a pervading symbol of the notion of death itself laying the seeds of life in Mesoamerican cultures,[16] sacrifice granted the soul the opportunity to live on precisely by offering up one's corporeal existence.

Rather than being a prison guard then, the Aztec captor was more akin to a custodian, perhaps even a guardian, bound to protect their captive's soul on its blessed path. As the other end of the bargain, the conduct of the prisoner in coping with his forthcoming sacrifice conferred a level of honour upon his keeper. Much as a parent is sometimes judged by their child's tantrums, the Aztec warrior could be dishonoured if his captive threw his toys out of the pram. Furthermore, it seems that the captor in some sense *became* his captive through this ritual. In the cannibalistic consumption of the body which followed the sacrifice, the captor would abstain from the meal in which his family partook: the reason, Pennock suggests, that to eat his prisoner would be to consume some part of his own self. And, in the most extreme form of the sacrificial ritual, the captor would even wear the skin of the flayed corpse, using the sacred mask to beg donations from members of the public in the days following the ceremony.[17]

Cacao was thus used to mediate the conduct by which the worth, the honour, of the sacrificial soul was determined. The very personal nature of the sacrificial rite, however, disguises a broader purpose. Despite its religious mysticism, the human sacrifice had a social function. For René Girard, this function was to protect society as a whole from the infectious tendencies of sacred objects. Blood and violence are included together in the realm of the sacred. They are dangerously virulent substances. Without intervention, one act of violence leads to another via the mechanism of reprisal, and an increasing measure of blood is spilt over what might at first have been a single, minor disagreement. For all its barbarity, the social function of human sacrifice was to provide an official, regulated channel for violent acts, thus preventing escalation. The imperative to stop one sort of violence in its tracks by means of another points to the dual attitude taken towards all sacred phenomena; towards what is called its *kratophany*: its encompassment of both 'desired goodness and feared evil power'.[18] It is this duality which meant that the sacred held together on the same plane disease and alcohol; blood and cacao; warriors and pregnant women.[19] These phenomena undoubtedly induced states which were spiritual, even if they were also painful or fatal. This is why it was not uncommon for particular diseases and alcohols both to have their own gods. Drunkenness was, for the Aztecs, a grave sin (punishable by death) for this very reason: not because it was a disgrace to society, but because society was a disgrace to it. As Sophie and Michael Coe illustrate, one of the reasons the Aztecs took to drinking chocolate at such a rate was that the other common beverage, the alcoholic wine *octli*, was incompatible with how they regarded both themselves – as a humble and hard-working people[20] – and humanity on the whole – as lowly tenants loaned their existence by superior beings. Intoxication was thus regarded as insulting the gods by taking on an inappropriate proximity to them, falling foul to the arrogance of thinking that humanity could fraternize with its divine creators.

Cacao was, as we have seen, also associated with the Mesoamerican deities, and there are suggestions that the role of the chocolate-like drink in the sacrificial rite resulted in cacao being viewed with the wariness and wonder of a sacred substance. The trance which the drink was supposed to induce in the sacrificial subject was not one of sedation – intended to quell consideration of the killing to come – but the generation of an elevated state, an initial step on the path to the afterlife. The ceremony in this way marked chocolate out as sacred; as a substance which would produce beneficial effects for society only if the gods were regularly reimbursed for its existence.

The structures of ritual both honoured and regulated the sacred. Simultaneous to being central to public life – witnessed by all – ceremonies of this sort served to insulate the effects of certain phenomena from spreading unfettered throughout society. This was accomplished by creating tight personal bonds between participants. Hence the captor-captive relationship among warriors, a perfect example of what Girard identifies as the tendency of some societies to systematically reserve 'whole categories of human beings...for sacrificial purposes in order to protect other categories': their duty was to die so that others would not.[21]

THE GIFT OF CHOCOLATE

Outside the institution of sacrifice, the bonds established by ritual took the form of elementary power relations. The theatre with which cacao-based beverages were prepared even prior to the Maya was a performance intended to form social debts in societies where relations of a monetary sort did not exist. The giving of a gift, distinguished by the grandeur of its presentation, created a quasi-hierarchical special relationship between host and guest. Just as inviting someone to a major social occasion (a party or wedding) places upon them an obligation to do the same for you in future, those who received the frothing drink of cacao would have been tied to returning the gesture, with one ideally even more spectacular than the last.

The Aztecs were not unique in their incorporation of trade within a religious or spiritual logic. The anthropologist Marcel Mauss, in his 1925 study of *The Gift*, argued that a number of tribal cultures in North America, the Pacific, and Siberia shared a system of exchange based upon the obligation of reciprocity. Simply, each time one was offered a gift (from another individual, family, or tribe), they were obliged first of all to accept it, and then, after a suitable period of time, to return another gift of greater symbolic value. The obligation was governed, not by rates of interest, fines, or threat of legal prosecution, but by honour, as witnessed by the thing given. The Maori, for instance, believe their gifts to be imbued with an individual spirit, *hau*, which, if it is not returned to its home, is possessed with the power to strip the perpetrator of their authority, their *mana*.[22]

In the terminology of the social theorist Jean Baudrillard, Mauss's study exemplified 'cultures in which the notion of value as we know it is virtually non-existent', in which the transfer of goods was conducted by a system of 'symbolic exchange' rather than commodity trade. For the Mayan and Aztec systems, cacao was similarly a being *beyond the value of objects*, viewed primarily within the context of sacred rites of offer and sacrifice.

In the Trobriand Islands of Papua New Guinea, the centrality of reciprocity to life was reflected in the fact that the chiefs of tribes were always the traders, the commanders of merchant fleets. Theatre was again vital, so the act of reciprocation often came in the form of great festivals, entire seasons of giving. It is here that the traders bear a striking resemblance to the Aztec *pochtecha*, the prestigious class of long-distance merchants responsible for operating the system of tribute. The island on which Tenochtitlan was located was not in fact a cacao producing region, so it was only by the labour of these men that the beans made their way to the capital from the cacao-rich provinces of *Xoconochco* (Soconusco) and Tabasco. Like the Trobriand traders, the *pochtecha* were required to throw grand feasts to give thanks for the gifts of cacao and other goods, and, while the Aztec merchants were not their society's leaders, they occupied a privileged position similar to that of the warrior. Despite their prestige, merchants were warned against the hoarding of things. This was a lesson taught, in the case of cacao, by another version of the Maize God's tale of regeneration. The Underworld Lord, known here as God L, appears as a richly-attired merchant whom retains possession of the Maize God's tree-hybrid for its wealth. In this and other versions he is punished and humiliated for the act of possession and accumulation: one vase shows the Hero Twins themselves forcing God L to surrender his wealth. As well as stripping the deity of his material riches, they enact an initial symbolic tribute by sacrificing the God's compatriot.[23]

The role of cacao drinks in the formation of semi-formal debt relations already suggests its potential for facilitating symbolic power on behalf of certain individuals by the fermentation of social obligations.[24] However, once confronted by the commodifying force of European merchant capitalism, cacao was slowly subjected to evaluation; it became *valuable* in a way that enabled monetary comparisons of wealth. The Aztecs were the first of the Mesoamerican civilizations to be widely troubled by this transition. Cacao was increasingly hoarded in the stores of the residents of the great cities. The court of Moctezuma II in Tenochtitlan alone was said to prepare 2000 jars daily to be consumed by the emperor and his guests.[25] This inequality began to affect a different kind of unease to that felt in relation to sacred substances: a propensity for violence that was socio-economic in its nature. It is clear that by the time Sahagún arrived in the Aztec world chocolate's consumption was considered a noble practice for which certain conduct was appropriate. In observing the customs of the elite regarding the drink, he tells us that:

> To carry it one placed the cup in his right hand. He did not go taking it by its rims, but likewise went placing the gourd in [his] palm.[26]

As if to foreshadow the rules which now govern champagne, Aztec chocolate drinkers were instructed in what manner it was proper to hold their glasses.

The commodity value of chocolate additionally led to a divide between two modes of consumption – one superior to the other – the application of which was bound inextricably to the way in which the drink was produced. However, it is evident from a recipe recorded by Sahagún that the split this time occurs within human society rather than beyond it. Unlike the Lacandón Maya recipe, the ingredients of the superior beverage are not blessed, and on the other hand only the inferior grade chocolate is now mixed with *nixtamalli* (maize) to form a thick gruel. What was previously exceptional to the sacred has disappeared, whilst what was previously normal for both secular and sacred has become a sign of frugality reserved for the inferior, an economisation not dissimilar from the use of other cheap carbohydrates as 'extenders' in modern kitchens, added to more precious ingredients in order to make them 'go further'.

As well as being representative of a crisis of Aztec identity that led ultimately to the civilization's demise, this early precursor to Brillat-Savarin's distinction between chocolates was just the first instance of chocolate's liminality; its position as an object in the midst of relationships both human and ethereal; forever something to be given and received.

The ancient civilizations set out the multitude of schisms that chocolate traverses. From their cultures of consumption, we can gather that chocolate is nothing if not a duality, a melding of oppositions; binaries such as life and death, pleasure and pain, luxury and humility, into a single object. By this ambivalence it has managed to resist, to some extent, the forces which seek to get the measure of it. History attests to its obstinacy, and in the following chapter we will see how it held its own even when confronted by the calculating violence of colonialism. As they came to be traded and consumed more widely by European societies – caught between religious piety and the temptations of material riches – the roles of cacao and chocolate shifted tumultuously, but the substances themselves strove to retain some semblance of spirit.

PRE-HISPANIC RECIPE

Since recipes written by the Maya or Aztecs themselves have not survived, they must come to us via European accounts. However, given that it was the ingredients rather than the method – with the exception of the temperature at which it was served – which varied most as a result of encounters with the Spaniards, the main test of authentication is the absence of Old World substances, notably sugar and cinnamon.

Chocolate recipes in the pre-Hispanic era were classified primarily as remedies, but it is worth questioning the assumption that what is medicinal cannot, at the same time, be enjoyed. In Ancient worlds, as well as in our own, many foods also serve as drugs. The potential of something ingested for reasons of health to become pleasurable to the palate means that the division between chocolate as medicine and chocolate as drink is not clear cut. Having said this, the strength of pure cacao is an acquired taste, as are the combinations of spices and herbs which traditionally accompany it. Though some of these flavours, such as the fragrance of vanilla and the hum of chilli, are familiar sensations to modern day chocolate connoisseurs, some others are less so. 'Ear flower', for instance, belongs to a native plant, and is unlikely to be found on any supermarket shelf, while annatto is an orange-coloured powder derived from the seed of the *achiote* tree, which we are indeed accustomed to consuming on a regular basis, only in our Red Leicester cheese, rather than in our chocolate.

Base
8-10 roasted seeds of cacao
5 seeds of tzapotl *(sapote – another soft native fruit)*
10-15 dried maize kernels

Flavourings
Annatto
5 hueinacaztli ('ear flower' – the petal of Cymbopetalum
penduliflorum, a tree of the custard-apple family)
1 tlilxochitl (vanilla pod)
½ dried ancho chili

water
honey, to taste

Method
According to the traditional method, the *cacao* seeds would be ground with the other base ingredients and the chosen flavourings using a *mano* and *metate* – the Mesoamerican equivalent of the pestle and mortar – and then beaten with the water and poured from one vase into another from a height, over and over, until the froth, considered the most advantageous element, rose to the surface. Though they did

not have sugar, honey was available to the pre-Columbian civilizations, and so was often added as a sweetener. The consistency should be that of a thin porridge, such that it has substance, but can still be drunk straight from the bowl.[27]

MODERN RECIPES

CHOCOLATE MUSHROOMS ON CORNBREAD

We have talked a lot of intoxicants in this chapter, of the importance of drugs both 'soft' and 'hard' to the workings of ritual. It is apt then that the first modern recipe should involve two ingredients employed to alter the mind: chocolate, whose enchanting functions we have discussed, and mushrooms, the 'magical', hallucinogenic uses of which do not need much introduction.

The union is not nearly as mad as it sounds. Mushrooms are very nicely suited to the fruit and bitterness of a cacao-rich chocolate, just as they are to a red wine or Madeira sauce. The cornmeal works especially well with the fungi, complimenting their earthiness with its own.

For the cornbread
160 g / 6 oz cornmeal
100 g / 4 oz strong white bread flour
2 tsp salt
2 tsp soft brown sugar
2 eggs, whisked
75 g / 2½ oz butter
180ml / 3½ fluid oz buttermilk
½ tsp baking powder
½ tsp bicarbonate of soda
100 g / 4 oz sweetcorn, well drained if tinned

Mix the cornmeal with the buttermilk and the salt and soak for a few hours to soften the corn.

Fry the butter with the sweetcorn and the sugar, then add to the cornmeal along with the flour, the raising agents, and the eggs. Mix well and pour into a small, lined loaf tin.

Bake for 25-30 minutes in a hot oven.

For the mushrooms
Knob of butter
300 g / 11 oz mushrooms – a mixture of chestnut and wild works
well – chopped or left whole depending on their size.
2 cloves garlic, chopped
Handful of tarragon and sage leaves, chopped
100 g / 4 oz extra dark chocolate, at least 80% cocoa solids, chopped
200 ml / 7 fluid oz double cream
Salt and pepper

In a pan, heat the cream until steaming and pour over the chocolate to melt.

Melt the butter in a frying pan on a high heat and then add the mushrooms, tarragon, sage, salt and pepper. Toast for a few minutes and then add the garlic. Once the mushrooms are caramelised take off the heat and fold three quarters of the mushrooms into the chocolate. Serve on a slice of cornbread, topping with the remaining mushrooms.

SEA BASS *MOLE ROJO,* CHORIZO AND BRAISED LEEKS

A book on the origins of chocolate would not have been allowed to go to press without at least one recipe for *mole*, the classic Mexican dish which excavated the chocolate-chilli combination favoured by the Mesoamericans in their cacao. People do not always realise that there are many different varieties of *mole*. Often they translate *mole* as *mole poblano*, the speciality of the state of Puebla, and assume that it accompanies turkey or chicken. In fact, *moles* of various kinds are paired with fish and seafood as often as they are with meat.

For the mole rojo

5 tbsp sesame seeds
1 tbsp sumac
½ tsp ground cloves
2 tsp dried oregano
1 tsp salt
Sesame oil
1 dried ancho chilli
5 cloves garlic, crushed
1 red onion, finely chopped
300 g / 11 oz cherry or small vine tomatoes, chopped in half
70 g / 2½ oz dark chocolate
500 ml / 17 fluid oz fish stock

Before you begin cooking, put the ancho chilli into a bowl or cup of boiling water. While it rehydrates (this should take about half an hour), make the spice mix.

Toast the sesame seeds in a small dry frying pan on a medium heat. Stir the seeds occasionally and watch carefully – one moment of inattention and they have the tendency to turn to tiny cinders. When they begin to take on a bit of colour, add the cloves and the sumac and toast for a further 30 seconds or so, until the spices start to give off a strong fragrance. Pour the seeds and spices into a mortar along with the oregano and the salt and grind to a fine powder.

Add the garlic and the onion to a larger pan with a drizzle of sesame oil and cook on a medium heat until soft, then pour in the spice mix.

Once the water in which it sits is a nice brownish red colour, remove the chilli, reserving the soaking liquid. Chop this finely before adding to the pan along with the fish stock, followed by the tomatoes and the chilli soaking liquid, filtered of any grit. After the mole has simmered for 15 minutes, add the chocolate. Leave to reduce, tasting occasionally to check that it is not becoming too strong or sweet.

For the braised leeks
4 leeks
150 g / 5 oz chorizo
50 g / 2 oz butter, cut into small cubes
1 tbsp fennel seeds

Trim the leeks of any tough bits, then slice each one in half, first horizontally, and then lengthways. Take each piece and roughly peel apart some of the layers, arranging them in an oven dish. Sprinkle with the fennel seeds and then dot evenly with the chorizo and the butter. Place the dish in a pre-heated oven at 170°C for about 15-20 minutes, or until the chorizo fat has rendered nicely and both the sausage and the leeks have gone crispy at their edges.

For the sea bass
4 fillets sustainably sourced sea bass
Salt and pepper
1 tsp extra virgin olive oil

When the mole has reduced and the leeks are almost cooked, remove the sea bass from the fridge and sprinkle both sides of the fillets with salt and pepper. Coat the base of a frying pan with olive oil over a high flame and wait until this gets very hot before adding the sea bass, skin-side down. As you place the fish keep your fingers pressed on the edges of each fillet for a few seconds to prevent the skin from curling up. Fry for around 4 minutes, until the skin is crispy and golden, and then turn and fry for another 2 minutes on a slightly lower heat to cook the fish through. Remove the sea bass from the pan onto some kitchen roll, skin-side up.

To serve
100 g / 4 oz tinned sweetcorn, drained

Add the sweetcorn to the hot pan from which you removed the sea bass, frying until charred.

Plate the fillets on top of a bed of leeks and chorizo and top with the reduced mole sauce and a sprinkling of sweetcorn kernels.

END NOTES

1. Coe, Sophie & Coe, Michael, *The True History of Chocolate*, 3rd edition, London: Thames & Hudson, 2013: 25; Henderson, John, Joyce, Rosemary, Hall, Gretchen, Hurst, Jeffrey & McGovern, Patrick, 'Chemical and Archaeological Evidence for the Earliest Cacao Beverages', *PNAS*, Vol. 104, Iss. 48, 2007.
2. Coe & Coe, *The True History of Chocolate*: 21.
3. Coe & Coe, *The True History of Chocolate*: 23.
4. Brillat-Savarin, Jean Anthelme, *The Physiology of Taste: Or Meditations on Transcendental Gastronomy*, Everyman's Library, 2009 (1825): 122 (emphasis mine).
5. Coe & Coe, *The True History of Chocolate*: 36.
6. Henderson et al., 'Chemical and Archaeological Evidence for the Earliest Cacao Beverages': 18938.
7. Henderson et al., Chemical and Archaeological Evidence for the Earliest Cacao Beverages': 18939.
8. Coe & Coe, *The True History of Chocolate*: 39.
9. Martin, Simon, 'Cacao in Ancient Maya Religion: First Fruit from the Maize Tree and Other Tales from the Underworld', in *Chocolate in Mesoamerica: A Cultural History of Cacao* , edited by McNeil, Cameron, University Press of Florida, 2006: 163-4.
10. Vail, Gabrielle, 'Cacao Use in Yucatán Among the Pre-Hispanic Maya', in *Chocolate: History, Culture, and Heritage*, edited by Grivetti, Louis & Shapiro, Howard-Yana, John Wiley & Sons, Inc., 2009: 5.
11. Coe & Coe, *The True History of Chocolate*: 62-3.
12. Pennock, Caroline, *Bonds of Blood: Gender, Lifecycle, and Sacrifice in Aztec Culture*, Basingstoke: Palgrave Macmillan, 2008: 29
13. Pennock, *Bonds of Blood*: 2.
14. According to the Codex of the Dominican friar Fray Diego Durán, in the fifteenth century the Aztec Triple Alliance signed a treaty committing them to instigate perpetual conflict (*xochiaoyotl*: the 'flowery wars') with neighbouring city-states for the primary purpose of supplying sacrifices to alleviate drought (*see* Durán, Fray Diego, *The History of the Indies of New*

Spain, translated by Doris Heyden, University of Oklahoma Press, 1994).

15. Grivetti, Louis & Cabezon, Beatriz, 'Ancient Gods and Christian Celebrations: Cacao and Religion', in *Chocolate: History, Culture, and Heritage*, edited by Grivetti, Louis, & Shapiro, Howard-Yana, John Wiley & Sons, Inc. 2009: 30.

16. Flowers were commonly pictured at the foot of the Mayan maize trees, and there was even one name given to Sustenance Mountain by the Tz'utujiil Maya which translates as 'flowering mountain earth' (Carlsen, Robert & Prechtel, Martin, 'The Flowering of the Dead: An Interpretation of Highland Maya Culture', *Man*, Vol. 26, Iss. 1, 1991: 27. *Cited in* Martin, 'Cacao in Ancient Maya Religion': 164).

17. Pennock, *Bonds of Blood*: 17; 19.

18. *See* Belk, Russell, 'The Sacred in Consumer Culture', in *Consumption and Spirituality*, edited by Rinallo, Diego, Scott, Linda & Maclaran, Pauline, London & New York: Routledge, 2013: 72.

19. Women who died in childbirth were one of the only other groups of Aztec society (in addition to those who died of certain diseases) that were granted reprieve from Mictlan, instead being sent west to the setting sun.

20. Coe & Coe, *The True History of Chocolate*: 75.

21. Girard, René, *Violence and the Sacred*, translated by Patrick Gregory, London: Bloomsbury, 2013: 11.

22. Mauss, Marcel, *The Gift: The Form and Reason for Exchange in Archaic Societies*, London: Routledge, 1954: 11.

23. Miller, Mary and Martin, Simon, *Courtly Art of the Ancient Maya*, New York: Thames & Hudson, 2004.*Cited in* Martin, 'Cacao in Ancient Maya Religion': 170.

24. Henderson et al., 'Chemical and Archaeological Evidence for the Earliest Cacao Beverages': 18939.

25. Prescott, William, *The Conquest of Mexico*, London & New York: J.M. Dent & Co. 1909: 30. *Cited in* Walvin, James, *Fruits of Empire: Exotic Produce and British Taste, 1660-1800*, Basingstoke: Macmillan, 1997: 90.

26. Sahagún, Fray Bernadino de, *General History of the Things of New Spain*, translated by Arthur Anderson & Charles Dibble, School of American Research and University of Utah, 1950-1959 (12 Volumes), Vol. 9: 35. *Quoted in* Coe & Coe, *The True History of Chocolate*: 98.

CHAPTER TWO

THE IMPERIAL BEAN
CHOCOLATE AND COLONIALISM

EUROPE'S ENCOUNTERS WITH CACAO

The story of cacao is deeply intertwined with European colonialism. In 1492, Christopher Columbus, a Genoese navigator, was sponsored by Isabella I of the Crown of Castile to set sail across the Atlantic. As is well known, what he initially sought was safe passage to Southeast Asia, his 'discovery' of the Americas coming about only as a result of erroneous geography.[1] Once found, however, the New World became the object of desire for the Spanish Crown. Columbus undertook three further voyages over the next decade, the stated purpose of which was religious education – to bring Catholicism to the idolatrous, backward peoples of the globe. Columbus certainly believed whole-heartedly in this holy calling, yet it is likely that, for the mission as a whole, the word of God served simultaneously as a true motive and as a convenient veil for less pious objectives. It may have been a mission of discovery, but first and foremost of all things the Crown had tasked Columbus with discovering was gold. A merely curious quest this was not, and the Spaniards showed little appreciation for discoveries that they could not exploit.

One of the most illuminating studies of Columbus himself is Tzvetan Todorov's *The Conquest of America*. Especially potent in his analysis is the portrayal of European arrogance, which reveals the blindness of Columbus to the subjectivity of language, and in particular to the notion of foreign languages. Columbus's own letters describe his futile first attempts at communication with the native populations. His Latin tongue is greeted with understandable bemusement by the locals, who respond in their own Nahuatl. But Columbus nevertheless seems adamant that they must understand him, and that they themselves must be practicing some corrupted version of his language – for him, the natural language; the language of God. In a delusion reminiscent of the most brash and ignorant of modern tourists, he insists in thinking that he can make out, in their speech, familiar words and phrases, and on occasion even corrects them on their pronunciation.[2] However, once forced to admit that he cannot understand the locals, Columbus' theorizing lurches to the other extreme. Since language is something which he, a civilized individual, would surely be able to understand, his conclusion is that the Indians must not be capable of language *at all*. What they are communicating with has to be something more primal and animalistic, something somehow below speech. What is different to Columbus must be inferior; what he does not comprehend he seeks to destroy.

It is reasonable to hazard that the closed-mindedness of the invaders contributed to their initial failure to realize the significance of the cacao fruit. On his fourth voyage of 1502, Columbus aimed for Jamaica, but landed instead at Guanaja, the Eastern-most of what we now know as the Bay Islands of Honduras. It is here that Columbus, if we are to trust the account of his son Ferdinand, first laid his eyes on cacao beans, preciously stowed within a trading canoe of the Putún

Maya. Yet it is telling that, unable to communicate with the natives concerning the nature of their cargo, Ferdinand satisfies himself with a description gleaned exclusively from a European standpoint. The canoes are like 'Venetian gondolas', whilst the cacao beans themselves are 'almonds'.[3]

Though it is understandable, when we come across something peculiar to us, to compare it to a more familiar object, the conquistadors displayed a stubborn refusal to enquire into cacao's difference. Ferdinand's almond conflation came to be a symbol of this lack of recognition, habitually reproduced by visitors and settlers alike over the following century. The first reference to cacao in France for instance may have been in the 1532 translation of the Milanese writer Pietro Martire d'Anghiera's tour of the West Indies. Something he calls '*cacap*' is mentioned, and said to be akin, again, to those teardropped nuts.[4] The result of this unfortunate habit was that these foreigners, and those who read their words, remained none the wiser as to the unique properties of the cacao crop cherished by the natives. It is hardly surprising that the Europeans, who had arrived with the idea that they were to teach these barbarians the correct ways of religion and civilization, had difficulty comprehending this thing which they did not know, and yet which seemed to be of great worth. Their response to cacao was a precise microcosm of the double movement which Todorov portrays the colonialists taking with regard to Mesoamerican culture as a whole: at first, in an attempt to fit it into their existing vocabulary of the world, they tried translating cacao into almond, but, when this did not make adequate sense of the object, they rejected it with vehemence, demoting it to a standard undeserving of European attention, let alone consumption. If cacao was not European, they concluded, it (and those whom treasured it) must be barbaric. The reactionary attitude applied not only to cacao, but also to its liquid form. As late as 1575 therefore the Italian Girolamo Benzoni writes of chocolate that 'It seemed more a drink for pigs, than a drink for humanity.' A harsh assessment, particularly given that he had not yet actually tasted the beverage.[5]

The desperation to know, to know even the unknown, derived

from the fact that the European desire for the New World was a fearful desire: the will to secure a land onto which a wild and frightening image had been projected. This paranoia led both Columbus, and that other great figure among the ranks of conquistadors Hernán Cortés, to seek certainty at every turn. For example, when Cortés broached the shores of Mexico on the 22 April 1519, it is undeniable that his arrival was timely. As wealth concentrated at the centre of the Aztec empire, those at the periphery were concerned by what they perceived as a deterioration of morals. Amid the discontent, Cortés garnered allies, his forces growing as he moved inland. According to Cortés's own account, however, the newly-acquired manpower was not required. As he approached the capital, the story goes that word travelled from Moctezuma's court in Tenochtitlan informing the natives that Cortés was to be welcomed into the capital and given gifts. Famously, Cortés claimed that the show of kindness was the result of an Aztec prophecy in which his arrival had been pre-empted as the return of the god *Quetzacoatl*. His claim is dubious, and, if it was a fabrication stands as an indication that the conquistador was searching for legitimization of his own god-given delusions by projecting them into the minds of his victims. As Anthony Pagden says in his introduction to Cortés's letters:

> whatever its origins, the story...enabled him to allege and explain a "voluntary" submission of Motecuçoma (sic), and the "legal" transfer of his empire...to its rightful ruler, [the newly appointed ruler of the Holy Roman Empire] Charles V.

It is possible that the true reason for Moctezuma's generosity was a strategic one, intended to lull the foe into an alliance by way of gift-giving. But if this was the case it did not have the desired effect since the conquistadors did not know the meaning of reciprocity. This European misconception informed their approach to cacao as it did the other Mesoamerican treasures. Once they had sampled cacao's value, the merchant capitalists' only thought was to accumulate and profit by it.

The initial European recoil from cacao and chocolate was not to last much longer. This was thanks, primarily, to the work of Franciscan friars, who arrived in Central America with a similar ambition to the conquistadors, that is, to convert the local peoples to Catholicism, but who were far more open to difference than their blinkered predecessors. They too sought to change the New World, but by first understanding it, rather than simply commanding it to change. The work of one of these missionaries, Fray Bernardino de Sahagún, has already arisen in the previous chapter. Having learned Nahuatl, Sahagún communicated with a group of local informants whose insights he recorded in his *General History of the Things of New Spain* (1590). Contrary to its title, what sets this work apart from others is that it concerned not only the *things* of 'New Spain', but also the ways in which the native peoples *used* and *valued* them.

The relative sophistication of the Franciscan approach led to a gradual erosion, among the settlers, of the psychological barriers which had obstructed the conquistadors' understanding of cacao and chocolate. Sahagún and others came to appreciate cacao's rich and nourishing character, its role in sacred ritual, and its medicinal virtues. For those visitors who lived on the European mainland however, the reactionary impulse remained. From the knowledge that Spanish settlers apparently approved of the beverage, the conclusion deduced was not that chocolate might be civilized, but that the settlers, in their Creolization, must have been converted to savagery. Having a taste for barbaric objects meant being barbaric, and barbarians, of course, did not possess the adequate expertise to mediate the object's value.

THE NEW VALUE OF CACAO

> Whether a tyrant or a lawmaker, he who holds the power is the surveyor of the city: the measurer of the land, of things, wealth, rights, powers, and men
>
> Michel Foucault, 2011 (1970): 132[6]

Among the many elements of nature harvested by the early European settlers in the Americas for the purpose of trade, cacao held a special place. One could not shake off the mystical significance which the Maya and the Aztecs had granted it. For them it carried the heavy weight of religious ritual symbolism; *a weight that might, paradoxically, have dissipated if actually weighed.* The Europeans measured by weight all that they traded, yet the first attempts of Spaniards to subsume cacao into the established commodity system; to reduce it to a measurable standard – comparable to all other goods – were in vain. It is true that the Mesoamerican populations had never possessed scales, but this absence is largely irrelevant, a symptom rather than a cause of their societal structure. Rather, what mattered was that neither this, nor any other instrument of homogeneous measurement, could ever hold the authority to determine cacao's meaning. When European merchants in the New World tried exchanging cacao beans by weight, local traders expressed the inadequacy of their methods with daily acts of resistance, turning the crude measuring techniques against their makers by means of counterfeit. They substituted the real thing for pretenders – from something called 'wild *cacao*' mentioned by Sahagún (likely *cacao*'s close relative *Theobroma bicolor*), to unripe seeds and ground avocado stones – in the knowledge that the undiscerning European would not be able to tell the difference until much too late.[7] This subversive conduct showed cacao to be more than an object or a commodity. As with everything and everyone in Aztec culture, cacao was *tonacayotl*: the spiritual flesh of gods on earth. As such, it had an agency of its own. It demanded recognition, and for a long time was granted it. The Spaniards even resolved reluctantly to make an exception for cacao, maintaining the Aztec method of trading it: by number rather than by weight. Though still a method of quantification, this meant that value – not only cacao's value but the value of everything (and everyone) to be traded – was to be assessed in terms of cacao itself. This was the privileged position of a currency. For instance, even if it was not one of the commodities in a transaction, cacao would be present as a mediator between parties, and if one good being traded (a slave, for example) was worth more than the other (a quantity of maize, say), then the difference – the 'change', as we would call it – could be made up in cacao beans.

When Marx, some years later, spoke of the reification of money in the capitalist system, he was observing the elevation of a medium of exchange to an almost sacred state. Through its self-referential momentum, the accumulation of money had become an end in itself, independent of the production of value. In the initial trading of cacao, this process is inverted: *the object is moving in the opposite direction.* Cacao, previously a symbol of the gods, hangs onto its reified status above all other commodities, but it has nonetheless been brought down to earth from the heavens, made to interact (if not merge) with its associates in the marketplace.

Cacao was not considered merely valuable; it had become a physical mediator of value itself, a primitive form of money. The currency even held denominations – the change from a transaction could consist of a certain number of ripe seeds, or a greater number of unripe ones. The strange irony is that, in preserving itself, this seed, which was such an important component of the Aztecs' ritual culture, became, simultaneously, the predominant means of that culture's erosion. The sweet fruit of success is pregnant, it is said, with the seeds of its destruction. And so it was with cacao. Except of course, in its case, the seeds *were* the success, and they were not sweet, but bitter.

Cacao in the Colonies: The Diversification of Supply

The other unforeseen consequence of cacao's eventual recognition was that Europeans embraced it as an ostentatious good, an exotic jewel of the New World. Like the t-shirt designers who first realized the universal draw of Ernesto 'Che' Guevara's disembodied profile, colonial merchants slowly found that cacao's very spirit could be marketed. Having constructed missions in areas of Gautemala inhabited by the Kekchi Maya, Dominican friars journeyed, in 1544, on a royal visit to the court of Spain's Prince Philip. They were accompanied by a group of Kekchi nobles, who presented gifts including cacao beans to the Spanish nobility.[8] This was doubtless a cultural exchange, but we may also imagine it as an unintentional trade exhibition. In 1585, 41 years after cacao's debut, the first official shipment arrived in Seville, and from then on the European palette slowly developed a taste for chocolate.

The growing demand for cacao increased its price, incentivizing the entry of new suppliers into the market from the colonial branches of the New World. This fuelled an economic expansion which, alongside the corresponding growth in popularity of tea, coffee, sugar and tobacco, played a leading role in the purpose and power of empire. At this early stage, the Spanish Crown was the main beneficiary of the trade, but as the value of the industry became apparent, the other great powers of western and southern Europe – the Portuguese, the Dutch, the French and the British – set their sights on a market share.

Typically, the initial splicing of this market had been conducted before its contents were known. In 1493, Pope Alexander VI Borgia carried out the unfeeling surgery of the colonial geographer, ruling an arbitrary line on a map which had itself been arbitrarily drawn, to divide the Americas neatly between the Spanish and the Portuguese. In 1500, the Portuguese unwrapped their prize, stumbling upon the coast of Brazil, and here, much like in Central America, Catholic orders begun erecting missions. South America was, however, not to be associated so much with the Franciscans or the Dominicans as with the Society of Jesus, soon to be a global and notorious presence. If the conquistadors were the soldiers of empire in the New World, and the Franciscans and Dominicans its scholars, then its politicians were surely the Jesuits. Where the other European settlers embraced force for the sake of force or knowledge for the sake of knowledge, the Jesuits recognized the advantages of combining the two.

The Jesuits of Brazil found trees of *Theobroma cacao* to be growing wild, predominantly in the northern territories of Grão Pará and Maranhão.[9] Unlike in Central America, where the *cacao* was of what we now call the *Criollo* variety – today considered the premium bean – this was different: what we know as *Forastero*. It was bitter, and the bitterness was considered unpleasant, so to cover it required the addition of greater quantities of sugar. However, there was little trouble finding a considerable market for the Brazilian beans. This was due not only to the burgeoning demand for chocolate in Europe and its colonies, but also the growing problems of Central American production during the seventeenth century. Its crops and labour force having suffered at the hands of Cortés, Mexico became dependent on imports from surrounding areas such as Ecuador.[10]

The freedom of trade at this time was restricted by the Spanish, who tried to exercise control over the continent by the *encomienda* system, insisting that all trade be filtered through the port of Cádiz. However, they lacked the maritime presence to govern the waters effectively, and as a result fell victim to both buccaneering and covert trading by the other imperial trading companies. The Portugese were the first to plunder the contents of Spanish ships and their American trading partners, but after King Phillip II of Spain inherited the Portuguese throne, the two countries became allied – the so-called 'Iberian Union' – and the Dutch, the French, and the English became the most troublesome rogue traders. In 1572, Dutch ships appeared off the coast of Panama, and begun trading clandestinely with Brazil and Venezuela. By 1599, the situation had escalated: in this year the Spanish Samuel de Champlain spotted, off the coast of Española, 'thirteen great ships, French, English, and Flemish, half armed for war, half with merchandise'.[11] The extent of this rebellion against Spanish monopoly power was to lead, eventually, to the proliferation of both the crop of cacao, and the drink of chocolate, around the globe. The diversification of supply quickened the pace of uptake via a long series of discoveries and cultivations throughout the Americas and the Caribbean archipelagos. Following the Portuguese plundering of northern Brazil, the Dutch found and began to trade a variety from Caracas, the capital of their colony in Venezuela. And, shortly after Jamaica had been snatched from Spanish hands by the forces of Oliver Cromwell's England in 1655, the island became the main supplier of cacao to London's markets.

Whilst sugar was the initial impetus of this expansion for all the West Indian colonial companies, the creation of a monoculture proved an injudicious move. From the island of Curaçao, off the coast of Venezuela, Dutch traders brought in Spanish cacao, as well as silver and indigo, to bolster their trade. But it was the French who cultivated with the greatest diversity (particularly the British, whom relied heavily on a large-scale sugar plantation model). They began to grow cacao in Martinique in 1680, then later in Grenada and Dominica, and to this economy they added also tobacco, coffee, indigo and cotton. Their efforts were rewarded: by the end of the century the French colonies were considered the most profitable of the West Indian enterprises.[12] The position of currency held by cacao in Mesoamerica had evolved from an entrenched religious and social tradition in which the substance had been regarded as sacred, yet even when lifted out of that cultural frame and transposed into others, the potency of cacao and chocolate were such that they were quick to develop symbolic, as well as physical, roots. Reading the observations of the Martiniquais plantations made by Enrique Pacheco y de Leyva, we find a quote from the Jesuit priest Jean-Baptiste Labat that puts quite beautifully the all-encompassing presence of the commodities:

> The inhabitants use [chocolate] so commonly, along with brandy and tobacco, that these things seem to them as a clock and a measure; so that if you ask them at what time they left a place and when they arrived, they answer "I left at the stroke of brandy and I arrived at chocolate".[13]

Chocolate, then, had the capacity to be a measure not only of the monetary value of objects, but also of the concepts of time and space. In contrast to the modern day capitalist conviction that 'time is money', it is fascinating to think of life dictated, rather, by alternative formulas: 'chocolate is money', or, perhaps 'time is chocolate'.

Chocolate may have been a yardstick for living, but it was at the same time a medium for a form of domination that deprived so many of life. Maybe the two most vital formative moments for today's chocolate industry took place under this rubric of colonial domination: first in Trinidad, where the Spanish intention to diffuse their sources of imperial wealth led, in 1757, to the incidental mixing of different *cacao* varieties; second, in 1820, when a similar imperial imperative, this time Portuguese, necessitated a transfer that paved the way for a continental shift in production. Both of these moments will be more thoroughly addressed in the following chapter, but here we perform a shift of our own, from the supply to the demand-side of chocolate; to its growing commonality in the lives of European elites.

CACAO IN EUROPE: CHOCOLATE AND THE ELITE

Bearing in mind the tumult of the imperial economy, the relative continuity of chocolate is mightily impressive. As well as managing to hold onto its spirit; its aura, long beyond most other commoditized goods (albeit by becoming one of the orchestrators of that very commodification), the preparation of chocolate also remained largely consistent with the pre-Hispanic instruction earlier described. Still it was ground with the chosen spices before being furiously beaten and decanted to lure the foam out from the body of the liquid, and still the concoction was combined with a starchy grain, usually maize.

The most visible of changes to chocolate during the period of its introduction to Europeans was the variation in its ingredients. It is logical to begin with the most significant of the alterations, that of sugar. All of Europe's nobility added sugar to their chocolate, but it was the French who had the sweetest tooth, a hankering associated with the opulence of Louis XIV's Court of Versailles. Commentators at the time – mostly male - were fond of the idea that chocolate was something on which the opposite sex were helplessly hooked, and there is some evidence that chocolate came to Versailles, and then was gradually popularized in France, through Louis XIV's Spanish wife Marie Thérèse. Initially, she took her poison in secret. Like an addict getting her fix, she had the drink prepared in the Spanish style by her female court assistants, the backroom dealers in this clandestine affair.[14] Whether Thérèse's habit, once it had become an article of public knowledge, was as influential as is sometimes made out, it is not certain: it may simply have suited the patriarchal discourse to believe that feminine weakness and deception had brought the foreign substance into the country. Nevertheless, three years before her death in 1683, her personal obsession had clearly been embraced more widely.

In Pierre Richelet's 1680 *Dictionnaire Francois*, the word *chocolat* was listed for the first time.[15]

Sugar was also a foreign commodity, extracted from sugarcane which had until the discovery of the Americas been imported primarily from south Asia. Thus, manufacturing sweetened chocolate for Europe entailed a global network through which multiple cash crops were produced, exported, imported, cultivated and consumed. For early modern Europe, this network was a mercantilist one, premised upon ownership of the means of production. Possession – of objects; of territory; of people – was the key expression of power for empire. *Theobroma Cacao* was, however, less suited to being possessed than something like sugarcane. In addition to being difficult to grow anywhere but the equatorial wilderness, the plant was sensitive to neglect. This meant that, for the majority of the sixteenth and seventeenth centuries, locals – experts by virtue of their knowledge of the environment – were considerably more adept than their colonial rulers at finding and harvesting cacao without damaging either the fruits or the trees from which they were severed. These indigenous experts were, of course, themselves owned as slaves, but the diffuse nature of cacao forced captors to allow their labourers more freedom than they would have considered ideal. In Portuguese Brazil, the Jesuits initially sent enslaved local índios out into the forest, but this strategy had to be rethought when the natives developed the tendency of using the excursions to make a dash for freedom. It is an indicator of the Jesuit talent for governance that they recognized quickly that the only way to maintain their grip would be to loosen it. They divided the labour force, employing a small number of free men to act as supervisors of the enslaved.[16]

Meanwhile, the system by which the conquistadors, and thus the Spanish Crown, were fed their beans relied, likewise, upon government at a distance. Not only had the Aztec system of numerical measurement been maintained; in Mexico, Cortés also kept in operation the tributary network which obliged rural communities to pay cacao to the great cities. Though they did not believe in the reciprocal function of tribute between man and gods – and it was precisely their mission to abolish such beliefs – Cortés and his men saw the economic usefulness of preserving this particular ritual. The soldiers had, it seemed, eventually come to understand the ways of the politician: the strength granted by the alloy of power and knowledge.

THE TAMING OF NATURE AND THE EUROPEANIZATION OF CHOCOLATE IN BAROQUE EUROPE

The consumption of chocolate was ritualized not, as one might expect, as a sweet treat, but as a breakfast staple. Where the first meal of the day had previously consisted of meat and grains, often washed down with wine or ale, the taste for chocolate influenced its evolution into the lighter combination of a hot, sweetened drink – chocolate, tea, or coffee – served with bread.[17] As opposed to the two caffeinated colonial beverages, which were drinks of the middle classes, chocolate was, according to many accounts, deemed aristocratic. Chocolate was associated with the image of how it was served, presented to lavish individuals – often female – by their lowly chamber attendants.[18]

This reputation remained a barrier to chocolate's popularity through the seventeenth and well into the eighteenth century. In his study of 'Life and Manners in Madrid' from 1750 to 1800 for example, Charles Kany observes that although 'the use of this beverage had spread even to the common people', it was perceived by them to be a 'regrettable extravagance', a sin of the rich that was often claimed to be responsible for their pallid complexions and bodily weaknesses.[19]

Chocolate was publicly available, in England, Spain, and France, at chocolate or coffee houses. In London, it was either drunk on the premises, thickened and enriched with milk, eggs, and sometimes sherry, or taken home in 'cakes' which could be ground and mixed as the customer so chose. The chocolate houses, the first of which was opened, by a French immigrant, in Queen's Head Alley, Bishopsgate, in 1657, were highly sociable establishments, but their very publicity excluded certain groups. The public sphere was a male-dominated environment, and the chocolate houses were, at least according to the image they put forth, where men talked seriously about the most prescient issues of society. Women were not permitted to enter, meaning that, if they wanted chocolate, men would have to buy it for them. In Madrid, in addition to the coffee house, chocolate could also be purchased from *botillerías* (small shops selling drinks and snacks), and outside the famous *botiellería Canosa*, women waited in their private coaches for chocolate to be brought to them by their male companions.[20] It should be clear from these accounts that the tradition of giving women gifts of chocolate has not necessarily evolved from some natural female inclination towards it, but rather from the historical restrictions on women to acquire it for themselves.

In its continued exotic connotations, chocolate's prestige went beyond a show of material wealth to a display of knowledge. To drink the dark, oily drink was not just to say that one had the money to afford it, but that, in the first place, one had the option to purchase this particular good; this strange and foreign substance. In other words, by drinking chocolate, the man or woman of Europe could show themselves to be a man or woman of empire, and thus of the world. Moreover, the lacing of chocolate with sugar and spices made it a drink in which the products of the East and West Indies were blended together. Consider this with the fact that it was often served, in the chocolate houses, alongside tea and coffee – or, in Madrid, alongside beverages flavoured with cinnamon, saffron, and amaranth seeds[21] – and we get an even more eclectic substance, a veritable 'empire soup'.

The status symbolism of chocolate invoked a mental separation of a different sort to that which had previously rejected it, but nonetheless still based upon the same old civilization-barbarian schism. Chocolate inferred an element of the wild. But for the drink to be deemed acceptable, never mind expedient, it would have to be adequately 'Europeanized'; cordoned off from its savage origins, whilst retaining its air of romance.

The native peoples of the Americas had, by the end of the seventeenth century, been well and truly conquered, their population reduced to a tenth of its original number. The force that accomplished such destruction – so dramatic that it is often described in the language of genocide – was twofold: on the one hand, a force of straightforward exploitation and brutality, subjecting the Mesoamericans to poor working conditions and inhumane treatment; on the other, a less direct, but nonetheless purposeful violence of a viral sort. It was Old World-borne diseases, to which the immune systems of the native Americans were not accustomed, that accounted for the spiralling rate of mortality. In 1518, a smallpox epidemic broke out on the island of Hispaniola (now Haiti), and in a matter of months had taken the lives of all but 10,000 of the island's indigenous population, which prior to the catastrophe had stood at as many as 4 million.[22] Though it might seem unjust to attribute accountability to the Europeans for the illnesses they carried, this was far from an unfortunate coincidence of different bodies. First of all, there is the obvious point that, was it not for their imperialist intentions, the Europeans would not have contaminated the continent to such an extent – it could be argued that contact could have been made even if the intentions were entirely benign, but the intermingling would not have taken place at anywhere near the intensity of invasion and occupation. Secondly though, there is the fact that what made the Europeans into imperialists rather than mere explorers; the motivation for their expeditions, was economic expansion. Specifically, it was the quest for a bounteous supply of commodities for which they could then stimulate demand, selling them back to Europe and lining their pockets with the gains. And what event had set them on this path to a global, market-oriented vision; what enterprise birthed the predecessors of capitalism? The answer: none other than the commodification of farming, an industry which, having learned how to produce food surplus to that required for subsistence, then learned how to sell that surplus and use the excess money for investment in capital and in labour. But here is the turn from coincidence into causality with respect to what might be termed a microbiological imperialism: the farm, upon which the idea of trade evolved, was also the space in and through which Europeans built up immunity to disease. The sheer concentration of biomass that large-scale agriculture entailed meant that the populations of farming societies were exposed to bacteria in a way that the native people of the Americas were not. In other words, it was manure that proved

European colonialism's most potent weapon.

In spite of the death of the population, there was a lingering apprehension in Europe that, even without its people, the environment of the New World itself remained a threatening presence. Since to know was increasingly to secure, the second way by which dominion was established involved a great project of knowledge. Simultaneous to chocolate's appearance on European breakfast menus, *Theobroma cacao* appeared in Linné's binomial schema. However, the scientific classification of the plants of the New World was the fulfilment of a process that had begun much earlier, in the second chapter of *Genesis*, with the Garden of Eden. For as soon as the Americas were discovered, they were envisioned, in their natural abundance, as Paradise on earth. Like Eden, the narrative attached to this Paradise was also burdened with the anxiety of original sin; the fear that the wild forests of these strange and beautiful lands were full of forbidden fruit, harbingers of Paradise lost. In response to the uneasy atmosphere of the forest, the ornamental garden increasingly became the spatial expression of imperial utopia – Paradise without its beguiling serpent.

Gardens, and the botanical or zoological garden in particular, were thus important to the psychological companion of what Alfred Crosby called 'ecological imperialism'.[23] Mirroring the transfer of European weeds, animals, and diseases to the American continent, New World crops including *Theobroma cacao* were taken back home to be buried in the flower beds of European gardens. The particular function of a botanical garden differed according to whether it was located at the European centre – in which case its borders quarantined the wild from the civilized world outside – or in the colony – where it created an ordered, ideal version of that which outside the garden was present, but threateningly untamed. In either case, it allowed the products of the New World to be civilized in the minds of European consumers. Then, once the wilderness of these foreign lands had apparently been tamed, they were no longer feared, and could instead be looked upon with a nostalgic eye.[24] Though seemingly a less destructive gaze than that of the conquistadors, this exoticism was really only an inversion of the identical logic: fearful ignorance swapped for patronizing arrogance, without departing from the imagined hierarchical binary of the animal versus the human. Exoticism's effect was to uphold the discursive distance between nature and culture, which in the case of cash crops like cacao meant a radical separation of the product from its producer. Chocolate was consumed as an innocent and civilized product, even if the methods used to reap cacao were ensnared in exploitation and slavery.

The extent to which the ideological binary of civilization and barbarism allowed Europeans to turn the blindest of eyes even in the face of the most obscene abuses is related aptly by the diaries of Thomas Thistlewood, the British overseer of the *Egypt* sugar estate in Jamaica during the second half of the 18th century. On Tuesday the 24 May, 1768, he records sending a letter to his sister Anne Haddon. He encloses, with his message, an artefact that represents well the character of exoticism. Where one might send a postcard, Thistlewood stocks the envelope with 'the wings of a long-tailed humming-bird...2 inches and a half long'. Then, without warning, he notes that, on his journey home that day 'they were hanging two Rebel Negroes'. This is shocking to the modern reader, but Thistlewood's diary shows little sign of emotional disturbance. He proceeds as if nothing were amiss – because, to him and to many others, nothing was – and the next day returns, where else, but to the civilized space of the garden, where he plants 'mahogany seed, cocoa or chocolate nut, and 4 of the best sorts of Mr. Barton's cashews'.[25]

Thistlewood's is the final episode in a series of colonial attitudes towards cacao which have in common exploitation as a particular kind of mediation. Understanding the consequences of this detached gaze is vital to confronting the present ethical issues of the chocolate industry, first and foremost because it forces us to recognize the relation of the consumed product – chocolate – to its source, cacao.

HISTORICAL RECIPE

The chocolate manufacturer Richard Cadbury (1835-99) – son of the Cadbury's founder John – recorded this early chocolate recipe, dated from Madrid circa 1664.[26] The method is almost unchanged from that of the Aztecs, but its ingredients list is peppered with substances of the Old World: most importantly sugar, but also aniseed, cinnamon, roses, and even those almonds with which cacao was initially conflated.

One hundred cocoa beans, roasted and ground
Equal weight of sugar
12 ground vanilla pods
2 grains of chili
Aniseed
6 white roses
Cinnamon
24 almonds and hazelnuts
Achiote

MODERN RECIPES

BRAZILIAN PIG'S CHEEK *CROQUETAS* WITH *CHIMICHURRI*

Croquettes are a dish shared across the Hispanic-influenced world. In Spain itself, the most traditional are the *croquetas de jamón*, a filling of ham hock in a *béchamel*-style sauce, while in Brazil they have the *coxinhas*, mounds of pulled chicken and cream cheese in the shape of Hershey's Kisses. But deep-fried breadcrumbs are a delicious vehicle for (almost) anything, and certainly for anything that melts. Into this category – 'things that melt' – we can put chocolate (the infamous deep-fried Mars Bar springs to mind) as well as any other ingredients high in fat, from dairy to meat.

In the case of meat, the fattier a cut, the cheaper it tends to be, and, of all the South American cuisines, Brazilian in particular knows how to use its humble cuts. As well as the *croqueta* and the *coxinha*, this recipe is part-inspired by *feijoada*, the Brazilian stew which often contains sausage, bacon, trotters and tongue. But pig's cheeks are something a little bit special: just about as cheap as mince, and with much more flavour, they're well worth the few hours of patient simmering.

For the *croqueta* filling
1 tbsp rapeseed oil
6 pig's cheeks (roughly 500 grams-worth)
1 tbsp plain flour
Pinch of salt
4 cloves of garlic, chopped finely
1 tsp ground coriander
2 tsp ground cumin
1 tsp paprika
2 tsp cocoa powder
25 g / 1 oz dark chocolate, at least 75% cocoa solids
Juice of 1 large orange
2 shallots
150 ml / 5 fluid oz white wine
400 ml / 14 fluid oz vegetable stock

For deep-frying
150 g / 5 oz breadcrumbs (you could use panko breadcrumbs for added crunch, but they do not stick so well, leading to a slightly erratic look)
2 tbsp plain flour
1 tbsp cocoa powder
½ tsp salt
2 large egg yolks, whisked
2 litres / 2 pints oil (olive is best, but vegetable or rapeseed will do)

Coat the pig's cheeks in the flour and then brown in a wide-bottomed pan with the oil. Once the meat is sealed, remove the cheeks onto a couple of layers of kitchen towel. Add the shallots and a drop more oil if necessary and fry for a couple of minutes, then add all the other croquette ingredients and return the cheeks. Turn the flame onto a low heat and cover to simmer for 2½/3 hours, checking occasionally to see if more water is needed.

Meanwhile, make the *chimichurri*.

For the *chimichurri*
Large bunch of parsley
Small bunch of coriander
6 cloves of garlic
150 ml / 5 fluid oz extra virgin olive oil
30ml / 1 fluid oz red wine vinegar
Sea salt
Juice of half an orange
Juice of 1 lemon

Add all the ingredients to a pestle and mortar and pound together, adding more salt and black pepper to taste. In the time it takes to prepare the *croquetas*, the liquids will draw out the flavour from the herbs and garlic.

Once you've almost chewed off your own hand waiting for the allotted time to pass on the braising of the cheeks, lift the lid from the pan and push at the meat with a fork. They should fall apart with relative ease. If they don't, cover again and wait just a little while longer. Fork the meat apart, taste for seasoning, and then leave the filling to cool. Once it has reached room temperature, lay out a long length of cling film and pile up the meat into 12-16 portions (depending on what size you want your croquettes to be), with plenty of space between each one. Cut the cling film between the portions and then wrap around each one, twisting the cling film at each end to condense the meat into a solid sphere. Put the *croquetas* into the fridge (or the freezer if you are feeling impatient) until they are firmly set (from ½ and hour to an hour).

Lay out three small bowls, one containing the flour, cocoa powder, and salt mixed together well, another containing the egg yolks, and a third containing the breadcrumbs. Remove the *croquetas* from the fridge, unwrap each one and coat in the contents of the bowls (in the order above).

Put the oil into a very big pan, so that the oil is deep enough to entirely submerge the croquettes, but nowhere near the pan's rim. Turn onto a high heat and wait until it gets extremely hot. Test the oil with a small piece of potato or bread. If it bubbles furiously, then the oil is ready to cook with. Lower each croquette into the oil with a slotted spoon, cooking them for 4-5 minutes in batches so that the pan doesn't get too crowded and confused. Because the filling is already cooked, all you are looking for is a crunchy golden exterior. Once each is ready, lift out of the oil and onto kitchen roll to drain and cool slightly.

Serve the *croquetas* warm with the *chimichurri*.

CACAO SOUP, CARDAMOM AND ORANGE CHALLAH, CANDIED PEEL AND ALMONDS

This is my take on the early modern European breakfast. It unites New and Old World ingredients – including that symbol of ignorance, the almond – for an aromatic and not oversweet afternoon treat.

For the orange and cardamom bread
225 g / 8 oz strong white bread flour
20g / ¾ oz dried active or 40g / 1½ oz fresh yeast
60 ml / 2 fluid oz warm water
1 tsp crushed cardamom
Grated zest of 1 orange
30 g / 1 oz unsalted butter
90 g / 3 oz caster sugar
¼ tsp salt
1 large egg (plus another, lightly whisked, to glaze)

In a large mixing bowl, dissolve the yeast in the warm water and combine with 40g of the flour. Do not be concerned that the mixture is fairly dry at this point – this is due to the large quantity of yeast required to offset the moisture of the egg and the butter. Cover and leave in a warm place to ferment for 30 minutes.

Meanwhile, melt the butter and sugar on a low heat. Watch

carefully and stir to make sure the sugar doesn't burn and, once dissolved, add the cardamom, followed by the orange zest and salt. Once aromatic, remove from the heat and leave to cool. Once the 30 minutes has passed, whisk the egg into the aromatic butter, and then add this wet mixture to the yeast, along with the remaining flour.

Bring together into a dough, cover, and rest for 15 minutes in a warm place. Knead for a mere 30 seconds inside the bowl, then cover and let it rest again for 10 minutes. Repeat this process of kneading and resting a further three times, after the fourth knead covering and resting for 1¼ hours, or until the dough has risen to roughly twice its original size.

Once the dough has risen, uncover, transfer to a lightly floured work surface, and 'knock out' the dough by punching down on it.

If you are electing not to plait, flatten or role the dough softly into a rough oval, then take one of the longer edges and fold into the middle, before taking the opposite long edge and doing likewise, forming a cylindrical shape. Roll and tuck in the ends with your hands to give a smooth finish, then transfer to your prepared baking sheet.

If plaiting, divide the dough into precise quarters and roll out each in turn into a rope of dough around 30cm in length. Do this using your hands on a well-floured surface, starting with your thumbs together at the centre and then rolling outwards, pressing evenly, in both directions.

Once you have four lengths of dough, lay them out vertically so that they are parallel to one-another, then bring the ends furthest away from you together and press lightly to form your starting point. The ropes should now look like an octopus with its tentacles opening out towards you. First, number the positions of the ropes (not the ropes themselves) 1 to 4 from left to right, then plait by following this pattern:

1 over 3
2 over 3
4 over 2

Continue until you run out of dough, and then tuck the loose ends into the loaf to neaten it up, before transfering to the prepared baking sheet.

Cover and rest again for 30 minutes, preheat the oven to 180°C, and then brush your loaf with the remaining egg.

Once the oven is hot, put the bread in and then pour a cup of cold water into an oven tray in the base of the oven to create some steam. This will give the loaf a firm outer crust.

Bake the challah for 20 to 25 minutes, remove from the oven and leave to cool slightly. Tap the bottom of the loaf: if it is cooked, this should make a hollow knocking sound; if it needs longer, you will hear more of a dull thud.

For the honeyed almonds and candied orange peel

75 g / 3 oz almonds
1 tbsp honey (or vegetarian equivalent)
Peel of 1 orange, cut into thin slices
Juice of ½ lemon
Boiling water
100 g / 4 oz sugar

Preheat the oven to 100°C (80°C if using a fan oven). Lightly grease and line a large oven tray with baking parchment.

Place the honey in a pan on a medium-low heat. Once it has lost its viscosity, pour in the almonds and stir gently to coat. Tip the pan's contents onto one half of the oven tray.

Wipe and rinse the pan to get rid of any remnants of almond, then add the orange peel and enough water to submerge. Bring to the boil and simmer for 10 minutes, then drain with a sieve, and add the peel back to the pan along with 50ml more boiling water, the sugar, and the lemon juice. Simmer for a further 5 to 10 minutes until the orange slices are translucent.

Remove from the heat and transfer the peel onto the other half of the oven tray holding the almonds. Put the tray into the oven and cook for roughly 15 minutes, until both the almonds and the orange peel are sticky and glistening.

For the cacao and vanilla soup

40 g/ 2 oz cacao
80 g / 3 oz dark chocolate (minimum 75% cocoa solids)
1 tsp vanilla bean paste
40 g / 1½ oz soft brown sugar
150 ml / 5 oz double cream
100 ml / 3½ fluid oz semi-skimmed milk
¼ tsp salt

Grate the cacao into a bowl and add the chocolate, broken up roughly, and the salt. Notice that cacao, though it looks like chocolate, hardly stains even the fingers of the warm-blooded.

Place the double cream, milk, vanilla bean paste and sugar into a saucepan on a medium heat, stirring to dissolve the sugar and disperse the black seeds. Wait patiently until the mixture is lightly steaming and, when settled, small bubbles appear around the edge of the pan. Take the pan off the heat and pour its contents over the cacao and chocolate. Stir until the cacao and chocolate ripple into the cream and eventually succumb to it.

Serve in a small bowl, alongside a couple of freshly sliced wedges of the bread, half a dozen slices of candied peel, and a handful of almonds.

END NOTES

1. Columbus used the calculations of Alfraganus as his guide, but, in failing to account for the astronomer's use of Arab (rather than Italian) nautical miles, underestimated the length of the journey by about a third (Todorov, Tzvetan, *The Conquest of America: The Question of the Other*, translated by Richard Howard, University of Oklahoma Press, 1984: 29)
2. Todorov, *The Conquest of America*: 29-30.
3. Columbus, Ferdinand, *The Life of the Admiral Christopher Columbus: by his Son Ferdinand*, translated and edited by Keen, Benjamin, Rutgers University Press, 1992: 232.
4. Gordon, Bertram, 'Chocolate in France: Evolution of a Luxury Product', in *Chocolate: History, Culture, and Heritage*, 569-593: 569.

5. Benzoni, Girolamo, *History of the New World*, Hayluyt Society, 1857 (1575): 150

6. Foucault, Michel, *Leçons sur la volonté de savoir (Lectures on the Will to Know)*, 1970-1, Paris: Seuil, 2011. *Quoted in* Lazzarato, Maurizio, *The Making of the Indebted Man: An Essay on the Neoliberal Condition*, Los Angeles, CA: semiotext(e), 2012: 81.

7. Sahagún, *General History of the Things of New Spain*, Vol. 10: 65. *Cited in* Coe & Coe, *The True History of Chocolate*: 100.

8. Coe & Coe, *The True History of Chocolate*: 130-1.

9. Walker, Timothy, 'Establishing Cacao Plantation Culture in the Atlantic World: Portuguese Cacao Cultivation in Brazil and West Africa, Circa 1580-1912', in *Chocolate: History, Culture, and Heritage*, 543-558.

10. Walvin, *Fruits of Empire*: 91.

11. *Quoted in* Davies, David, *A Primer of Dutch Seventeenth Century Overseas Trade*, Springer, 1961: 113.

12. Boucher, Philip, 'The French and Dutch Caribbean, 1600-1800', in *The Caribbean: A History of the Region and Its Peoples*, edited by Palmié, Stephan & Scarano, Francisco, Chicago & London: University of Chicago Press, 2011: 219-20.

13. *Quoted in* Coe & Coe, *The True History of Chocolate*: 194-5.

14. Gordon, Bertram, 'Chocolate in France: Evolution of a Luxury Product', in Grivetti, Louis, & Shapiro, Howard-Yana (eds), *Chocolate: History, Culture, and Heritage*, John Wiley & Sons, Inc. 2009: 570-1.

15. Perkins, Suzanne, 'Is it a chocolate pot? Chocolate and its Accoutrements in France from Cookbook to Collectible', in Grivetti, Louis, & Shapiro, Howard-Yana (eds), *Chocolate: History, Culture, and Heritage*, 157-176:159.

16. Walker, 'Establishing Cacao Plantation Culture in the Atlantic World': 547.

17. Goodman, Jordan, 'Excitantia: or, how enlightenment Europe took to soft drugs', in *Consuming Habits: Global and Historical Perspectives on How Cultures Define Drugs*, edited by Goodman, Jordan, Lovejoy, Paul & Sherratt, Andrew, Routledge, 1995: 131.

18. See for example Jean-Baptiste André Gautier d'Agoty's late eighteenth century engraving *Madame Du Barry à sa Toilette (Madame du Barry at her Dressing Table)*. *Cited in* Perkins, 'Is it a chocolate pot?: 168.

19. Kany, Charles, *Life and Manners in Madrid, 1750-1800*, University of California Press, 1932: 150.

20. Kany, *Life and Manners in Madrid, 1750-1800*: 149-50.

21. Kany, *Life and Manners in Madrid, 1750-1800*: 148.

22. Monzote, Funes, 'The Columbian Moment: Politics, Ideology, and Biohistory', in *The Caribbean: A History of the Region and Its Peoples*, edited by Palmié, Stephan & Scarano, Francisco, Chicago & London: University of Chicago Press, 2011: 90.

23. *See* Crosby, Alfred, *Ecological Imperialism: The Biological Expansion of Europe, 900-1900*, Cambridge University Press, 2004 (1986).

24. Ritvo, Harriet, 'At the Edge of the Garden: Nature and Domestication in Eighteenth- and Nineteenth-Century Britain', *The Huntington Library Quarterly*, Summer, 1992: 369.

25. *Quoted in* Hall, Douglas, *In Miserable Slavery: Thomas Thistlewood in Jamaica, 1750-1786*, Kingston, Jamaica: The University of the West Indies Press, 1998: 165.

26. I have adapted this recipe from that quoted in Cadbury, Deborah, *Chocolate Wars: From Cadbury to Kraft: 200 Years of Sweet Success and Bitter Rivalry*, HarperPress, 2010: 35-6.

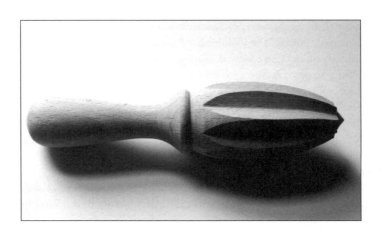

CHAPTER THREE

DEFINING 'FINE FLAVOUR'
CACAO VARIETIES AND THE CONTINENTAL SHIFT

> Classification and hierarchy are operations of naturalization *par excellence*...the projection of historical and social differences into the realm of an imaginary nature.
>
> Etienne Balibar, 1991: 56[1]

The previous two chapters have shown that conflict is inherent to the journey from cacao to chocolate. In some ways, cacao has proved itself defiant, resisting the efforts of those who have looked to get its measure. But in others it has seemed to beckon, even instigate, its own commodification precisely by being so mystical and unique. Though cacao might easily and simply be portrayed as a kind of victim in the way it was cultivated by European colonialists – exploited by external forces; snatched from the freedom of nature's bosom and enslaved like so many of the men and women that perished harvesting it – this would be to ignore cacao's conditions of reproduction: its requirement for animal intervention. That the means of dispersal – through the direct digestion of the seed itself rather than its indirect passing through the consumption of the fruit's flesh – was different from that originally intended does not invalidate the fact that it was helpfully disseminated, the species' diversity increased and its resilience thus emboldened.

For the sake of classification, *cacao* is typically divided into three main varieties: *Criollo*, *Forastero*, and *Trinitario*. However, the cleanliness of names disguises the fact that each denotes only a point on a spectrum. The first two varieties, *Criollo* and *Forastero*, were, along with the Americas themselves, 'discovered' and labelled as 'pure' or natural types. However, their names were given to them only to assert a negative distinction; a differentiation *from*. More specifically, these titles were conjured as a method of differentiating the known from the unfamiliar; the new from the old, and the borders along which the battle-lines were drawn are a source of both controversy and confusion. Like the corrupt colonial Pope ruling arbitrary lines on an arbitrary map, the three-strand classification of *cacao* frequently and without much thought cuts through the heart of villages, cleaves sons and daughters from their parents, and in general denies the imminent versatility of plant life.

PROPER NAMES: THE DISCOVERY OF CACAO'S IDENTITY

The proper name can be nothing more than an extreme case of the common noun, containing its already domesticated multiplicity within itself and linking it to a being or object posited as unique. This jeopardizes, on the side of words and things both, the relation of the proper name as an *intensity* to the multiplicity it instantaneously apprehends.

Deleuze & Guattari, 2012: 31[2]

The usage of the words *criollo* and *forastero* are not specific to *cacao*, and they were certainly not invented to describe it. Rather, both are staples of the Spanish language which precede *cacao*'s classification, which continue to bear other meanings outside that of *cacao*, and which would continue to exist if *cacao* were to fall into obsolescence. For the Spanish word *criollo* means both 'Creole' and 'native', while *forastero* translates as 'foreign'. These terms, which are words in their own right, are further subjective units: they interchange freely according to the positionality of whoever uses them. Put simply, one person's *criollo* is another person's *forastero*. Thus, these names were not intended to be fastened to *cacao* so much as to float in front of it. They are adjectives and yet, like so many adjectives, they have come to be used as if they were nouns. They have even come into the possession of a capital letter to become *proper names*. As Gilles Deleuze and Félix Guattari argue in their critique of Freud's method, the consequence of this linguistic mutilation is inevitably reductive, and may in the case of *cacao* be considered offensive to the diversity, the variable 'multiplicity' that constitutes the plant.

Now that their relativity has been elucidated, it will come as no surprise that the *Criollo* and *Forastero* varieties were conjured at the same time, and on the event of the first congregation of two *cacaos* – one familiar; the other alien – in the same place. Trinidad is known as the site of this first instance of hybridization. Venezuelan *cacao* had been introduced to the Spanish possession by Capuchin friars (a branch of the Franciscan order) during the seventeenth century, and had grown successfully, but in 1727, some form of natural disaster, either of weather or disease, it is not clear which, struck and the crop was decimated. Not to be deterred, in 1757 the friars returned with more Venezuelan seedlings, this time from the valley of the Orinoco River. It is said that these were of the *Forastero* variety, and that their intermingling with the litter of the dead (*Criollo*) crop incidentally created a novel family, aptly named *Trinitario*, which possessed some of the productivity and hardiness of *Forastero* without its bitterness. But this idea has only been registered retrospectively, after the process of classification and in simplified form. As Deleuze would say, identity (as signified by the name) proceeded from difference, not the other way around. For instance, the friars who brought the cuttings did not think that they were bringing *Forastero* with a capital 'F'; only that they were bringing *more cacao*; *new cacao to replace the old;* new *cacao* which, by virtue of necessity, had to be brought from *elsewhere*.

So though there were, according to the modern identification, two varieties existent in Trinidad by 1757, one was only a lingering, underground presence, in the form of remnants from the dead crop. There was little purpose in giving name to an invisible (if not extinct) variety, and neither was there any reason to name the import called upon to replace it. As a matter of fact, the Venezuelan cultivators had already given the new import a name: it was *Calabacillo* (Little Calabash), a positive description based upon its shape, rather than on its supposed nativity. It was therefore only once the hidden debris begun to mix with the *Calabacillo* cuttings that the terms *Criollo* and *Forastero* were put into use on the island.[3]

Given that it was unique to their country, we could easily assume that the Trinidadian population themselves named the hybrid 'Trinitario' after their own soil, and thus that *Criollo* and *Trinitario* emerged at this time as interchangeable terms for their 'native' crop. Yet this train of thought is derailed when it is discovered that, when it entered the vocabulary of the Spanish Trinidadians, the word *criollo* was attributed not to the hybrid variety, but to the imported Venezuelan *Calabacillo*. This is because the Trinidadians were not the first to attribute the name *Criollo*: they had inherited this nomenclature from other groups of Spaniards, who had unearthed Venezuelan *cacao* before any other, and therefore thought it the most authentic, *most native* type. Meanwhile, it was the Trinidadian hybrid that was dubbed *forastero*; 'foreign' not in a geographical sense – that is, because it came from overseas – but because it was new and unfamiliar, emerging unannounced and unrecognizable from the soil. As it is for the modern reader, this system of names soon became confusing for Trinidadians, and *Forastero* in particular was a chronically misused category holding various and often contradictory meanings.[4] Since the hybrid was, to the farmers and plantation owners of Trinidad, known as *Forastero*, it was not called *Trinitario* until later. For only once the highly productive Trinidadian germoplasm was transported back to Venezuela in 1825 did further differentiation became necessary.

The Venezuelans, observing the differences of this *cacao* compared to that which grew on their own lands, once more separated out the foreign from the home-grown. This is where *Trinitario* most likely came into usage, not quite as a distinct third type of *cacao*, but as a particularly intriguing (not to mention potentially profitable) subcategory of that vague negative classification of foreignness. In his 1922 treatise on tropical agriculture, J.C. Willis commented on this all-encapsulating characteristic of the *Forastero* name that 'The term Forastero includes all the varieties other than the Criollos. The chief ones, in order of merit, are Cundeamor, Liso or Trinitario, Amelonado, and Calabacillo'.[5] Gradually, as numerous other 'foreign' varieties have come to the attention of the industry – in other West Indian islands, but also as far afield as Java and Indonesia – *Trinitario* has earned its own place outside of *Forastero*.

It is made clear from this treacherous mire that, when giving names to anything (whether a commodity or a human being) that moves from place to place, and that reinvents itself in those places, transforming itself as it does so, it is extremely foolish to talk in terms of 'native' and 'foreign'. And yet the terms *Criollo* and *Forastero* have undeniably congealed in the vocabulary of *cacao*, attaining meanings which it would be just as foolish to ignore.

With scientific means of justification, the strange linguistic history of *cacao* continues to emerge with new denominations. An apparently 'new' variety was, for example, found in Peru in 2009. The unfamiliar fruit, when spotted, was taken to a laboratory, where it was likened chemically to another *cacao*: a type of *Forastero* present across pre-twentieth century Ecuador. However, the DNA of this particular tree was found to be of such a pure composition that it was judged to deserve its own class.[6] Adding to the strange technical vocabulary of 'native' and 'foreign', this new-found family of *cacao* was called *Nacional*. Even more bizarre is that, before being given the privilege of its own category, it already held this name. It was the variety *Nacional*, a member of the family *Forastero*: thus it was, taken by its proper name, a 'national foreigner'. There is no need for us to pick apart the precariousness of naming any further when the name betrays itself in this way. This is the thing with names: although the classification may contain contradictions, putting on a convincing façade, so one thinks it was at all times set in stone, names, because they are also words, leave traces of their making in the wet cement for the curious to discover upon careful excavation.

THE CONTINENTAL MIGRATION OF FORASTERO

What *Criollo* means now is, as a result of the categorical confusion, an extremely difficult question. Some scientific classifications demand a clean definition, using distinctive and observable characteristics, such as the red or yellow colour of the pods (whereas *Forastero* can also be purple or orange), and their pointed, uneven shape (whereas *Forastero* is smoother and more stocky). However, because it is almost inevitably looked at as the precursor to chocolate, the most readily-noted feature when talking of *cacao* is, unsurprisingly, taste. *Criollo* is commonly held to be less bitter and more complex in flavour than either *Forastero*, which is the most astringent, or *Trinitario*, which sits somewhere between the two.

The biochemical association of levels of bitterness with each of the three categories formed the basis, in 1925, for the development of a further, economic classification: a standardized grading system that denoted 'fine flavour' and 'bulk' varieties.[7] According to this commodity categorization, *Criollo* and *Trinitario* are 'fine flavour' *cacaos*, while *Forastero* is 'bulk' *cacao*. Notable exceptions, however, include the *Nacional* which, despite starting out as a member of the *Forastero* family (by virtue of its Ecuadorian origin), is denoted 'fine flavour', and Cameroonian *Trinitario*, which is deemed 'bulk'. *Criollo* is the category which is deemed 'fine flavour' without exception, but its purity is nonetheless a myth, infected as it has been by a slow yet inevitable genetic mixing with the other varieties, and as a result *Criollo* and *Forastero* both are converging toward *Trinitario*'s blurred make-up.[8]

The industry definition reflects a historical timeline of demand and supply. *Criollo cacao*, a range of varieties which were not sufficiently different from one-another to require separation, was the predominant export up until the nineteenth century. During the 1700s for example, *cacao* supplies from Venezuela and the Amazon basin region accounted for as much as 90 per cent of Europe's chocolate, despite the fact that European consumption increased more than 6-fold over the course of that century, from 2 million to 13 million pounds.[9] Even as other, more resilient and higher yielding varieties – those latterly grouped under the *Forastero* label – were cultivated, for example by the Jesuits in Portuguese Brazil, the original *Criollo* regions proceeded to hold their own. But a twin supply-side jolt changed all this: within a period of thirteen years, one family of *cacao* was disseminated, while another suffered a demise from which it would struggle to rebound. These opposing fortunes occurred in response to the self-same problem: that of labour. The initial labour question, posed by the collapse in the indigenous populations of America, had been answered with economic intervention of a very colonial sort: the importation of labourers in the form of African slaves. The Middle Passage, as it was known, referred to the triangle created on the map by the hulls of merchant ships which first took European goods to West Africa to be exchanged for slaves, then took those slaves to America where they were sold for raw materials, and finally returned those raw materials to Europe. Before the impact of the forced labour itself is taken into account, the journey alone was viciously inhumane: it is estimated that 35 per cent of the Africans perished prior to reaching their destination.[10] The slave traders did not impose or invent slavery. What they did was change its form. Models of enslavement based on social debts already existed in West Africa. But these were instances of forced, unwaged labour instigated among families. The young were often the victims of these lineage customs, acting as pawns on behalf of more senior family members. In order to extend these bondage systems to an international trade therefore, colonial officials acted as pawnbrokers, monetizing the system and thus inserting currency as an intermediary to enable the distancing of the enslaved from their initial enslavers.[11]

This inhumane solution was, however, interrupted in the early nineteenth century by the legal abolition of colonial slavery, entering law first among the British colonies following the Slavery Abolition Act of 1833. Interrupted, but not eradicated, for, to put it in the language of the entrepreneur, the colonial administrators of the time innovated their way out of, or rather, *around* the new regulations, weaving cruel threads through loopholes left wilfully unsecured. This required a great number of winks, bribes, and turned cheeks, but it could not be accomplished quite so brazenly as with the previous system. Though the three-way trade continued to ship slaves sporadically to the Americas in spite of the illegality of the commerce, it was soon found to be much easier to slip under the nose of the law than through the fingers of its long arm. The initial grand display of force over men would have to be substituted for a more subtle implement of power, operated at close quarters, and under the pretence of legitimacy. This would require that the human cargo move less, and, correspondingly, that the *cacao* move more.

The mission to transplant *cacao* and cultivate it artificially had always met with difficulty, for no matter the willingness to invest and experiment, even empires could not be hegemons of the weather. The first systematic cultivation of *cacao* in Portuguese America took place in Brazil, around the colonial capital of Salvador de Bahia, in the sixteenth and seventeenth centuries.[12] From here, numerous efforts were made to transfer the crop to other climates, but the majority failed. Cuttings shipped to the island of Madeira in 1762, for instance, refused to bloom because the Portuguese territory off the coast of Africa was too far north, while those sent to the capital Rio de Janeiro in 1880 would not grow because the city was too far south.[13]

It was in the end that notorious breeder of innovation, necessity, which came to the crown's rescue. Toward the conclusion of the eighteenth century, the fear of Brazilian independence loomed over the Portuguese kingdom. Without their largest colony, the empire would be bereft of its economic heartbeat. Out of this desperate situation came a lone success. In 1820, following a royal order issued by King João VI, Portuguese imperial subjects found the equatorial conditions of São Tomé and Príncipe, a two-island territory off the coast of Gabon, to be to the Brazilian *cacao*'s liking.[14] The Portuguese had shifted their eggs from their sole basket just in time – Brazil broke the colonial shackles in 1822. Yet the transfer turned out to facilitate more than mere survival: the island territory was to become one of the most prolific cacao-producing regions, albeit also one of the most controversial. By the early twentieth century it had, despite its diminutive stature, overtaken all regions of the Americas to become the world's primary producer.

Previously slave ports in a trade which was now declining, São Tomé and Príncipe were reinvigorated by their pioneering roles in a new game, a global game whose rules they had themselves helped to devise. Now, from sounding the death knell of the trade which took the enslaved to the New World, they emerged, resurrected, as the epicentre on which *cacao* cuttings descended, to be met by plantation labourers from the West African mainland. Islands are so often grey areas in their relation to law, and former slaves were delivered to São Tomé and Príncipe under a number of seemingly legal rationales. First, at the conclusion of slavery, former slaves were obliged to serve a further twenty years of forced labour. Second, the islands served as a penal colony, the place to which convicts would be taken to serve their time and payback to the community. Third, and most sly, was the apparently 'free' employment of these men and women. After being officially freed, the *libertos* signed contracts, with a duration of five years, agreeing to work as paid labourers in order to earn enough money for repatriation to the mainland. The cruel hitch: the vast majority could not understand what they were signing themselves up to because they were illiterate. The repatriation funds promised rarely materialized, meaning that come the end of their five years the labourers were left with no real choice other than to carry on under the 'employment' of the plantation owners.[15] In 1894, the British Consul at the Angolan capital of Luanda Clayton Pickersgill quoted, in a report to the Foreign Office, a song he heard drifting eerily across the island plantations. As they worked, the cacao farmers voiced the hopelessness of their predicament: 'In São Tomé there's a door for going in, but none for going out'.[16]

Though it did so with great difficulty, and by a large dose of inhumanity, *Forastero* did succeed in migrating, and once it had survived the initial voyage, took to its new home with vigour, moving swiftly across the continent from São Tomé and Príncipe to the Côte D'Ivoire, Ghana, Nigeria, Cameroon, Sierra Leone, and a number of other soils. Given its homesick tendencies, *Criollo* was not capable of such adventure, and thus the share of the *cacao* supplied by that famed family dropped dramatically, from 90 per cent in the eighteenth century, to as little as 0.1 per cent by the beginning of the twenty-first. *Forastero*, by contrast, now accounts for upwards of 80 per cent of supply to the chocolate market.[17] And the impact of its 1820 migration is clear, with today's top two producers – the Ivory Coast and Ghana – both situated on the West African mainland.

EXCEPTIONAL TASTES: THE RARITY AND BITTERNESS OF CACAO

It is in the interest of the producers of the few remaining 'pure' *Criollo* varieties that it not be contaminated. For some, this is because they are trying to retain its distinctive flavour, but besides this there are two other motives. First of all, because of *Criollo*'s unfortunate history, it is comparatively scarce. There is a part of its value which may be attributed to this scarcity, and so there is an interest in maintaining it. Secondly, it is rare. Rarity is not unlike scarcity, but is subtly differentiated by its social function. While scarcity concerns demand, rarity concerns desire. Rarity is a condition reserved for the luxury good. For Brillat-Savarin, *Criollo* would be the delicacy to be eaten rather than the food to be used.

Rarity is a social and cultural phenomenon. It is linked to such emotionally loaded terms as authenticity, prestige and tradition. As such, it is a phenomenon which is deeply embedded in place.

The rarity of *Criollo* cacao, as the 'first' cacao, is associated with *T. Cacao*'s historic origins in Central and South America. The maintenance of this link therefore contributes to its desirability as a rare and authentic variety.

When the absence of bitterness fails to coincide, for example, with the particular tree's historic origin in denoted regions of Central or South America, it is nonetheless relegated to *Forastero* in order to maintain the integrity of the traditional geographical order.

This is what in the field of international relations John Agnew calls the 'territorial trap', a geo-scientific determinism resolved to keep hold of pre-given spatial boundaries, discounting evidence to the contrary as an exceptional case. Such a static position is far from unusual in the world of food and drink. Rachel Laudan calls it the 'French terroir strategy', and indeed the position of *Criollo* is, in everything but law, simply the most prestigious Appellation d'Origine Contrôlée (AOC) of the cocoa industry.[18] Just as the finest sparkling wine is culturally incomprehensible without allusion to a certain French region, so the geographies that make up *Criollo* are synonymous with the production of high quality chocolate. To extend the comparison, if that region of France were to expand – even if according to a reasonable logic (for example because the grapes and producers in a neighbouring region were found to create sparkling wine of an equal quality) – then the market value of a bottle of champagne would decrease, not only due to the rules of supply and demand, but also because of the loss of prestige that comes with rarity.[19] As a consequence of the authenticity of place, the 'quality' of a cacao variety does not always correlate (negatively) with its bitterness, though it is nonetheless one of the most important determinants. There are two principle chemical sources of the bitterness of the cacao seed. One is an alkaloid which, after being identified as *Theobroma cacao*'s most significant ingredient – that which lends it its stimulating qualities – was named 'theobromine'. However, it is the degree to which a second group of compounds is present which accounts for the disparity in astringency between the different cacao varieties. The group is that of *anthocyanins*, a particular form of flavonoid occurring in plant tissue. Since *anthocyanins* affect not only flavour but also colour – they are a pigment – it is possible to make a rough estimation of a variety's bitterness by the shade of the raw seeds extracted from the cacao fruit. With such a heartless name, one would not guess *anthocyanins* to be producers of beauty, but these compounds are in fact what give to our eyes the brooding romance of autumnal foliage. In the same way, if the inside of a cacao fruit is reminiscent of autumn – its seeds blushing dark reds, purples, blues and browns – then the quantity of *anthocyanins* is likely to be high and the taste sharp; if more like spring – a significant number of the seeds of a light hue, or even white – then *anthocyanins* are scarce and the flavour mellow.[2]

However, much as one can make remarkably unpleasant sparkling wine from the finest champagne grapes, it must not be assumed that the raw seed counts for everything. The flavour of the final bean, as described in the introductory pages of this book, relies heavily upon the processes of fermentation and roasting. It is also significant that, for all the fuss that is made over the genetic purity of beans – the (re)discovery of the *Nacional* being a prime example – there are few unadulterated varieties remaining, and what's more few plantations that can afford to run their production along such stringent lines. A more relevant word than 'purity' here is 'blend', indicative of the fact that the production of cacao today is, much like the brewing of beer or the distilling of gin, as much an art as a science. A blend may be unique to a particular plantation, such that we might think of each producer as a new variety, but of course, in the age of capital, great corporations have come to standardize such blends across the plantations they control so as to benefit with greater ease from technical economies of scale, and ensure the brand consistency of which we consumers have proved to be so fond. Where small-scale individual producers – the self-proclaimed 'bean to bar' industry – are enjoying a resurgence, we see evidence in the growing range of chocolates available to us, and specifically the names on their wrappers. Survey the supermarket shelves, and it will be found that the multiplicity of cacao is slowly revealing itself to us: first in the form of bars that, rather than being called merely 'dark', 'milk', or 'white' chocolate, also display a percentage indicating the proportion of 'cacao solids' present – either in the form of the fatty cacao butter or that dark powder which we know as 'cocoa'. Second, we have the slow emergence and recognition of individual producers of cultivated varieties, as recorded in the formula of a place-name followed by a number. The name *Ocumare 61* for instance, signifies one of the most sought-after varieties, a vintage of sorts: the 61st of the *Ocumare cacao*. Unlike a vintage of the wine variety however, the place-name does not demand that this is where the fruit was grown, only that this is where the original genetic material – in the form of seeds or a cutting – originated. Thus, all chocolate bearing the words *Ocumare 61* has been manufactured from cacao beans whose ancestors were the 61st variety to be plucked from the Ocumare Valley in Venezuela, but which themselves may have been grown in Ecuador, before being roasted, ground, defatted, moulded and packaged in Devon.

The spirit of experimentation has, in turn, been taken up in the laboratory, where those in the profession of hybridization seek to splice *cacao* varieties, genetically engineering new breeds with specific characteristics. This may facilitate an opening up of the classificatory dogma, but it may also fall back towards an even more universal homogeneity. Running parallel to the grand narrative of genetics – that of finding a way of constructing, from a selection of previous 'imperfect' specimens, the 'perfectly healthy human' – is a project intent on finding the perfect cacao. The end result of this project of genetic improvement would possess all the mellow complexity of *Criollo*, and all the productivity and hardiness of *Forastero*, but it would also be more than this; more than merely the sum of its parts. It would rather be a super-cacao; the Vitruvian cacao to da Vinci's Vitruvian Man. *The* Cacao, a proper name with a capital 'C', on which no further variation, no further guess-work, would be necessary. This is, of course, a dystopian vision, but it warns of a very real threat: the reduction of cacao's diversity by the preference of one variety over others.

A NEW CLASSIFICATION: EMBRACING BITTERNESS

Science has its engineered three- of four-strand classification; the chocolate industry its simple binary, but if we are to get the best out of cacao, we need our own, much more ingenious system. If the varieties of *cacao* are to be differentiated, it would serve us better to do so on a fluctuating basis, ranking each according to their suitability to the use in question, rather than attempting to draw a solid and immobile partition between a superior and an inferior grade, with the inevitability of numerous exceptions. A good comparison here is pasta. There is fresh pasta and there is dried pasta, and it is assumed – perhaps because of the connotations of 'fresh' in the age of anxiety concerning use-by-dates and contamination – that fresh pasta is at all times the superior type. Yet dried pasta has its uses. In fact, as a companion to a strong tomato or meat-based sauce, it is to be preferred. Similarly, *Criollo* and *Trinitario*'s flavours may be more complex and less bitter – preferable characteristics for eating alone or pairing with equally subtle ingredients – but it is also less robust than *Forastero*. This latter variety might be bitter, but it is only in the context of a culture that consumes cacao as chocolate, that is, predominantly in solid bars and almost exclusively as a dessert, that bitterness is considered a vice to be covered up. Though our palates may not be accustomed to enduring much of the raw astringency of cacao, all who delight in raw chillies will know that what at first may be a strangely painful experience can over time turn to a strangely joyful obsession. It may be customary to bury lemons, like cacao, in sugar, but we recognise that citrus has more in its armoury than the ability to act as a foil to sickly sweetness; it is just as fitting as a compatriot to roasted chicken or any number of cheeses. In short, any bold and unique flavour opens up a whole field of opportunity for a cook, and cacao is no different. We should not feel obliged to sugar-coat it.

BEEF, ANCHO AND BITTER CHOCOLATE STEW

In response to the new opportunities granted us by cacao, this simple, South American-style one-pot pairs the ingredient with flavours that are intense – salty bacon and smoky, hot ancho chillies – but that work with rather than against its bitterness.

400 g / 14 oz beef braising steak, cubed
1 tbsp flour

6 rashers smoked streaky bacon, cut up with scissors
2 whole dried ancho chillies
30 g / 1 oz cacao (or 50 g / 2 oz dark chocolate, 85% cocoa solids)
1tsp smoked paprika
1 cinnamon stick
3 shallots
1 red onion
4 cloves garlic
A few sprigs of thyme
250 ml / 8½ fluid oz red wine
500 ml / 1 pint water, plus the chilli water
400 g / 14 oz black-eyed beans

15 minutes before you start cooking, place the ancho chillies in boiling water to rehydrate.

Meanwhile, brown the braising steak with a little oil in a pan over a high heat. Do this in batches if necessary, so that all the meat is in contact with the surface of the pan. When the steak has a good colour on all sides, transfer it from the pan into a dish and set aside. Placing the pan back on the heat, add the bacon and fry it until crisp.

Reduce the heat and add the shallots, the onion, and the finely chopped chillies (reserving the soaking liquor), cooking for five minutes before adding the garlic, paprika, herbs, and the cinnamon stick. Cook for another five minutes until the onions are soft, before adding the water (including the chilli water), the wine and the cacao or chocolate and leaving to simmer for 1-2 hours.

Around 15 minutes from the end of the cooking time, just as the sauce is beginning to grow slightly glutinous in spirit, add the black-eyed beans to soften.

To serve
Soured cream/crème fraiche
2 tsp chipotle paste

Combine the ingredients and serve with the stew, and rice or potatoes if you like.

CRÈME DE CACAO

The idea of making your own liqueur sounds intimidating. It sounds like something which would involve hundreds of fiddly processes and thousands of pounds of specialist equipment. But it is, in fact, utter simplicity, merely a matter of flavouring a flavourless alcohol.

750 ml / 1½ pints good vodka
200-250 g / 8 oz cacao nibs
250 ml / 8 fluid oz water
250 g / 8 oz caster sugar

Pour your vodka into a thoroughly clean, roughly sealable vessel and add the nibs. Because they need to break down and diffuse into the liquor, you will have to endure a wait of twelve days or so for the drink to be ready. However, you want the cacao to have as much exposure to the alcohol as possible during this period, so at any spare moment take the bottle from the fridge and give it a shake and a swirl, disturbing the nibs from their refuge at the foot of the container. As the days go by and the nibs surrender themselves to the vodka, the liquid will take on a deep caramel hue.

Filter the liquid through a fine sieve or cheesecloth to remove the nibs.

To make a sugar syrup, combine even parts of caster sugar and water in a pan and bring to the boil, dissolving the sugar, and then take of the heat before the sugar starts to caramelize. The quantities above will make more syrup than what is required for the liqueur itself, but the excess can be stored in the fridge and used for any number of cocktail recipes, including the one that follows.

After being allowed to cool, add between 100 and 200ml of the syrup to the cacao infusion. Whether you use the lower or upper limit depends on how alcoholic you like your liqueur. Put back in the fridge for a couple more days for the liqueur to settle, then remove and enjoy in whatever way you see fit.

COCKTAIL: CHOCOLATE AND CHERRY PORT SOUR

Southern Europe shows much greater appreciation for the bitterness of cacao than other parts of the continent. The Portuguese, the Spanish, and the Italians have long preferred to drink (and eat) their chocolate, like their coffee, in short-form: a small, intense cup or bar 'cut' (*cortado*), or just 'stained' (*macchiato*) with a very small quantity of milk or cream.

If you have been to Lisbon, you will probably have sampled the local liqueur, *Ginjinha*, famed for being served from delicate cups moulded out of dark chocolate. The role of the chocolate component is to counteract the sweetness of the alcohol, so it only works if bitter. I, unfortunately, have not yet had the opportunity to experience *Ginjinha* for myself, so I owe it to my friend Jess for making me aware of this tradition, and urging me to make a cocktail based upon it.

Ginjinha is usually made by soaking *ginja* berries (what we know as Morello cherries) in an alcoholic spirit. Here the cherries are soaked in port wine, the jewel of that other great Portuguese city, *Oporto*, before being combined with our crème de cacao and lime juice for a sour early evening cocktail.

Makes 4 glasses
400 g / approx. 1 lb cherries, Morello if possible.
200 ml / 7 fluid oz white port
200 ml / 7 fluid oz crème de cacao
120-160 ml / 4 fluid oz lime juice (from 6-8 limes)
Sugar syrup, to taste

Put four whole cherries to one side and halve the rest, discarding their stalks and stones. Add the halves to a pan with the port and place on a low heat, crushing the cherries with the back of a wooden spoon as the liquor warms. Once all the blood of the cherries has leaked out into the port, turning it a brilliant red, remove the pan from the stove and pass the liquid through a sieve, crushing the cherry skins one last time to persuade any lingering juices.

Leave the juice to come to room temperature and then shake with the crème de cacao, lime juice, and ice.

Serve over plenty more ice with fresh lime and a whole cherry dangled from the rim of the glass.

END NOTES

1. Balibar, Étienne, 'Racism and Nationalism', in *Race, Nation, Class: Ambiguous Identities*, edited by Balibar, Étienne & Wallerstein, Immanuel, London & New York: Verso, 1991. pp. 37-68: 56.

2. Deleuze, Gilles & Guattari, Félix, *A Thousand Plateaus: Capitalism and Schizophrenia*, translated by Brian Massumi, London & New York: Continuum, 2012 (1987): 31.

3. Bartley, Basil, *The Genetic Diversity of Cacao and Its Utilization*, CABI Publishing, 2005: 17-8.

4. Bartley, *The Genetic Diversity of Cacao and its Utilisation*: 18.

5. Willis, J.C., *Agriculture in the Tropics*, Cambridge University Press, 1922 [1909]: 70.

6. Fabricant, Florence, 'Rare Cacao Beans Discovered in Peru', *New York Times*, 11th January, 2011.

7. Daviron, Benoit, 'Small Farm Production and the Standardization of Tropical Products', *Journal of Agrarian Change*, Vol. 2. Iss. 2, 2002: 162-184. *Cited in* Cidell, Julie & Alberts, Heike, 'Constructing Quality: The Multinational Histories of Chocolate', *Geoforum*, Vol. 37, 2006. 999-1007: 1000.

8. Wood, George, & Lass, R., *Cocoa*, 4th edition, Abingdon: Blackwell, 2001: 6-7.

9. Alden, Dauril, 'The significance of cacao production in the Amazon region during the late colonial period: an essay in comparative economic history', *Proceedings of the American Philosophical Society*, Vol. 120, Iss. 2, 1976, pp. 103-135: 132. *Cited in* Goodman, Jordan, 'Excitantia': 121; 124.

10. Boucher, 'The French and Dutch Caribbean, 1600-1800': 236.

11. Getz, Trevor, 'British Magistrates and Unfree Children in Early Colonial Gold Coast, 1874-1899', in *Child Slaves in the Modern World*, edited by Campbell, Gwyn, Miers, Suzanne & Miller, Joseph, Athens: Ohio University Press. pp. 157-172: 159.

12. Walker, 'Establishing Cacao Plantation Culture in the Atlantic World': 544.

13. Walker, 'Establishing Cacao Plantation Culture in the Atlantic World': 547; 549.

14. Walker, 'Establishing Cacao Plantation Culture in the Atlantic World': 549.

15. Clarence-Smith, William, 'Labour Conditions in the Plantations of *São Tomé and Principe, 1875-1914*', in *The Wages of Slavery: From Chattel Slavery to Wage Labour in Africa, the Caribbean, and England, edited by Twaddle, Michael, London & New York: Routledge, 1993. pp. 149-167: 149.*

16. *Quoted in* Higgs, Catherine von, *Chocolate Islands: Cocoa, Slavery and Colonial Africa*, Athens: Ohio University Press, 2012: 11-2.

17. Coe & Coe, *The True History of Chocolate*: 197.

18. Laudan, Rachel, 'Slow Food: The French Terroir Strategy and Culinary Modernism', *Food, Culture & Society*, Vol. 7, Iss. 2, 2004: 138-9. *See also* Heath, Deborah & Meneley, Anne, 'Techne, Technoscience, and the Circulation of Comestible Commodities: An Introduction', *The American Anthropologist*, Vol. 109, Iss. 4: 596.

19. In the case of Champagne an expansion of this kind is in fact currently underway, with the INAO (*Institut National des Appellation d'Origine* – France's AOC validating authority) approving plans to increase yields and the number of producing villages – from the original 319 to 357 – in 2008.

CHAPTER FOUR

CACAO ECONOMICS

The nineteenth century saw chocolate losing ground to rival beverages. When Queen Victoria came to the throne in 1837, Britain was importing less than 5,000 tons of cocoa per year for domestic consumption, and half of this was destined as rations for the Royal Navy.[1] Furthermore, by 1880 it was estimated that chocolate was the favourite hot drink of 50 million people worldwide, in comparison to 200 million people for coffee, and 500 million for tea.[2] This global hierarchy partly reflected the cultural preference for tea and coffee consumption in regions of the world, such as the Middle East and South-East Asia, together with other substances which fulfilled the similar role of a soft drug ingested via the mouth. Various masticatories were prevalent in a number of societies, and the African habit of chewing on kola nuts, which like cacao seeds contain both theobromine and caffeine, may help to explain why chocolate did not take hold in the new epicentre of its cultivation.[3] But even in Europe, where the drink had not faced such pre-existent barriers to entry, and where trade liberalization had brought down the cost of cacao by abolishing the excise duties on its import, chocolate makers found themselves struggling to make ends meet. It was becoming painfully clear that, as cacao's exotic lure waned with that of empire itself, chocolate in its current form – a liquid with the remarkable tendency to be both gritty and oleaginous – would not be able to stand up to its competitors.

Chocolate was exposed to the forces of the free market, to the global reverberations of the transition from merchant trade to a liberal form of capitalism among the European economies. The exact rhyme or reason of this historical moment is one of the most contentious issues in discussions of economic history, and a thorough analysis would lead us far from chocolate's path. Nonetheless, the seismic transformation in economic logic, followed by the further evolution of capitalism over the next two centuries, is crucial to our story in a couple of ways, one having to do with the process of production; the other with the value chain which connects cacao with those who wish to purchase it. This era was a pivotal one for cacao in that it involved a wholescale physical transformation of the object: from liquid to solid; from the cacao drink to the chocolate bar. Furthermore, this transformation was performed via a regular set of processes, the end result being the rise of the chocolate industry.

CACAO ON THE ASSEMBLY LINE

Of the countless ingenious innovations of industrial production, one of the most fundamental was that of division, or more accurately the relation between division and exploitation captured by Fordism. Besides its employment of the strategy of standardization which marked the advent of mass-produced goods, the assembly line model of Fordist production meant that both the thing being produced and the labour producing it would be internally split according to its minute attributes; the workforce divided and *specialized* according to its alignment with each component part of the eventual object.

Thanks to the development of colonial trade networks since the

Columbian exchange, cacao had become an ingredient – relegated, despite its protests, to one good among many – for which the purposes, the *recipes*, were multiple. Some were gastronomic; others medicinal; still others a combination of the two. But prior to the industrial revolution it had almost always been a single ingredient, marketed as a single, relatively unprocessed good: that of fermented, roasted, ground beans. It was, like the labourer then, a unified individual, and was put to work as such: it had its own particular *techne* or *craft* (chocolate), and was present all the way through the process of production. Different effects on both body and mind were thought achievable depending on what other ingredients one added to cacao to make the drink, but little question was made of cacao itself. Whatever else it contained, it was self-evident that chocolate had, as its base ingredient, the cacao bean.

The process most representative of cacao's industrialization was therefore that which made cacao's presence throughout its own craft unnecessary. The making of chocolate – now envisioned not as a smooth craft but as a chain of many links – may not be possible with cacao altogether absent (just as the factory required some form of human labour), but, by performing the bean's internal split, cacao could be separated out into necessary and unnecessary parts. This would not have been achievable without standardization, since it was this that facilitated the exorcism of the whole in favour of a limited range of standardized hybrids. The inspired logic was that the unnecessary components could then be considered for alternative uses, allowing for a higher level of overall economic efficiency. For the labourer, since she could not remove the now unnecessary creative parts from her body whilst her still necessary limbs worked the factory floor, the consequences of this division manifested themselves in a newly intensified divide between work and leisure time, the latter intended to be spent restlessly consuming the goods restlessly produced in the former. That most famous quotation, from the autobiography of Henry Ford himself, that '[a]ny worker can have a car painted any color he wants' followed by the qualification, 'so long as it is black', illustrates the pairing of standardization and its societal effect, enabling every individual (including the builders of the cars themselves) to be split into a productive and a consumerist part.[4]

For cacao, no such temporal measures were required. The split could be imminent and permanent. In 1665, with the publication of *Micrographia*, Robert Hooke brought public attention to a new scientific way of seeing; a movement, as Aristotle had it, beyond the generalities of raw sense-perception. In so doing, he laid the foundations for a revolution in deconstruction: the microbiological discipline. By the late 1600s, the Dutchman Antony van Leeuwenhoek had constructed microscopes which could achieve a magnification of up to 500 times. One of the first substances subject to van Leeuwenhoek's newly concentrated technological lens was in fact coffee, but the deconstruction of cacao was not far behind. Its division into a composition of cacao butter: a fat that makes up around half of the fermented, roasted nib, and cacao solids: starch, protein, and a huge number of other chemical compounds (including a range of flavonoids, theobromine, and small amounts of caffeine), was a crucial change in perception. From now on, when eyes were set upon the bean, they perceived not a ritual symbol (a thing far greater than itself), nor a single commodity (a thing far smaller than the network of trade of which it was a part), but a conglomeration of commodities, *a thing of many other things*.

This scientific advance allowed two questions to be posed by those of an entrepreneurial spirit. First, 'What can each of cacao's component parts be used for?' and second, 'how can these parts be distributed most efficiently, such that the bean is working to the limits of its productive capacity?'. Vitally, this imagination would then be realized through an industrial innovation: the capacity to take the elements which had been partitioned in theory and separate them physically. In 1828, the Dutch factory owner Casparus van Houten (probably in collaboration with his son Coenraad Johannes) developed a procedure by which the ground cacao nibs, often referred to as the 'liquor', could be defatted, extracting the majority of the cacao butter and leaving behind a cake of the dry powdered substance we commonly refer to as 'cocoa'. The van Houten method was mechanical, using a hydraulic press to force some of the butter from the mass, thereby reducing the fat content to around 27 per cent. Where economization had previously only been possible by dilution – the addition of maize, cassava, or more sinister adulterants that soaked up the fat and added bulk – it was now possible to practice *extraction* and *substitution*: to give each part its respective value, and then to *lift out* the most precious elements, replacing them with less expensive substances. The mechanical invention was coupled with a chemical process, devised by Coenraad Johannes, which treated the cocoa mass with alkaline salts. This latter innovation – known as the 'Dutch process' – increased the solubility of the powder, enabling it to be more easily combined with water or milk.

The physical act of substitution was achieved separately to that of extraction. In 1847, the prominent Bristol-based chocolate makers J.S. Fry & Sons – who in 1795 had acquired that emblematic technology of the first industrial revolution, a Boulton and Watt steam engine, for use in their factory – discovered a method of returning fat (along with sugar) to the dry cocoa solids.[5] This momentous discovery excavated a double-opening, at once creating the first truly modern chocolate bar – their 'chocolate *delicieux a manger*' – and the means by which such chocolate would come to be maltreated. Though prior to this moment certain types of chocolate may have been considered inferior as a direct result of the quality of the cacao used in its production, the moment of substitution was what ultimately opened up chocolate to the possibility of abuse in the manufacturing process itself, the possibility for the creation of what we might call 'artificial chocolate'. This is because, although Fry's method would initially have re-imparted a proportion of the previously extracted cacao butter, it almost immediately acquired a second function, that of replacing the valuable butter with cheaper fats. The good news was that chocolate could now achieve a palatable ratio of fat without resorting to additives. The adulteration of chocolate with absorbent starches to soak up cacao's oily residue, which had been common practice – even our beloved Cadbury contained sago or potato flour, while less morally virtuous manufacturers used brick dust, iron filings, and lead[6] – was no longer necessary. The bad news: this form of adulteration nonetheless continued in shady corners of the market, whilst another, the use of vegetable and even animal fats as cacao butter replacements, ensued.

For chocolate – one of the many industries beginning to thrive under liberal European governments – the processes of division, extraction and substitution had altered its product from one made up of cacao and a variety of other ingredients, to one consisting of a quantity of unspecified 'cocoa solids' varying in relation to the proportion of fats, milk solids and sugar.

In terms of value, Fry's discovery represented the first shift in the focus of consumer judgements and marketing strategies concerning chocolate's quality and appeal onto considerations of the chocolate itself (in particular, the nature of its processing) rather than its agricultural beginnings. The consumer at this point abandoned the art of preparation so prized by previous cultures, forgoing their direct involvement in even the final flourishes of the productive process.

SUPPLY AND DEMAND – THE ASYMMETRY OF THE CACAO MARKET

The interwoven fabric of cacao and chocolate's at once physical and cultural entry into European society demonstrates that the value of a commodity depends upon an integration of supply and demand-side models. We can claim that supply must come 'first', in that there can be no demand for a product that does not exist. Yet the economist would likely say that a product supplied but unwanted is not a commodity so much as it is a vanity project. And likewise we might say that demand is most 'fundamental', but then again there are many desires which go unrequited, and these are not commodities either but dreams, utopias, fantasies. Neither demand nor supply alone can attribute commodity value; it is only the interaction of the two which has this capacity.

THE SUPPLY OF CACAO

From the golden age of colonialism to the present, the wellsprings of cacao have migrated dramatically. *Theobroma Cacao* has been transplanted, with varying degrees of success, to parts of the world other than its Amazonian origins. However, the changes are bridged by an overarching continuity: cacao's supply has, at each pause in its travels, remained highly concentrated, even if the site of the concentration has changed. To give the journey a general schema: for the sixteenth and seventeenth centuries, cacao production was dominated by the Amazon region; for much of the eighteenth and nineteenth centuries by colonial powers in South America and the Caribbean more widely – including the Portuguese in Brazil and the Dutch in Venezuela; and for the twentieth and nascent twenty-first centuries, by West Africa.

According to the estimations of the International Cocoa Organization (ICCO), 72 per cent of the world's cacao production for the season 2013/14 was supplied by African plantations, with just 16 per cent coming from the former hub of Latin America, and the remainder from Asia and Oceania.[7] The title of the world's greatest cacao-producing nation, having been held by São Tomé and Príncipe in the mid-nineteenth century, passed to Ghana, and then, by the 1980s, to the Côte D'Ivoire, which by the end of the millennium was consistently yielding over one million tons each year.[8] This sort of concentration is on its own a matter for only minor concern, and would usually be more of an issue for the economies of those countries excluded from the concentration in question. However, it is when three appendages are added that the situation becomes more worrisome for West Africa itself.

First of all, cacao's fussiness and vulnerability translates into a commodity characterized by frequent supply-side shocks. The unidentified 'blast' which struck the Trinidadian plantations in 1727 is just one of many similar incidents by which whole harvests have been destroyed. As well as diseases, especially 'witches' broom' (*Crinipellis perniciosa*) – so called because it develops when organisms alter the internal structure of the tree, causing it to sprout dense clumps of branches from the same spot – and 'pod rot' – a fungal infection responsible for much of the irreparable damage to tropical American plantations in recent decades – *Theobroma cacao* may be affected by pests such as mirids (small mosquito-like insects), and by adverse climatic conditions of both an acute and a chronic kind.[9] With regard to the factor of climate, supply in West Africa is rendered a more serious issue because of certain weather episodes that affect the region. The Harmattan trade winds, which plague the winter months with dry and dusty air blown north from the Sahara, can have severe impacts upon the moisture-reliant crop, as can the unusually high temperatures brought about by the El Niño effect.

The volatility of cacao production is given a general model, that of the 'cocoa cycle'. Much like the parallel economic cycle, this theory is premised on the notion of a regular pattern of boom and bust. In a given region, production can grow at a rapid pace, but after a certain time tends to plateau, before falling into crisis. It is wise to be wary of models, for to give something the reassuring structure of a model has a dangerous naturalizing tendency. In other words, the second half of the model – crisis – is only inevitable because of the way in which the initial surge is conducted. The demanding nature of *Theobroma Cacao* presents a challenge to agriculture. Because it grows much more easily – as do many other crops – on virgin soil (that which has not been previously cultivated) it is difficult to sustain the yield of the peak harvest in following years. But there can be different responses to this challenge: either the land is handled carefully, with a view to maintaining a lower but more stable yield over the long-run, or it is intensively farmed, pushing out as high a yield as is possible for each harvest until its nutrients are eroded. In the latter case, cacao goes hand in hand with expansionism as a system of accumulation, a dramatic departure from the cyclical attitudes of subsistence in traditional agrarian societies. Life does not arise from death anymore as it did for the Aztecs. Rather, life is piled on top of life. Death is postponed for as long as possible and, when it can be postponed no longer; when death bursts the seams of life, is abandoned, left behind. The accumulation of life simply begins again somewhere else. The temptation to exploit and abandon in this way has proven especially strong in West Africa, where there has usually been an abundance of 'idle' land onto which to expand. Unsurprisingly, this abundance did not last long. Since the late twentieth century, virgin soil has been in increasingly short supply, and many West African governments, including that of the Côte D'Ivoire, have reversed their expansionist policies.[10] But while expansion has slowed, the expectations of consumers have not, and these expectations continue to impart huge pressures on the environment. Despite the policy reversal therefore, deforestation rates in the Côte D'Ivoire remain high. Between 1990 and 2007, the country is said to have lost on average more than three per cent of its forested area every year, contributing to ever-faster rates of soil erosion.[11] Our second troubling appendage is the extent to which farming communities in the main African cacao-growing nations are dependent upon the undependable crop. In contrast to the cocoa industry, cacao continues to resist the grand mechanized structures and technologies of large scale agri-business. The French word spoken in West Africa to describe the farms, *plantation*, misleads us here by its association in English with dramatic expanses of sugarcane patrolled by countless toiling bodies. In fact, approximately 85 per cent of global supply is harvested from family-run smallholdings, and the majority of West African cacao farms measure just three to four hectares in size.[12] Across these many smallholdings, the World Cocoa Foundation (WCF) has put the number of cacao farmers worldwide to be between 5 and 6 million. This does not seem a large number considering the scale of the industry, but given that in many cases the money earned by these farmers will account for over half of their household's income, and that these households are often large, it is estimated that this equates to 40 to 50 million people reliant on the crop for their livelihoods.[13] This time around, the natural preferences of *T. Cacao* can potentially be of help. Whilst many crops crave sunlight, cacao requires shade and shelter. In the wild, it nestles beneath other larger trees. It is therefore what we might call a social plant, and it encourages its farmers to create a diverse multi-culture. Ideally, this leads to security by allowing cacao farmers to benefit from the best of both worlds: accessing the cash flow of global commodities markets with an export crop while securing immediate needs with a food staple. However, cacao can often get its shelter from another export crop. Wild oil palm, for instance, has proven a successful cohabiter of cacao smallholdings.[14] This still diversifies the farmer's portfolio, but leaves them with a diversity that is nonetheless wholly dependent on the global market.

The third concern follows from the stark divide between supply and demand; the fact that there is little overlap between the extremities of the value chain. The divide is both structural and geographical. In contrast to the instability of the supply laid out above, the demand-side of cacao tends to be relatively reliable. Though it suffers small fluctuations in the short term according with price and the current economic climate, it is in the long-run characterized by steady growth. Demand for cocoa products has grown steadily over the past decades, and the Fairtrade Foundation predicted back in 2011 that there would be a further 30 per cent expansion by 2020.[15] It is precisely the contrast between this stability and the unpredictable nature of supply which constitutes the issue. The names of continents affected by the unstable side of the market are notably absent from the list of chocolate's primary consumers. In 2011/12, Europe accounted for around 46 per cent of world consumption, with North America ingesting 24 per cent. The only exception is the Asia-Oceania region, which appeared as a producer above, and is third on the consumer list with 16 per cent of the global total.[16] Being so far removed from the sources of cacao, consumers have little concept of the difficulties of its production. Having grown accustomed to the high yields of the boom years, they are therefore struggling to come to terms with the bust.

Africa consumes very little of its own export, a mere 4 per cent of the global sum.[17] Cacao is by no means a unique commodity in this respect. Rather, it is one of a number of agricultural export industries established by the African 'cash crop revolution' of the late nineteenth and early twentieth centuries. Ghana's experience of the revolution warns of the risks of the cash crop. The entrance of Ghana – then the British territory of the Gold Coast – into the global industry was extremely rapid, going from a country which exported no cacao at all in 1892 to the largest supplier in the world just nineteen years later.[18]

Some of this expansion was made on the initiative of the farmers themselves but, once all the suitable land was occupied, the colonial administration incentivized further planting on less appropriate plots. The nation's dominance was short-lived: by the 1930s, the cacao crop had peaked and began to stagnate.[19] It is likely that one factor compromising the longevity of the success was the very rapidity of it: an intensive expansion which spared no time for soil to recover or for careful replanting on old plots. Here there is a connection between the third and the first appendages: the way in which the relation between the markets was conducted – in the manner of coercive pressure imposed on producers by the colonial consumer – led to the creation of a deeply unsustainable industry.

In this sense cacao as a cash crop bridges the colonial and post-colonial eras, the transition from an imperial to a humanitarian framework as the mediating paradigm for the relationship between cacao and chocolate; supply and demand; West Africa and the West. The humanitarian framework is an alloy of trade and aid, of charitable aims and neoliberal methods. Thus, while development programmes emphasize education as a way of fostering independence, in West Africa the lessons are often focused on developing farming best practice and efficiency in the production of cacao and other export crops. They look to ensure quality, increase yields, but most crucially to establish the sustainability of the crop. This may well be to the benefit of West African farmers, but a large part of the impetus and funding for such charitable enterprises derives from the fact that they are also beneficial to European and American buyers; from the fact that the sustainability of cacao (a crop) means the sustainability of cocoa (an industry).

Building resilience to pests and diseases has grown to be a priority within this framework. The failure to contain such scourges has been a common factor in the cacao crises of West African nations. For instance, after overtaking its neighbours once more to become the world's largest producer in the middle decades of the twentieth century, Ghana's cacao crop fell to ruin due to the combined effect of mirids and 'swollen root' disease. The crisis was in fact of a political origin, the corrosive effect of another gnawing pest, that of corruption.

Under colonial rule, cacao farmers in the Gold Coast had accused the agents of international exporters – including those employed by Cadbury – of fixing prices at artificially low levels. The socialist Nkrumah government that had led the country to independence in 1957 looked to clamp down on this rogue activity by giving the state-owned Cocoa Marketing Board ('Cocobod') the power to act as smallholder representatives, but this, as it turned out, was the spider swallowed to consume the fly. Taxation of farmers was high and, when world prices for cocoa fell during the 1960s, Ghanaian smallholders had to cope not only with the direct impact of this external factor but also with the fact that Cocobod, unwilling to take an equal haircut (let alone to absorb some of the losses as might have been considered their duty) reduced the share of revenues doled out to farmers.[20] By 1979, when a *coup d'etat* was staged by the Armed Forces Revolutionary Council, suspiciously wealthy Cocobod managers were the ones facing accusations of skimming more than a little off the top.[21] These consecutive episodes of corruption meant that scarce money was made available for investment in extension services. Without either effective farm management or new planting, cacao trees grew old and fragile, with each crop more susceptible to diseases which their farmers did not have the means to protect them from.

Given that this was a political as well as an economic problem, it was fitting that the solution should be of a similar inclination. From the 1980s onwards, international agencies like the International Monetary Fund (IMF) and the World Bank stepped into the vacuum left by inadequate local authorities not only in Ghana, but throughout sub-Saharan Africa. They were short of neither advice for farmers on how to protect their crops, nor cash to facilitate its implementation. The capital offered was in the form of loans rather than grants, and these loans were conditional on the recipient's participation in programmes of structural adjustment. The IMF and World Bank issued 378 of these loans between 1975 and 1990, aiding 71 countries on the condition that they would adopt the preferred neoliberal market ideology.[22] For the cocoa-producing nations of West Africa, adjustment tended to mean the abolition of national marketing boards and so the full subjection of cacao producers to the vagaries of the global price.

CORPORATE RESPONSIBILITY AND THE CACAO TRADE: ETHICS OR ADVERTIZING?

The ability to specialize the functions of the commodity and its labourer helped to engender the mammoth transitions of power which took place during the nineteenth and twentieth centuries. The extraction of cacao butter allowed for the medicinal and culinary merits of cacao to be divided into two specialized products. Colonial merchant enterprises initially benefitted from the division: the Jesuits for one stocked their mission *boticas* (pharmacies), as far afield as Goa in Portuguese India, with cacao butter, selling it as a remedy for shingles.[23] But the two products were rapidly aligned with two separate industries, and industrialization as such spelt the end of the road for Baroque enterprises like the Society of Jesus. The Jesuits suffered persecution from the middle of the eighteenth century onwards, and the order was officially dissolved in 1773.[24] The new force, coming to the fore via the turmoil of social unrest in Enlightenment Europe, was the capitalist bourgeoisie, a professional class of entrepreneurs tuned to the management of labour processes. Iconic to this groundswell was a revolution in political thought: the radical voices of the French Revolution's *philosophes* (including Voltaire, a chocolate-lover himself). But in England, a nation already – as Adam Smith had proclaimed before Napoleon more famously spoke – 'governed by shopkeepers', it was another society: the Society of Friends, the Quakers, whom spearheaded the industrial transformation.

The Quaker model of business taught that the basis of every successful enterprise should be the principle to avoid biting off more than one could chew, and that wealth should be spread, not accumulated. As befits the Quaker philosophy of plain living, industry should be pursued only so far as it produces necessary goods, and certainly not for the love of the money that it may give rise to. A number of the most influential British chocolate manufacturers, including York's Joseph Rowntree, and Bristol's Joseph Fry, were

Quaker capitalists. Most famously, on Birmingham's Crooked Lane in 1831, John Cadbury set up his factory in the hope that chocolate, still an unknown quantity to most, could capture the imagination of the British public. The Cadbury business started promisingly, benefiting from the relative novelty of the mysterious product to the masses, as well as from its position as official supplier to Queen Victoria. But by the mid-1800s this novelty had worn off, tea was finding its place as a stalwart of British identity, and Cadbury was in a grave financial state.[25] Effective control of the factory at this point was handed down from John to his two sons Richard and George. In terms of the chocolate itself, the Cadbury brothers were able to profit from its division and multiplication. After their acquisition of the van Houten defatting machine, they diversified their enterprise with the release, in 1866, of Cocoa Essence: Cadbury's first cocoa powder. But this would not be enough by itself. The struggling demand for chocolate was also associated with two counts of immoral repute: on the one hand, the frequent adulterations of the product, and on the other, the enslavement of its farmers. The resurrection of chocolate's appeal would therefore not have been possible without the ethical work of its manufacturers.

The Quaker families had long been heavily involved in social activism, the Cadbury's in particular with their mission to lift the residents of Birmingham's slum districts out of destitution.[26] However, the most important ethical mediator of chocolate was Richard's son William, who took a frontline role in fighting the lingering remnants of slavery in the colonial cacao trade. As a member of the British and Foreign Anti-Slavery Society, there were numerous instances to be struggled against, but the labour contracts of Portuguese São Tomé and Príncipe were of particular concern to William since, until now, over half of his factory's cacao had been imported from the islands. Cadbury funded trips to Lisbon and the colonies to inspect the operations and interrogate its officials. Notably, he was part of the quartet of chocolate makers – alongside the Frys, Rowntrees, and the German company Stallwerk – that assigned fellow Quaker Dr Joseph Burtt to the case in 1905. This lead to the publishing of a report which was extremely influential in raising awareness of the trade's corruption, and which by 1909 had pressured all major English manufacturers to boycott its proceeds.[27] The reputation which this achieved for the company gave Cadbury's chocolate an appeal which remains today. It was, as such, a form of advertizing; the construction of a desirable image. In the liberal capitalist period, advertizing as a medium of communication supplemented the 'word-of-mouth' transfer of information which had spread the popularity of chocolate among the Baroque nobility.

Advertizing looked to purify chocolate not only in moral terms but also with regards to health. It sought to delegitimize the competitors by exposing the adulteration of their products. Cadbury thus heavily publicized their adherence to the first UK food standards regulations, established in 1860 as The Adulteration of Food and Drugs Act, to expose the non-adherence of others. This new approach was summed up in their newly-devised slogan: 'Absolutely Pure, Therefore Best', tying quality explicitly to the ideal of purity. The company was active in pressuring the government into further regulatory steps over the following decades, leading eventually to the inscription in law of a now very familiar phenomenon: the obligation to list the ingredients of a product upon its packaging. Other chocolate manufacturers were caught on the back foot by the shift in emphasis, scrabbling to clean up their supply chains so that they could match Cadbury's pledge.

This method of advertizing is now part-and-parcel of the message of 'corporate responsibility' necessary for the success of the modern Transnational Corporation (TNC). According to the WCF, the chocolate industry has invested around $75 million over the past decade to improve the conditions under which their cacao is grown and harvested.[28] In addition to increasing resilience and productivity, the focus of this investment is on eradicating forced labour practices, particularly those that employ minors.

In sub-Saharan Africa one in every four children between the ages of five and seventeen are in work.[29] As well as making school attendance difficult, this labour is often hazardous. Cacao farming, still a low-tech, physically intensive industry, takes its toll on the body, and harvesting is often carried out using machetes or even chainsaws. The development programmes usually come in the form of public-private partnerships (PPPs) between national governments, inter-governmental and non-governmental organizations (NGOs), and the chief global corporations of the sector. The WCF's Cocoa Livelihoods Program – a four year project that was responsible for the training of around 106,000 farmers between 2009 and 2013 – its African Cocoa Initiative – running from 2011 until 2016, with a focus on sustainable productivity growth – and the International Labour Organization's (ILO) project to eradicate child labour from the cocoa industries of Ghana and the Côte d'Ivoire, have all taken this collaborative approach, while the giant corporations themselves employ organizations such as the ILO and the Bill and Melinda Gates Foundation to monitor their practices. However, slavery's definition is by no means stable, and, as in the aftermath of colonial slavery's formal abolition, it has changed its appearance once more. It is now even more subtly disguised. There are, for one thing, no physical shackles to be broken. Furthermore, the smallholder culture makes the ethics of cacao farming especially murky. Not only is it difficult in practice to regulate such a great number of individual farms; the legal status of smallholders, often categorized as self-employed or informal labourers, also makes things problematic on a theoretical level. When the Cote D'Ivoire outlawed the employment of under-fourteens in 1995 for instance, this applied only to the formal business sector.[30] Likewise, when children are forced to work on farms owned by members of their own families, the point at which this should be considered child labour is still under debate.

Vanquishing child labour is framed by the language of human rights, but improving working conditions is also crucial for the industry. Faced with the push of low pay and exploitation on the plantations, versus the pull of opportunity – the so-called 'bright lights' of the city – more and more young West Africans have been choosing urban over rural life. As a result, the industry itself is at risk: while demand for cocoa grows, the suppliers of cacao grow old and frail. Along with the ageing trees come ageing farmers: the average age of the West African cacao grower is now over 50.[31] Humanitarianism and international development set out to communicate a particular message, but the centrality of communication; of raising awareness, to their initiatives is such that the message is at constant risk of being subordinated to the medium. The Fairtrade Foundation is a case in point. Fairtrade originated as an informal movement among coffee farmers in the late 1980s, and was institutionalized in 1997 with the formation of the Fairtrade Labelling Organization (FLO). The first cacao growers to apply for recognition from Fairtrade were a Ghanaian farmer co-op, Kuapa Kokoo. In 1998, alongside the British alternative trading group Twin Trading, Kuapa Kokoo went on to found the Day Chocolate Company (now Divine), and has since been adopted as Cadbury's Fairtrade supplier.

Fairtrade's ambition must be to raise awareness for its products so that there is higher demand for Fairtrade beans, equating in theory to a higher return for farmers. But the humanitarian stage is a crowded one: competition for the attentions of the Western public, and the contents of their wallets, is fierce. The consequence of these scarcities, according to Lilie Chouliaraki, is that the aid and development sector has undergone a process of marketization.[32] The imperative to be heard above the rabble has necessitated that organizations like Fairtrade make use of all the promotional tools available to them, from social media to celebrity advocacy. The Divine annual report for 2013/14 for instance promotes its activities with the aid of a celebrity ambassador:

> Star of reality show *Made in Chelsea*, Cheska Hull, visited Kuapa with the Fairtrade Foundation and Divine and her trip was covered in *Good Housekeeping* and *Hello!*, helping to introduce us to their audiences. Cheska tweeted about her trip to 306,000 followers.[33]

Cheska Hull is not the first celebrity ambassador to visit the Kuapa Kokoo cooperative – Chris Martin made an appearance on behalf of Oxfam in 2005[34] – and in many ways these individuals are seen as necessary representatives of cacao farmers, using their global following to attract attention to the issues residing at the base of the chocolate industry. However, the danger that always lurks in representation – that the voice of the person or thing being represented is drowned out rather than being amplified – is intensified by the fact that the representative is a celebrity. Even as they try to focus the world's attentions on cacao farmers, it is precisely the celebrity's fame and glamour that risks simplifying, even beautifying, the image of the industry, drawing our attentions away from the complex issues that affect its participants.

A similar conundrum faces Fairtrade itself. When Órla Ryan asked a Cadbury's representative, Alison Ward, why Fairtrade was the chosen vessel for the company's investment, she replied by referring to the brand power of that name.[35] This is not particularly shocking: the ability of a strong brand – like a famed celebrity – to communicate instantaneously with a large number of consumers by the evocation of a single word or image gives it budding potential as a tool for spreading awareness. And yet the fact that Ward did not feel the need to refer instead to the particular values and practices underlying Fairtrade reveals the hazardous implications of the humanitarian brand. In short, the more powerful the Fairtrade logo, the easier it is for consumers – as well as investors such as Cadbury – to buy (into) the brand, and the chocolate bars on which it is stamped, without feeling it necessary to consider the ethical principles of production which that brand claims to stand for. The mass appeal of Fairtrade chocolate lies precisely in the fact that one does not need to envelop oneself in the murky world of ethical choices in order to be ethical.

UNCERTAIN FUTURES: CACAO AND THE GLOBAL COMMODITIES MARKETS

Given the various 'blasts' which may destabilize the crop, producers of cacao seek stability by participating in the larger marketplace. This is the same stability as that which was sought by maritime traders in the 1700s. The voyages they undertook to source commodities were often long and treacherous, so sailors wanted a guarantee that what they brought home would be purchased for a reasonable price. To provide this guarantee, buyers established forward contracts which arranged for the acquisition of a quantity of the traders' goods at a pre-agreed price. This was a 'futures price', a prediction of what the price of a commodity would be in a certain period of time. Fittingly, in England the value of these contracts was determined by the congregation of buyers in London's coffee and chocolate houses, where, standing in a circle, they would shout their predictions until an average value was reached.[36] This method of agreeing futures prices, known as 'open outcry', still operates on certain commodities markets.

What forward contracts mean for farmers is that, rather than growing, harvesting, and then selling the resultant crop to the market – before apportioning the revenue to other labourers, the maintenance of equipment, etc. – they are able not only to count but also to sell their chickens before they've hatched. As with the possibility of spreading growth across a diversity of crops, a cacao farmer could minimize risk by hedging: selling only a proportion of their expected harvest on a forward contract, then waiting for the crop to materialize before selling the rest for the current ('spot') price. This way, if the price of the commodity had fallen lower than predicted by the time of the harvest, the farmer would gain back on the forward contract some of the losses they suffered on the spot price, while if the price had increased higher than predicted, the farmer could still benefit from 'discovering' this higher value.[37]

However, the smallholder complex of cacao production makes the use of hedging more difficult. Individual farmers do not have the collective bargaining power needed to negotiate directly with the international traders and manufacturers, so their crop must be entrusted to middlemen. These middlemen vary depending upon the extent to which the market is liberalized. Thus in Ghana, farmers sell their harvest to the state-owned Cocobod buying centres in the local community, where it is weighed, graded, and paid for at a fixed price decided by the government. From here it is sold onto the Cocoa Marketing Company (another Cocobod-operated organization), who in turn export it to cocoa grinders and chocolate manufacturers around the world.[38] This government regulated buying chain contrasts with the more free-market model of Ghana's neighbour, Côte D'Ivoire. Here, rather than nationally-owned bodies, the crop is sold to private agents known as *pisteurs* who, along with the next link in the chain, the *traitants* (middlemen), are under the employ of the large exporters.

In free market systems where prices are not fixed, middlemen will try to ensure a relatively stable spot price by restricting the supply of beans. This is facilitated by buffer stocks, which in periods of over-supply (such as that faced by the cocoa industry for much of the latter half of the twentieth century) take up as much of the excess cacao production as possible, releasing it again when yields fall back to an acceptable level.

This is one approach to abundance and glut, a situation which, throughout the history of the traded commodity, has caused just as much, if not more panic than scarcity. For though economics is indeed the science of distributing scarce goods, what the text books curiously omit is that, if this scarcity had not naturally existed, it would have been found necessary to invent it.

In the East Indies during the seventeenth century for instance, merchants of the Dutch East India Company frequently found that the Indonesian Moluccas – the Spice Islands, as they were known - contained more spice than was convenient. Throughout the 1620s, on the urgent instructions of the Company's directors, the Dutch governors of the archipelago burned tens of thousands of clove trees to the ground, later repeating the trick with nutmeg in the Banda islands to the south.[39] The air must have been soaked with the perfumed stench of the crime; the 'invisible hand' of the arsonist correcting the economic naivety of the land. But this is not a strategy reserved for mercantilist greed. It is a modern practice. In 1887 the accessibility of sugar to North American households, approaching a dangerously non-profitable state due to improvements in transportation, was brought under control by The Sugar Trust, an oligopolistic union of eight large refinery companies who kept the price sufficiently high by colluding on production levels. And, even more dramatically, in 1931 the Governor of the State of Oklahoma declared martial law in order to forcibly prevent the overproduction of another dark and luxurious substance:

oil.[40] By artificially restricting the supply of cacao, buffer stocks perform a function that is similar to, if not quite so dramatic as, these interventions. The 'synthetic scarcities'[41] they create facilitate insurance, stability, yes; but they also facilitate control. Those who control the stocks have the last say on cacao's supply. They can employ them as a means of hording; of creating the impression of greater scarcity than actually exists. This can work to the advantage of producers. When OPEC restricted the output of oil in 1973-4, causing a dramatic price hike, it raised hopes among other developing nations that they might use their position at the start of the value chain to negotiate a better deal for themselves. However, the difference with cacao is that control of the crop is not in the hands of those that produce it. Given their lack of both unionisation and any means to warehouse beans for long periods, smallholders themselves are unable to withhold supply. It is only the middlemen – the cocoa industry buyers, grinders, and manufacturers – who are able to influence the market in this way.

While the WCF estimates the production of the cocoa industry to be worth around $12 billion annually, the volatility of that production is worth even more. The trading of cacao futures contracts has become a more profitable enterprise than the production which those contracts were drawn up to guarantee. In the midst of cacao's long value chain is the financial commodities market, connecting smallholders not only with our supermarket shelves but with the City of London and Wall Street. In 1925, cacao varieties were graded so that they could provide two stable standards for the trading of cocoa futures. These futures are now bought and sold – along with a number of other 'soft' commodities (those which are grown, as opposed to mined) – on the InterContinental Exchange (ICE), which determines the price of the average cocoa contract: the amount in US Dollars for which ten metric tons of cocoa is purchased. Together with the commercial traders that purchase cocoa futures contracts with the intention to buy the cocoa itself and turn it into, say, a chocolate bar, the financial markets also host non-commercial speculators that, beyond the return they might get from betting correctly on the direction of cocoa's value, have no long-term commitment to the crop. The interest of this particular middle man lies therefore not in maintaining a certain, stable, value or price – the high price favoured by producers or the low price favoured by consumers – but on predicting instability. Their section of the market deals only in the notional realities and values of commodities yet to be produced, yet to be *made real*. The scale of this notional activity is suggested by the fact that only a very small proportion of futures trading – sometimes as little as two per cent – ends with the physical transfer of cacao.

While the financial markets provide welcome liquidity to the cocoa industry, speculation can come at the cost of increased price volatility. In contrast to the Quaker model founded on aversion to the vices of risk and debt, the financial model is based on profiting from those very same vices. It bets on the outcome of future crops. Given the range of factors which can affect these crops, this is a bet on the weather, on disease, on conflict, and many other futures besides.

Consequently the futures market can at times throw up strange augmentations. If one looks at a graph of global cocoa prices for the year 2014, for example, you will notice a sharp price spike for the month of September, from around $3000 per ton to almost $3400 per ton, and back. As a number of economic journalists observed, it is no coincidence that this is the same month when the West African Ebola outbreak took on the prospect of a full-blown epidemic.[42] The disease had originated in Guinea, and had begun to spread like wildfire across Sierra Leone and Liberia, leaving thousands dead. At this point there seemed a considerable chance that Ebola would continue to expand its grip on the region, continuing into the Côte d'Ivoire and other prime cacao-producing regions. Speculating on this macabre possibility, which, given the high fatality rates, would have caused a decimation of the labour supply on almost the scale (and at an even faster rate) of that which occurred in Mesoamerica four centuries earlier, cacao buyers frantically bought up stock to bolster their stocks, thus driving a surge in demand which pushed up the commodity price to a level almost twenty per cent higher than the previous year. Despite the fact that these predictions turned out to be false – Ebola did not get as far as Côte d'Ivoire on any significant magnitude – the market acted according to them, causing a distortion in cacao's value with the result of intense short-term volatility.

The problem is that speculation is not merely speculative. As well as being in some sense detached from reality, it is in another way all too attached to it. It suffers from an unhealthy concoction of anxiety and the observer effect. That is, it makes the events which it predicts come to pass.

Expressing the gravity of speculation's impact on the commodity today is not easy because we are by now so accustomed to the language of credit and debt. It is therefore helpful to put ourselves in the position of the first industrialists – the Quakers in particular – for whom the potential of credit still rung alarm bells. As the moment of payment was pushed further and further into the future, an ever-longer period of uncertainty opened up. And within this period, the value of the product in question was indeterminable. In the words of the economic historian James Thompson, 'disturbing new forms of paper money provoked a semiological crisis over the concept of value.'[43] This rupture of semiotics manifested itself in the distancing of the signifier from the signified value of the commodity. In other words, price bore increasingly less relation to the present value of the good in question, relocating value itself to an entirely different characteristic of the object under consideration, to its potential. This relocation is achieved precisely by the anxious logic of the signifier; the paranoid proximity of the speculator to its object. He is too close, too preoccupied – constantly forecasting and pre-empting – to register and react to events as they unfold.

In view of the long-term supply deficit, forecasts indicate that the price of cocoa is likely to rise in the coming years. In another world, this would constitute a seller's market, but, by virtue of the power relations of the industry's value chain, it is the middlemen who hold the greatest influence.

Cadbury has, ultimately, always been one of these middlemen, but the end of the Quaker model, even if already surpassed in practice, was heralded symbolically by the most spectacular demonstration yet of financial sway in the chocolate industry: the hostile takeover of

Cadbury by Kraft Foods in 2009/2010. Cadbury, together with the other British Quaker chocolate firms, had been threatened by financial aggression from larger corporations for the past three decades. Market predators employed almost every trick in the book to take control of the companies from under the noses of their current management. In 1988, for instance, a 'dawn raid' – the tactic of buying a significant proportion of another company's shares first thing in the morning, immediately after the stock markets have opened – was made on Rowntree by the Swiss-German Jacobs Suchard, acquiring fifteen per cent of the company on one April morning. The covert move started a bidding war with Nestlé, eventually ending, late in 1988, with the pure Swiss coming out on top.[44] This set the tone for an era in which, prior to its takeover of Cadbury, Kraft absorbed (in 1993) the York company Terry's. What matters here is not the fact that these were friendly British companies being gobbled up by heartless global giants – Cadbury's was, at the time of its consumption, no minnow, with branches in India and China, and had itself captured J.S. Fry & Sons in 1919. The significant point is that, across the confectionary sector and the food and drinks market in general, predators were being snapped up by, or were merging with, other predators, even higher up the food chain. Since their takeover of Cadbury, Kraft have expanded even further, spinning out their food division from the main company so that it could merge with Heinz in July 2015 – forming the Kraft Heinz Company, the fifth largest food producer in the world[45] – while the division responsible for snacks and confectionary now goes under the name Mondelēz International.

The repetition of manoeuvres of this kind across the industry has led to an increasingly concentrated centre of power, a select group of apex predators. But this concentration is also increasingly being funded and managed by speculative stakeholders. The £11.7 billion deal which eventually secured the sale of Cadbury was accepted by a 71 per cent majority of Cadbury's shareholders. The problem is that this statistic was representative of only an ephemeral majority, a fleeting commitment that was itself not necessarily fit to mediate the value of the company. The majority consisted largely of short-term shareholders rather than long-term investors, mindful only of the quick buck to be made, and with scant regard for the history, the quality, or the morality of the product. By the end of the saga, in early 2010, nearly a third of Cadbury was owned by hedge funds, the managers of which showed their indifference by standing idle as Kraft crossed a supposed red line of the deal, closing down the Somerdale factory near Bristol (the historic home of Fry's), eliminating 400 jobs in the process.[46]

THE VALUE OF CHOCOLATE, THE VALUE OF CACAO?

In 1988, the total global consumption of cocoa stood at 2,015,100 metric tons. At the time, this figure was less than one tenth of the quantity of cacao exported worldwide in the form of beans and cocoa products, which stood at roughly 24,605,000.[47]

The cocoa industry has quickly turned from a market trying to deal agitatedly with the burden of glut to one looking fearfully towards the hovering spectre of a structural supply deficit. Supply for the growing season of 2014/15 was expected to fall approximately 100,000 tonnes short of demand, and the largest manufacturers are full of woeful foreboding. Barry Callebaut, the world's largest chocolate producer (with a 40 per cent market share as of 2012[48]), has cautioned that stores are fast being depleted, while Mars. Inc. has predicted the deficit to grow by a factor of ten by 2020.[49] In the opinion of the ICCO however, chocolate producers are exaggerating the shortfall. They estimate that, though supply deficits may be experienced over the coming few years, the resultant higher price for cocoa will incentivise and fund productivity growth in the long-run.[50] Either outcome is possible. While it is likely that chocolate producers are amplifying the scale of the issue in order to prepare consumers for higher prices, for the alternative, best case scenario to be realised requires that farmers themselves, rather than just manufacturers like Mars, get a return for the present scarcity.

The new problem emanates from the contrasting fortunes of the two sides of the market, whereby supply is concentrated and unstable, while demand is steadily growing and increasingly diverse.

Though parts of Asia and the Pacific, notably Malaysia and Indonesia, represent the best current hope for the supply-side, the mammoth growth in demand from another Asian nation, China, will likely only exacerbate the imbalance in demand in coming decades. It is hoped that 'productivity' and 'sustainability' will provide the answers, but where these have the tendency to be buzzwords one must accept that these terms can both elucidate and veil what is actually going on.

There is a more fundamental problem which must be addressed if these words, and the ICCOs optimism, are to mean anything: the structure of the value chain itself. As cacao has been divided up into fractions, brought under a variety of complex industrial, scientific and financial procedures, the mediation of its value has been reallocated to the agents in control of these processes. Furthermore, the determination of quality rests in the hands of an increasingly powerful few. This model is not a conventional oligopoly – it does not take power from the consumer and hand it to the producer. Influence gravitates towards the centre, sucked inwards like interstellar dust into a black hole. As such, it is possible that a rise in the price of cacao would hit the pockets of both consumer and producer, without those of the middlemen – the shareholders and traders – being any less well-lined.

WEST AFRICAN COCOA-ROAST COD, PEANUT SOUP, SWEET PEPPERS

Dishes across West Africa use the combination of tomatoes, onion, and the fire of the scotch bonnet pepper as the base of their sauces. Peanut soup is a particularly popular variation. and its sweetness is paired here with a heat from the spices, and the saltiness of the anchovies coating slippery peppers.

For the peppers
10-12 small sweet peppers
3 anchovy fillets, chopped
1 tbsp olive oil

Toss the peppers in the anchovy and olive oil, then arrange in an oven dish and roast for 30 minutes at 180°C. Remove from the oven, cover tightly with cling film and leave to sweat until you are ready to serve.

For the peanut soup
4 cloves of garlic, chopped
1 large onion, chopped
1 scotch bonnet chilli, finely chopped
1 tsp dried shrimp (optional)
400 ml / 14 fluid oz vegetable stock
6 tomatoes
2 tbsp crunchy peanut butter

Fry the onion for a few minutes, then add the garlic, the shrimp, and the chilli, cooking until the onion is translucent. Add the tomatoes, vegetable stock and peanut butter and simmer for 10-15 minutes.

For the cod
4 sustainably sourced cod fillets
2 tbsp black onion seeds
2 tbsp mustard seeds
1 tbsp good quality natural cocoa powder
2 tsp cayenne pepper
2 tsp salt
1 tsp caster sugar
1 tbsp red pepper paste
1 tbsp olive oil

Lightly toast all the spices (excluding the cocoa powder) in a hot pan for a few minutes, until the pungent aroma hits your nostrils, then transfer to a mortar along with the cocoa powder, salt and sugar, pounding to break down the seeds and combine. Add the oil and red pepper paste, mix, and then coat the cod.

Leave half an hour for the spices to permeate the fish, then place in an oven at 180°C for 15-20 minutes.

Remove the cod from the oven and serve in a shallow bowl, ladling the soup around the fish and finishing with the whole peppers.

SPICED SWEET POTATO AND CHOCOLATE CAKE, CHOCOLATE AND GINGER GLAZE

The sweet potato is one of the most important crops in Africa, and unlike cacao, it is grown for domestic, as well as foreign consumption. The continent as a whole accounts for over 95 per cent of global production, and the top three producing nations – Nigeria, Ghana, and Côte d'Ivoire – are all West African.[51]

The use of vegetables in sweet cakes is something which (with the notable exception of carrots) continues to split opinion. But sweet potato, being, well, sweet – and without being insipid – is a winner in my opinion. The potato gives the sponge a closer texture than a cake made exclusively with flour, a stickiness which is well suited to the autumnal spicing, while the icing, made with fresh root ginger (another West African staple), adds a vibrant edge.

For the cake
325 g / 12 oz sweet potato
150 g / 5 oz flour
50 g / 2 oz ground almonds
300 g / 10 oz caster sugar
½ tsp salt
75 g / 3 oz high quality, natural cocoa powder
1 tsp ground cinnamon
1 tsp allspice
3 eggs, lightly whisked
1 tsp baking powder
1 tsp bicarbonate of soda
75 g / 3 oz butter, softened

Cook the sweet potatoes in the oven for around 40 minutes, or until tender, and leave to cool. Keep the oven on, at around 170°C, to preheat in advance of the cake.

In a bowl, cream together the butter and the sugar until light and fluffy. Add the eggs gradually, mixing as you do to prevent the mixture from curdling (if it does, add a spoonful of flour to bring it back together).

Sift the flour into another bowl and combine with the ground almonds, cinnamon, allspice, salt and raising agents.

Scoop out the innards of the potatoes into the bowl with the wet ingredients and mix before adding in the dry ingredients, combining well, and pouring into a lined cake tin to bake for around 40 to 50 minutes.

For the glaze
2 tbsp golden syrup
100 g / 4 oz dark chocolate, 70% cocoa solids, roughly chopped
40 g / 2 oz salted butter
Small thumb root ginger, very finely chopped

In a saucepan, melt the butter into the golden syrup with the ginger and, once hot, pour over the chocolate. When the cake has cooled, tip the glaze over its rippled surface, leave it to firm up a little, then serve.

END NOTES

1. Walvin, *Fruits of Empire*: 98.
2. Clarence-Smith, *Cocoa and Chocolate, 1765-1914*: 16.
3. Clarence-Smith, William, 'The Global Consumption of Hot Beverages, c.1500 to c.1900', in *Food and Globalisation: Consumption, Markets and Politics in the Modern World*, edited by Nutzenadel, Alexander & Trentmann, Frank, Oxford & New York: Berg, 2008: 37-8.
4. Ford, Henry, *My Life and Work*, New York: Page & Co., 1922: Ch.IV.
5. Othick, J., 'The Cocoa and Chocolate Industry in the Nineteenth Century', in *The Making of the Modern British Diet*, edited by Oddy, Derek & Miller, Derek, Totowa, NJ: Rowman & Littlefield, 1976: 79. *Cited in* Walvin, *Fruits of Empire*: 99.
6. Gordon, Bertram, 'Commerce, Colonies, and Cacao: Chocolate in England from Introduction to Industrialisation', in *Chocolate: History,*

Culture, and Heritage: 589-90; Cadbury, *Chocolate Wars*: 12-3.

7. ICCO, Quarterly Bulletin of Cocoa Statistics, February, 2014.

8. Robson, Paul, 'Ending Child Trafficking in West Africa: Lessons from the Ivorian Cocoa Sector', Anti-Slavery International, 2010: 10. Available from: http://www.antislavery.org/includes/documents/cm_docs/2011/c/cocoa_report_for_website.pdf.

9. Wood & Lass, *Cocoa*: 57.

10. Anti-Slavery International, 'The Cocoa Industry in West Africa: A History of Exploitation', 2004: 7. Available from: http://www.antislavery.org/english/who_we_are/resources/reports/english/who_we_are/resources/reports/child_labour_reports.aspx.

11. Food and Agriculture Organization (FAO), State of the World's Forests, Rome, 2008.

12. WCF, Cocoa Market Update, 1st April, 2014: 2. Available from: http://worldcocoafoundation.org/wp-content/uploads/Cocoa-Market-Update-as-of-4-1-2014.pdf; International Cocoa Initiative, 'Cocoa Farming: An Overview', 2011: 6. Available from: http://www.cocoainitiative.org/en/documents-manager/english/13-cocoa-farming-an-overview-2011/file.

13. *Cited in* 'Economics', *The Story of Chocolate* (website), available at: http://thestoryofchocolate.com/Who/content.cfm?ItemNumber=3450&navItemNumber=3481 [accessed 28th March, 2015].

14. *See for example* Ruf, François, 'Cocoa combined with Palm Wine in Côte D'Ivoire: An Unexpected Resilience', *Bois et Forêts des Tropiques*, Vol. 321, Iss. 3, 2014, 33-44. Besides chocolate itself, palm oil is utilised in numerous other food products, as well as household goods such as shampoo. Though its fast-growing and resilient nature make it a reliable source of additional income for farmers in west Africa, the growing global demand for it has been identified, in recent research by the World Resources Institute, as the key driver of deforestation in the region, as well as in Indonesia and Brazil (see Howard, Emma, 'Palm oil drives surge in west African forest loss', *The Guardian*, 2nd September, 2015).

15. Goodyear, 'The Future of Chocolate: Why Cocoa Production is at Risk'.

16. ICCO, Quarterly Bulletin of Cocoa Statistics, February, 2014.

17. Ibid.

18. Clarence-Smith, *Cocoa and Chocolate, 1765-1914*: 238-9.

19. Austin, 'Vent for Surplus or Productivity Breakthrough? The Ghanaian Cocoa Take-Off, c.1890-1936', *The African Economic History Network*, 2012 (working paper): 3.

20. Anti-Slavery International, 'The Cocoa Industry in West Africa': 7.

21. Ryan, Órla, *Chocolate Nations: Living and Dying for Cocoa in West Africa*, London & New York: Zed Books, 2011: 16-7.

22. Kapoor, Ilan, *The Postcolonial Politics of Development*, London & New York: Routledge, 2008: 83.

23. Walker, 'Establishing Cacao Plantation Culture in the Atlantic World': 546.

24. Clarence-Smith, *Cocoa and Chocolate, 1765-1914*: 9.

25. Cadbury, *Chocolate Wars*: 15-6.

26. Cadbury, *Chocolate Wars*: 101-2.

27. Anti-Slavery International, 'The Cocoa Industry in West Africa': 5.

28. *Cited in* 'Economics', The Story of Chocolate (website).

29. International Labour Organisation (ILO), 'Child Labour in Africa'. Available at: http://www.ilo.org/ipec/Regionsandcountries/Africa/lang--en/index.htm.

30. Anti-Slavery International, 'The Cocoa Industry in West Africa': 49.

31. Goodyear, 'The Future of Chocolate: Why Cocoa Production is at Risk'.

32. Chouliaraki, Lilie, *The Ironic Spectator: Solidarity in the Age of Post-Humanitarianism*, Cambridge: Polity, 2013: 6.

33. *Divine Chocolate Company*, Annual Report 2013-14. London. Available from: http://www.divinechocolate.com/uk/sites/default/files/img/AnnualReport1314.pdf.

34. Ryan, *Chocolate Nations*: 98.

35. Ryan, *Chocolate Nations*: 111-2.

36. Coote, Belinda, *The Trade Trap: Poverty and the Commodity Markets*, Oxford: Oxfam Publishing, 1992: 61.

37. Coote, *The Trade Trap*: 58.

38. Anti-Slavery International, 'The Cocoa Industry in West Africa': 19.

39. Davies, *A Primer of Dutch Seventeenth Century Overseas Trade*: 55-7.

40. Huber, Matthew, 'Enforcing Scarcity: Oil, Violence, and the Making of the Market', *Annals of the Association of American Geographers*, Vol. 101, Iss. 4, 2011. 816-826.

41. Davies, *A Primer of Dutch Seventeenth Century Overseas Trade*: 58.

42. *See for example* Spence, Peter, 'What chocolate prices tell us about the spread of ebola', *The Telegraph*, 7th October, 2014. Available at: http://www.telegraph.co.uk/finance/economics/11145266/What-chocolate-prices-tell-us-about-the-spread-of-Ebola.html.

43. Thompson's crisis, following Marx, began with industrialisation, with

money's 'transformation into capital'. This was the precondition for its development from a medium of exchange – a comparative measure of the value of things being traded or accumulated – into the means of value itself; an infinitely circulating medium, restless in its mission never to let value's dust settle in anything but the potential of its own creation (*see* Thompson, James, '"Sure I Have Seen That Face Before": Representation and Value in Eighteenth Century Drama', in *Cultural Readings of Restoration and Eighteenth Century English Theatre*, edited by Fisk, Deborah & Canfield, J. Athens, GA: University of Georgia Press, 1995. pp. 281-308: 283-4.

44. Cadbury, *Chocolate Wars*: 277-9.

45. Feeney, Nolan, 'Kraft and Heinz merge to become world's 5th largest food company', *Time*, 25th March, 2015, available at: http://time.com/3757678/kraft-heinz-merger/ [accessed 23rd April, 2015].

46. Cadbury, *Chocolate Wars*: 296; 300-1.

47. Coote, *The Trade Trap*: 174. Though the degree of difference is exaggerated by the fact that the export figure would inevitably have double counted some transactions, it gives an adequate inclination of the speed at which the situation has changed

48. 'Market Share of Global Chocolate Manufacturers in the Open Market, 2011/12', Statista (website), available at: http://www.statista.com/statistics/238854/market-share-of-global-chocolate-manufacturers-in-the-open-market/.

49. Goldberg, Shelley, 'Expanding Markets Drive Cocoa Futures', *Wall Street Daily*, 13th February, 2015. Available at: http://www.wallstreetdaily.com/2015/02/13/cocoa-market-futures/ [accessed 23rd May, 2015].

50. 'ICCO Statement on Reports of a Cocoa Supply Deficit in 2020', 21st November, 2014, available at: http://www.icco.org/about-us/icco-news/270-icco-statement-on-reports-of-a-cocoa-supply-deficit-in-2020.html.

51. Statistics for 2013, obtained from the UN Food and Agriculture Organization's 'FAOSTAT'. Available at: http://faostat3.fao.org/browse/Q/*/E.

Above: Chocolate mushrooms on cornbread - P. 30

Below: Brazilian Pig's Cheek *Croquetas* with *Chimichurri* - P. 53

Above & below: Cacao soup, cardamom and orange challah, candied peel and almonds - P. 56-9

Cocktail: Chocolate and cherry port sour - P. 78-9

Sea bass *mole rojo*, chorizo and braised leeks - P. 31-3

Above: Spiced sweet potato and chocolate cake, with chocolate and ginger glaze - P. 108-9   Below: Chocolate sorbet - P. 136-7

Above: Salted chocolate, lime and treacle tart - P. 163-6

Below: Molasses and Chocolate brownies - P. 165-6

Above: Chocolate and Sultana rolls, spiced maple butter - P. 137-9

Below: Chocolate and malt *Alfajores* - P. 166-8

Above: Beef, ancho and bitter chocolate stew - P. 75-6

Below: Filipino *Tsokolate* - P. 193-4

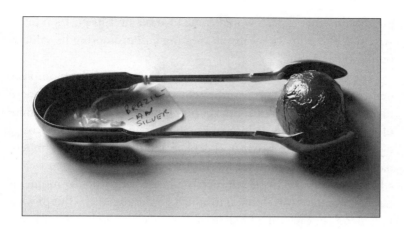

CHAPTER FIVE

'THE FOOD PRESCRIBED BY DOCTORS'

CHOCOLATE AND HEALTH

In AD 129, while in Mesoamerica Maya tribes were coming to grasp the significance, both medicinal and ritual, of the cacao seed, 6800 miles east as the crow flies, at Pergamum – a large city of the Roman Empire at the western edge of modern day Turkey – a boy named Claudius Galen was born. Despite the gulf between them, Galen and cacao would form a bond of sorts; their histories would intertwine without touching. That boy grew to be one of the most influential physicians who ever lived, famed above all for his development of the Hippocratic theory of the four humours into a comprehensive system of nosology which dominated European medical thought and practice for the next 1600 years. Thus, though Galen himself would never know of cacao, a wealth of physicians, priests and other experts would come to argue over its position in his system as the primary means of assessing and promoting its value as both food and drug.

The Galenic system of thought may have been unceremoniously dethroned by Enlightenment thought and the discoveries of modern medicine from the seventeenth century onwards, but it is the premise of this chapter that something of its logic remains prescient in debates over the relationship between chocolate and health up to the present day. This debate is still, as it was in Ancient Rome, a moral as well as a biological tussle. Diet is not merely a matter of particular moments – those moments (meal times) in which food is ingested – but of what in Galen's era they called a dietetic 'regimen': a whole way of living in which food, drink, exercise, sleep, sex, and almost everything in between were to be practised in moderation and in perfect balance with one another and with nature.

THE GALENIC SYSTEM OF THE FOUR HUMOURS

Galen portrayed himself not as a prophet, but as a simple messenger, a conduit for two other much more resourceful and profound beings. First of these was the Ancient Greek physician Hippocrates, whom Galen looked to as a model of perfection in his field. He was by no means alone in idealising a Classical Greek thinker, for this was a common tendency of the 'Second Sophistic' in which Galen was raised and educated, a Greek cultural movement which referred nostalgically to the era prior to that nation's incorporation into the Holy Roman Empire. Thus Galen, so he himself claimed, was the most skilled physician of his time principally because he understood the Hippocratic teachings better than all others. Secondly, Galen declared himself as an interpreter for the body, which through a variety of perceptible signs spoke of its afflictions and its needs. The sole task of the doctor was to listen carefully to its voices, an industry for which none other than Hippocrates provided the appropriate set of tools.

The voices of the body spoke of the need to balance the distribution of four fundamental substances, known as the humours, within its cavities. The four humours – Blood, Phlegm, Black Bile and Yellow Bile – were at the same time sources of health, and of illness and death. None was essentially 'bad' or 'good'; whether they beckoned benevolence or malady depended entirely upon their relative quantity and their mixing with the other humours. Thus pain and disease were the result of the *excess* of one humour in relation to the others, either in the body as a whole, or more often in one of its regions. Excess of, say, Black Bile, in an arm would be capable of causing two separate pains: one pain in the arm as a direct result of the excess; another in the part of the body where Black Bile was, correspondingly, lacking in relation to the other humours. The pain would be exacerbated further by the isolation of a substance, that is, where multiple humours may be present in a region but are, like communities in a dysfunctional urban area, nonetheless segregated.

Health was envisioned as an ideal balance, but maintaining equilibrium was problematic due to the inescapable fact that the body is not a closed circuit, that it must open itself to the uncertainties of the world in order to survive. Accordingly the pragmatic thrust of the Galenic system was towards the interaction of the humours with the external qualities, of which there were also four: hot, dry, cold and moist. These qualities constituted nothing less than the relation between body and world, the forces which passed across between the elements (earth, fire, water and air) of which nature had been crafted, and the composite of flesh and blood, mind and soul that was man. One of the most commonly recurring of the things to make this passage across the corporeal limit was of course food.

Though not possessing the complexity of modern medicine, the Galenic system was in no way rigid or simple. In fact, its structure was designed specifically so as to provide guidance in frequently shifting circumstances. The four qualities affecting the humours resided on either end of two intersecting axes. One held the qualities of hot and cold; the other of dry and moist, and each person, place, or thing occupied a certain point between them, indicating their 'constitution'. What's more, these occupations were transient: the constitution of a person could alter with age, with mood and with activity, a place with the weather and the seasons, and a thing (a food for instance) with how it was prepared. According to one of Galen's apostles, changes to the qualities might even cause a 'particular humour [to]…metamorphose into one or another sort of humour'.[1] Health was, then, a question of reacting to a nexus of destabilizing factors via a delicate programme of adjustments.

The durability of the Galenic system is quite remarkable. Though elaborations were made – a division of the qualities into a number of degrees, for instance – its core elements remained largely unchanged. As such, Europe's 'discovery' of the Americas and the process of gathering knowledge of these new territories involved the complete integration of every aspect of that continent into Galen's theoretical framework. Alongside a myriad of other ingestible plant species, cacao was subjected to a flurry of descriptions and categorizations within the humoral logic; that is, as possessing a certain set of qualities. For once it was known, cacao could be demanded, supplied and consumed.

CHOCOLATE AND THE HUMOURS IN COLONIAL LITERATURE

The choice earlier expressed by Brillat-Savarin – that between the utility and the luxury of food – foreshadows the language in which the modern relationship between food and health is often phrased. Yet not more than two centuries earlier, the preparation of chocolate would have been based on a more specifically medicinal evaluation of humoral health.

In this way the physician Henry Stubbe, in his 1662 work *The Indian Nectar*, cautions those making chocolate to 'consult your own Constitution and Circumstances, and vary the Ingredients according to the Premises'.[2] The range of preparations possible for chocolate was key to its medical functionality. As well as additional ingredients, the constitution of the final drink could be influenced by processes, such as mixing and cooking, which accentuated certain properties of the cacao bean. Consequently, there was not much in the way of a general consensus on chocolate's effects. Francisco Hernández, Royal Physician to King Philip II of Spain, gives one of the first classifications of cacao within the humoral register, propounding that it is on the whole 'cold and humid'. Yet Juan de Cárdenas, a Spanish Jesuit physician and theologian writing in 1591, observes a warm and humid oiliness to the bean emphasized by toasting, and the French chemist Nicolas Lemery, turning the original diagnosis on its head in 1698, argues that, being hot and dry, chocolate should be imbibed by the elderly, and in winter (both of which were considered cold and wet), whilst being avoided for the main part by the 'hot and bilious' young:

> Chocolate agrees, especially in cold Weather, with old People, with cold and phlegmatic Persons, and those that cannot easily digest their Food, because of the Weakness and Nicety of their Stomachs; but young People of a hot and bilious Constitution, whose Humours are already too much in Motion, ought to abstain from it, or use it very moderately.[3]

Depending on its make-up then, chocolate was associated with a diversity of curative and palliative functions: the easing of intestinal diseases, the encouragement of digestion and the flow of blood, the evacuation of phlegm, as well as treatment of skin conditions and psychological complexes including melancholia. It really was the pre-modern superfood in both the application and the believed range of its powers.

It is, however, not the truth or falsity of these fluctuating claims which is of concern here, but rather the logic in which such claims were shrouded. The Galenic system emphasized resilience, an idea which attained a renewed significance as increasing numbers of Europeans left their home continent as part of the project of colonial expansion. As was the case in any changes to circumstance, the effects of the New World climate on the humours needed to be accounted for so as to determine how they may be balanced out. For Cárdenas the drink of chocolate was a vital substance in this balancing act:

> Again, I say that in no land of the world is chocolate more necessary than in that of the Indies. Because the atmosphere is

humid and listless, bodies and stomachs are full of phlegm and excess humidity, which with the heat of the chocolate is fermented, and converts into blood.[4]

Chocolate is viewed here as a form of treatment for restoring the equality of the humours, compensating for the excess of phlegm with a dry heat, and thus acting as a preventative technique against disease. In this sense it was a typically fearful colonial medicine, offering a remedy to the threat which the New World posed for the body of the European by virtue of its unfamiliar atmosphere.

This particular idea also reveals the Platonic origins of diet, which attested to dietetics as a form of knowledge made necessary by man's diversion from the natural path. As such, the underlying message is a conservative one, strictly allied to a romanticized vision of Nature. For the colonial settler this naturalistic imagination had worrying implications. Having uprooted him or herself from the place of their birth, the migrant lived a deeply unnatural life, and as a result could expect the discordance between their body and its surroundings to be reflected internally by a humoral disturbance. Appropriate measures, in the form of adherence to a certain 'regimen', were necessary if the imbalance was not to escalate to a perilous magnitude.

Foucault, in *The History of Sexuality* (1976) sorts the vigilance required by regimen into two kinds: 'serial', an attendance to the effect of following one activity with another, and 'circumstantial', having to do with the impacts of changes to the internal and external qualities.[5] This perpetual state of alertness entailed a whole way of life (*techne tou biou*, translating as 'art of life' or 'aesthetics of existence') and as such aligned physical resilience with moral fortitude. Greek culture also summoned this dual conception of strength, for instance attributing the same appellation of 'exercise' (*gymnasion*) to the practice of the athlete or the gymnast to that of the philosopher or the physician. All involved the flexing of muscles, whether the biceps or the vocal chords. Linguistic synthesis of this sort was commonplace due to the centrality of gymnastics to the Greek identity, particularly in the Roman era. The festivals in which competitions of all kinds were played out on the amphitheatre's stage were the most formal and famed guise of this identity. But this institution and its pervading phraseology were indicative of a broader, integrated 'exercise' of everyday life.

Foucault chooses to identify the dietetic regimen as an 'art of living' because of both its perpetuity and its individuality. Humoral balance did not lend itself to sporadic application, allowing excess at times and then compensating for it with 'crash dieting' at others. Since compensations must be gentle, a boom and bust economy of the body could not be afforded. It thus required constant monitoring, but such regulation could not be imposed from the outside. Of course, a select few might be able to employ their own physician, a personal trainer of sorts (Galen himself was later appointed physician to the emperor, Marcus Aurelius) but the regimen was not intended as an exclusive privilege of the elite. It was, in theory at least, an agenda for the working man. Therefore, though the outline of the system originates in a number of public experts (notably Galen), it was integral to the regimen that it be practised at the level of individual lives, as a philosophy of the mundane, or what Foucault refers to as a 'care of the self'. Foucault argues that the banal philosophy was mobilized from the eighteenth century onwards as a form of 'noso-politics'. This was to enable the government of population health without coercion by teaching individual subjects how to regulate their own conduct.

EXPERTISE AND THE MODERNIZATION OF MEDICINE

Despite the stated intention that the humoral regimen apply to all, it nonetheless required a minimum level of prosperity. For food in particular, the capability of wealth lay at the juncture of two notions of strength: the Stoic strength exhibited by the mental restraint of moderation or abstinence, and the strength-giving power of food. Though not a way of life premised on opulence, for one to guard against excess they must in the first place have access to it – abstinence could mean little without temptation. As a result of it straddling the borders between necessity and luxury, drink and food, food and drug, chocolate has been implicated perhaps more than any other foodstuff in this quandary.

We have already mentioned that the Aztecs worried over the level of chocolate drinking in the cities and courts. The excess of its consumption in one part of the body – a political body this time – was seen to bring into disrepute the heritage of a civilization built on principles of humility and equality. And, in quite another world, that of early modern Europe, a similar altercation erupted among the Catholic clergy, who wrangled over whether chocolate's constitution came into direct contradiction with the fast, the religious festival of abstinence. The peculiar problem here was that chocolate, as described by colonial botanists and physicians, had been anecdotally endorsed on the basis that it was wholesome – both nutritious and fatty. Stubbe, for instance, relayed tales of women in the New World colonies eating so much chocolate 'that they scarcely consumed any solid meat yet did not exhibit a decline in strength'. Where the Stoic values of ecclesiastical law were concerned, this quality gave rise to a dilemma: if fasting derived moral fortitude and divine contiguity from the act of denying one's body earthly sources of strength, then chocolate's consideration as one of said sources outlawed its consumption. On the other hand, the religious order had grown quite fond of the beverage. Besides any personal taste for chocolate, it was held to be compatible with the social policy of the church. Even if the exact natures of its medicinal and moral worth were uncertain, chocolate was the least of all possible evils, and was promoted keenly, alongside coffee and tea, as a resolution to the 'demon alcohol' that plagued the condition of the poor. Additionally, a number of Catholic orders, the Jesuits in particular, were invested in the colonial cacao trade, and thus feared the considerable dent that chocolate's banishment would incur in their profits.

It was clear to most that chocolate broke the fast, and yet it remained exempt from church law. This was made possible, in large part, by the authoritative opinions given by a series of popes who were able to uphold the classification of chocolate as a drink rather than a food by dint of the expert knowledge passed down to them from the heavens.[6]

The Greek physicians of the Roman Empire could not speak with such unquestioned command on all things, but, depending on their individual esteem, could become an influential mouthpiece in the medical field. The expertise of a physician would be tested by way of public demonstrations held in baths and theatres, often in the form of competitions with rival practitioners. This contest structure gave the manner in which medical knowledge was substantiated the air of spectacle, a flamboyance which we would now tend to see as unbefitting of scientific practice. Indeed, were these physicians still performing today, their methods would most likely appear to us as an attempt to compensate for a lack of real expertise with amateur dramatics: the medical equivalent of the televangelist's overzealous illusions. However, spectacle lay at the heart of medical proof at this time, for it was only by the audience bearing witness to something – a diagnosis or a cure – that theories could attain the mark of truth. Galen's proficiency in evoking public testimony of this sort, his ability to work the audience into raptures with his demonstrations, was therefore crucial to the influence of his theories. Such was the importance of public demonstration to Galen's ideas that the process leading to the eventual rebuttal of the humoral system started with the discrediting of this method of truth-construction. Thus, the establishment of London's Royal Society in 1660 (followed by similar learned societies across Europe) was emblematic of a shift away from the subjective judgement of the audience as the trusted form of scientific proof. The idea of an inductive experimental method, as envisioned by Sir Francis Bacon, was to shed the preconceived opinions of the physician, and instead to let the object speak. This restructuring of medicine relegated anecdotal evidence to the trivial status of 'old wives tales', dismissing 'ordinary' in favour of 'ordered experience'; taking the perspective of the object as opposed to that of the subject.

But wait. Was this not also Galen's stated intention? He too referred frequently to objects – often the docile bodies of dissected animals or cured patients – in order to prove his theories. In a significant sense, it was the inner workings of these objects which he claimed to reveal to the audience by slicing them open. Thus, the fundamental difference between Galen's self-proclaimed objectivity and the officially sanctioned objectivity of inductive method lay elsewhere: not in the content of experiments but in their mode of delivery. Because the only mechanism of verification available to Galen was popular approval, his demonstrations were not only public but also dramatic. In them bodies did not speak so much as scream, and the reactions of the spectators were equally emotional, often gasping in awe and astonishment.[1] From the perspective of a modernising medical discipline, 'emotion' and 'truth' were incompatible terms. Emotions could not prove anything; on the contrary, they were an unfortunate trait of humanity that distorted scientific fact. By employing a visceral aesthetic to stir and persuade his audiences, the Galenic physician was seen to betray a reliance on emotion and therefore an unscientific approach.

In contrast to such theatrics, modern medicine would be deliberately unspectacular. It was the aesthetic of the method, its outward appearance, which would undergo the most complete transformation. The mode of demonstration would be sterilized; spattered blood expunged from the public imagination to be replaced with the cleanliness of ink. It was from this perspective that other forms of medicine, and indeed other forms of society, could be declared 'barbaric' by modernising Europe in spite of their continued use of many of the same practices. It was possible, for example, to decry the cannibalism of Aztec sacrificial ritual without any recognition that cannibalism was also practiced in Europe as late as the eighteenth century. 'Corpse medicine', as it was called, made use of almost every part of the dead human body to cure a wide variety of ailments. And this was not merely the dubious science of black market physicians but rather the recommended best practice of the pioneering minds of modernity themselves, Francis Bacon included.[2] Again, it was the sterilization of the method that separated this (European) from that (Aztec) form of cannibalism, making the former a permissible modern medical practice and the latter an act of primitive savagery. Oil taken from the brain (known as 'spirit of skull') was distilled; blood was dried to a powder; the heart was ground to an unidentifiable pulp. In contrast to the Aztec sacrifice – during which, you will remember, the blood was to be as fresh as possible - corpse medicine heavily processed the dead body to create an epistemological and aesthetic distance between the product and its grisly origins. It was civilized because it was, in the terms of the anthropologist Claude Lévi-Strauss, 'cooked' as opposed to 'raw'.[7]

Hypotheses, in the newly-conceived inductive method, could only be proven to a calculated level of probability, and only by reference to objects. Only these passive, non-sentient things could qualify as proof because, unlike humans, they were deemed not to have the wherewithal to deceive. The object, it was claimed, did not lie like the subject. Where human individuals were involved in medical experimentation, they were supposed to obey the principle of neutrality, imposing themselves – their opinions and emotions – as little as possible upon the results. However, this did not mean, either for chocolate or anything else, that the expert no-longer bore influence. Rather, expertise was made to alter its tact, but became all the more powerful for it.

While it had already been realized that knowledge was an important ingredient for power, it was the seventeenth and eighteenth centuries which proposed that the two might be one and the same. In *New Atlantis*, Bacon's utopian vision for a future shaped by scientific progress, published in 1627, the father of empiricism regales the narrative of a fictional isle named Bensalem off whose coast a crew of European merchants are strewn by a ferocious tempest. They are aided and brought ashore by the inhabitants of the island, a mysterious but generous Christian people, and there a Priest patiently explains to them the origins of the nation and its way of life. Bensalem is not a mercantilist society, and partakes little in global trade, but sends out two ships, once every twelve years, on missions of discovery:

> ...we maintain a trade, not for gold, silver, or jewels; nor for silks; nor for spices; nor any other commodity of matter; but only for God's first creature, which was *Light*: to have *light* (I say) of the growth of all parts of the world.[8]

The 'light' to which the priest refers is knowledge, and it soon becomes clear that this knowledge is of a scientific sort. Bensalem has as its most proud institution a society called 'Salomon's House', an enormous network of numerous different spaces of experimentation in which the treasures of nature are replicated, or perhaps even surpassed. Artificial metals are produced in imitation mines, 'divers plants rise by mixtures of earths without seeds', and brewhouses, bakehouses and kitchens concoct novel foods and drinks.[9]

But the utopia of a peaceful scientific Christian state was undermined by the roles that both science and religion continued to have in colonial exploitation. An instrumental figure here is Sir Hans Sloane (1660-1753), a man whose legacy turns, as James Delbourgo puts it, on 'the ambiguous relation between the production of natural knowledge and its commercial exploitation.' Sloane was one of the most prominent of those botanists who used scientific classification as a means to taming the New World environment, in doing so encouraging the exotic appeal of its products. As a botanist and a businessman both, he studied cacao simultaneously as an element of the natural world, and as a potentially profitable commodity. But this was not the limit of Sloane's talents. The primary role for which he was hired, and his famous expeditions funded, was as a physician to the governor of Jamaica Christopher Monck. He was a truly polymathic individual, the likes of which we do not see today, in our era of specialization. It was Sloane's multiplicity, coupled with that of cacao itself – a polymath in its own right – that allowed for the formation of *a composite mode of knowledge*. He became renowned for his detailed anatomical sketches of New World objects, documented together in his *Natural History of Jamaica* written during his voyage of 1687-1689, and in this sense he typified the scientific shift from spectacular display to careful observation as a method of acquiring knowledge. Yet however much the use of a 'dry' aesthetic and a discourse of objectivity veiled the part of the subject in the demonstration of knowledge, the hand of Sloane and other individuals was ever-present. Delbourgo points out for example that the anatomy of *Theobroma cacao* in the *Natural History* was drawn from the sketches of local Jamaican artist Garret

Moore and Dutch draftsman Everhardus Kickius, supplemented, at a later date, by Sloane's previously published annotations. What's more, these annotations were not of a singularly biological nature, but were adorned with historical, cultural, and economic contextualisation. In seeming contradiction to the inductive methodology, these were the subjective and preconceived opinions of Sloane himself, pasted onto an artist's impression of the plant. Not 'facts of nature', but theories moulded to resemble them – '*arti-facts*' in the most fundamental sense.[6] These opinions attained scientific significance through the expertise of Sloane, his reputable status in a plurality of pursuits and institutions. Precisely as Galen's demonstrations had relied upon his tricky rhetoric and visceral aesthetic to persuade the audience of the truth of what they were witnessing, Delbourgo talks of how Sloane's annotations implored readers 'to look, but then to be told what they had seen'.

The influence of Sloane in communicating cacao was attributable at first to his position as a representative of *episteme*, attached directly to his professional stature and botanical expertise. However, the way in which the knowledge-based source of authority was presented by Sloane, and the use of collage (the cutting and pasting of different knowledges onto one another), was in some way an aesthetic proficiency, a *techne* or art of visibility. As is evident in its use in the phrase *techne tou biou*, *techne* is a heavily ambiguous term. It at times refers to the formally technical; at others to a far more generic, moral sense of ability as *virtue*. Hans Sloane's promotion of chocolate, which had originally employed the authority of scientific theory, gradually diffused into a broader relationship of trust between consumer and producer based upon a virtuous or well-respected name. No more apparent is this diffusion than in the employment of the name itself as a brand after the departure of the expert himself: the *Sir Hans Sloane* brand of milk chocolate, which was not created by Sloane himself, but by a London grocer shortly after his death,[10] is successful to this day.

By showcasing the ability to move seamlessly from *episteme* to *techne*, Sloane serves as a microcosm for the diffusion of chocolate from a substance promoted for its medicinal benefits, to a product advertised according to a series of virtuous images.

When William Cadbury pulled his company from the ashes, he did so by drawing the British public's attention to his firm's newly determined purity. To begin with, Cadbury obtained the endorsements of qualified physicians to verify the medical and moral legitimacy of Cadbury's products; to substantiate the 'Absolutely Pure, Therefore Best' slogan. The strategy was soon picked up by other manufacturers. Baker's Chocolate (of the Baker Chocolate Company, itself founded by a doctor) was accompanied by the proud declaration that it had been 'recommended by the most eminent physicians', while a trading card for Van Houten's chocolate touted itself as *L'aliment Precrit Par le Medicin*: 'The Food Prescribed by Doctors'.[11]

It was not long however before the endorsement, in becoming a slogan, began to drift from the science to which it had first purported to allude. With the discrediting of the humoral system, the exact nature of chocolate's medicinal value became increasingly uncertain. Mottos continued to play on the historical status of chocolate as a drug, but the expert endorsements themselves referred only to a vague identification of strength and purity. In the advertisements of Cadbury's, these two themes were often invoked together, as in the 1888 poster which had, as its image, a group of boys playing rugby, and, as its twin mantras, 'Strength and Staying Power', 'Cadbury's Cocoa is Absolutely Pure'.

The peak of this particular discourse came in the context of twentieth century Europe's two major conflicts. When war was declared, chocolate was soon enrolled in the war effort, as it was believed to be a giver of strength and sustenance. During the First World War, Rowntree put added emphasis on its nutritional value, and also devised a service gift box which customers could send straight to their loved ones on the battlefront.[12] In 1937, Captain Paul Logan of the US army contracted the Pennsylvania chocolate maker Milton S. Hershey to design a bar, lighter and higher in calories than the civilian variety, to be sent out with the troops as emergency rations.[13] This was not the first instance in which cacao had been employed as military fuel. In fact, some of the first solid chocolate – though not of the smooth variety we are familiar with today – was created in the form of wafers for Aztec warriors, and chocolate was also issued to servicemen of the Royal Navy from the late eighteenth century onwards. However, it was the first instance in which chocolate's military deployment was itself employed as a promotional technique by manufacturers back home. Chocolate was profitably reimagined as a 'Fighting Food' by Nestlé, while Mars similarly employed military motifs in their advertising campaigns at this time.[14]

Advertising thus exploited the variety and the pliability of expertise, drawing upon a collage of knowledge appropriate to the meaning it currently wanted to construct. Hence, in times of peace, when speaking in terms of war did not capture the public spirit, chocolate's advertising strategy was directed not towards soldiers and violence but towards women and children, happiness and play. Like the Catholic clergymen of the seventeenth century, Victorian advertisers drew on the respectability associated with chocolate relative to alcohol and other drugs. But, again, chocolate's ambivalence with regards to hedonism and utility returned to split the practice of how it was to be portrayed. Advertising was doubly ambiguous when it came to images of women. Depending upon which side of chocolate's nature the advertisers decided to flaunt, the woman could be adapted to suit. The female on chocolate advertising posters therefore took two main forms: either she was deeply suggestive of opulent sensuality, all frills and winks, or she was one of two females in a homely mother-daughter scene.[15]

It was the latter of these female tropes that appeared most consistently. In particular, mothers were often depicted feeding their daughters, or else children were visualized playing with or for chocolate. The innocence of play was accompanied by allusions to health. In particular, these made reference to the know-how of the paediatrician, an expert not solely of children's health but of the transfer of health in the parent-child relationship. Chocolate was at this point often marketed to parents as a method by which they could fortify the health of their children, capitalizing on the pressure (increasingly falling upon the mother of the nuclear family) to take responsibility for the physical and biological development of their young.[16] It was in this paediatric context that the further scientific advances of the twentieth century, especially the observation of vitamins and minerals, were, in the words of Harvey Levenstein, 'an advertiser's dream'.[17] The product to which this strategy was best suited was milk chocolate, as the calcium content gave more certain form to the motif of strength. Milk was a perfect addition in that it enabled advertisements to confirm both of the virtues from which chocolate had historically been accused of straying. While calcium was proof of chocolate's benevolence to physical health, milk's associations with nature – commonly represented by the milk carton's depiction of a happily grazing cow – gave chocolate the impression of something pure and innocent.

In spite of claiming to let the object speak, the way in which advertising has employed endorsements in order to emphasize different aspects of chocolate to particular consumers demonstrates the complex role of the expert in determining how the meaning of an object comes to be perceived. The mobilization of female tropes is especially interesting. The fact that the woman was the motif of choice for the promotion of both of chocolate's quite polarized identities in Victorian society – promiscuity and hedonism on the one hand, purity on the other – reflects upon a fascinating continuity between these two dualistic figures.

Though the advertising of chocolate through the prism of femininity is often linked to the especially prudent atmosphere of Victorian society, this form of mediation has both ancestors and descendants. For the Mesoamericans female sexuality was, like cacao, filled with sacred ambiguity. And on the other hand it was less than fifty years ago that a TV advert for Cadbury's Flake – part of the 'Flake Girl' series in which female models were shown provocatively biting into the chocolate – was taken off the air following a spate of complaints, sparking a debate on the place of feminine sexuality in public life in the process. Was its appearance in the promotion exploitative? Was it inappropriate or over-sexualized for a company whose products were often geared towards children? Particularly given the viral influence of television advertising, the concerns underlying the complaints repeated the notions of contamination familiar to us from the theory of the sacred.

'RESPONSIBLISATION' AND THE GOVERNANCE OF PUBLIC HEALTH

The function of advertising for chocolate hints at a continuity between Galen's time and our own. Even modern medicine relies upon a certain degree of subjectivity. 'The facts, contrary to the old adage,' says Bruno Latour, 'evidently do not "speak for themselves"':[18] they are rather emphatically *spoken for*. The question to be answered is, therefore, who speaks for the facts? Who speaks on behalf of objects? This translator is most often an expert of some kind, a figure regarded as having some form of *techne,* or recognizable by their superior theoretical knowledge, a certificate of *episteme*. The physician was certainly not the first of these experts in the field of dietetics. In fact, all doctors were for a long time treated with a great deal of scepticism by the ancient masses, who much preferred the wisdom of herbalists and astrologers. And, though the physician was listened to for a great deal longer than most, this expertise in turn eventually diffused. In medicine, it would give way to an (allegedly) objective scientific voice, and in dietetics, to the mantric sloganizing of advertising in addition, as we shall see in the following chapter, to the patriotic advice of the housekeeper.

During the late twentieth and early twenty-first centuries, however, particularly in wealthier societies, the pressures to 'do something' about population health have intensified, and in response the dietetic expert has been called back into the fold. The difficulty is that, in contrast to the Renaissance Pope, the expert can no-longer dictate our behaviour to us. Every piece of advice must be weighed carefully alongside the imperative to maintain neoliberal freedoms. This is expressed in the recent turn towards Evidence-Based Medicine (EBM), an approach which sets out to combine the inductive method with the principle of individual rights. The task of Foucault's 'art of government' is precisely to traverse the impasse between government and freedom. Rather than proscribing actions, experts proscribe information.

In consequence, the lives which we hope to lead bear a strong resemblance to a regimen, reliant on our capacity to self-govern our everyday lives. A pertinent example is the UK National Health Service's (NHS) Live Well programme, which disseminates via its website information on over 100 topics referring not merely to food (including the '5 a day' healthy eating scheme), but to exercise, smoking, sleep, pain, dentistry, sex, and so on. Crucially, this is all couched in the language of freedom to choose. The NHS slogan is itself 'Your Health, Your Choices', and its structure is increasingly pointed towards a constant self-assessment for which it provides numerous 'tools'. Just as regimen had its humoral measure, dietetics today is premised on moderation and balance, including its own forms of vigilance. The main difference is that the measure is now expressed in predominantly statistical terms. Thus, the tools of self-assessment offer their targets and warnings, and most importantly their averages, by way of numeric data with which – through digital and interactive technologies such as podcasts, games, and smartphone apps – we are encouraged to engage.

Behind the scenes of this self-government by statistics, this process of what Btihaj Ajana has termed 'responsiblisation', the expert still holds an important role. The distinct character of expertise today is that it is diffused across a number of specialized professional agencies, and as a result our choices are that much more difficult to make. There is no one norm to which it is right to conform; no true Nature or true God to have the final say.

Symbolic of the renewed emphasis on the importance of regimen, one of the agents whose advice has been gaining influence in recent decades is the dietitian. Though dietetics is a theory of knowledge with a long history, the dietitian is a distinctly modern creation. The British Dietetic Association (BDA), for instance, was established in 1936, at St Thomas' Hospital in London, and, similarly, the American Dietetic Association (now the Academy of Nutrition and Dietetics) was founded in Ohio in 1917. As opposed to the nutritionist, the dietitian is regulated by law, and their profession is notable for its focus on the composition and definition of the field of health, as well as its work across that field's various scales and institutions, from 'the NHS, private practice, industry, education, research, sport, media, public relations, publishing, government and Non Government Organisations (NGOs)…from government, to local communities, to individuals'.

Once again, in the explanatory guide issued by the BDA, a discourse of choice is summoned:

Uniquely, dietitians use the most up-to-date public health and scientific research on food, health and disease which they *translate* into practical guidance to *enable people to make appropriate lifestyle and food choices.*

Despite the fact that the final choice is left to the individual, it is nevertheless the case that the information supplied to them is always already interpreted in a certain way; already spoken for. Precisely as Galen and Sloane accompanied their demonstrations with a commentary, informing the audience as to what they were, in fact, seeing, the field of nutritional research supplies the public with a set of numbers ascribed with a given meaning; a set of instructions on how to read and make use of them.

The Front of Pack (FoP) Labelling policy, introduced to the UK food industry on the advice of the dietetic profession in 2011, is a typical example of such a process. Displaying the contents of the food on the packaging is nothing new. Likewise, the integration of a Guided Daily Allowance (GDA) for each main ingredient has been in place since 1998. The novel aspect of the FoP programme is therefore its *aesthetic*; its emphasis on information that is both unavoidably visible and immediately comprehensible. Generally, the label is made up of five sections: kilojoules (kj)/calories (cal), fat, saturated fat, sugars and salt, for which both a quantity by weight and a corresponding percentage of GDA are displayed. But the latest development of the scheme has been one rendered to encourage a particular judgement based predominantly upon visual aesthetics. As of 2013, the presentation of the labels has been standardized. Each quantity is given one of three colours which correspond to its value relative to the GDA, an intake which has been deemed 'normal' and thus 'healthy'. The significance of the colours chosen – green (low), amber (medium), and red (high) – is to render the level of knowledge needed on the part of the consumer to a bare minimum. So familiar are we with the connotations of those shades through their presence in everyday life – green for 'go'; amber for 'wait'; red for 'stop' – that no education as such is necessary. The colour-coding reduces statistics to the universal language of aesthetics.

For Thomas Keenan and Eyal Weizman, the effect of this reduction is to bring about the decisive moment: 'Aesthetics, as the *judgement* of the senses…cuts through probability's economy of calculations', thereby encouraging a certain choice to be made *in spite of* the uncertainty of the situation.[19]

Though the healthy decision is determined in advance, the responsibility to make that decision is left to the individual. This is a kind of freedom – it does indeed 'enable' people to make 'choices' – but it is nonetheless a strange one, whereby we can choose whatever we want, but we are made relentlessly aware of our responsibility for the consequences of that choice. Given that the sources of expertise are diffuse, the message received is often contradictory. On the one hand the advertising of chocolate actively encourages consumption on the basis of purity, health, and sensuous luxury. On the other, the government and food industry partnerships focus on finding new and ingenious ways of helping people recognize the bad choice, but shy away from involving themselves in any restrictions on the industry itself.

Healthy Chocolate and the Responsibility of Industry

> At no other time has Nature concentrated such a wealth of valuable nourishment into such a small space as in the cocoa bean.

The words of the Prussian botanist Alexander von Humboldt quoted above may praise cacao at a time when, even as the Galenic system lingered, evidence for chocolate's nourishment came in primarily anecdotal form, but the past decades have witnessed a renaissance in this attitude towards chocolate within the turn towards EBM. As the scientific gaze has been magnified, cacao's healthy attributes have been rediscovered at a molecular scale.

One of the unfortunate consequences of a public health policy that reduces choices to a set of responses governed by the colours of traffic lights is that we begin to think in terms of a binary of 'healthy' and 'unhealthy' foods. Because of our love for chocolate, we feel an understandable urge to squeeze it into the former category. We remain faithful, in this way, to chocolate's mythological presence. And because cacao has an extremely complex chemical make-up, consisting of up to 200 compounds, we can remain faithful to myth without breaking our oath to science. The media has seized upon the opportunity cacao's multiplicity provides to lend scientific 'approval' to popular will, and declare chocolate 'good for you'. These declarations have taken a number of forms. The release of serotonin, a chemical representative of happiness, has been broadcast with expectant glee. Meanwhile, articles proclaiming the presence of phenylethylamine have appeared to confirm the long-suspected association of chocolate with love and lust, returning again to chocolate's identification with promiscuity.

It appears that the bug of advertising is infectious, for though these two substances are present in cacao, it is not likely that they reside in high enough quantities to have any significant direct effect.[20] However, myth and reality cannot be parted so easily outside the rigidly controlled experiment. The physiological impacts of chocolate's cultural associations to certain behaviours should not be discounted. Until science overcomes the public desire to believe in chocolate's numerous benefits our bodies will experience their placebo effects. This term 'placebo' is, in many senses, one of those scientific allusions to phenomena which it alone cannot explain; science's classification for *doxa*; for what is outside (its) classification. Thus, depending on the societal consensus on its functions, chocolate's placebo has ranged from our happiness and arousal, to the trance of the warrior awaiting sacrifice.

Screened from the blurred science of placebo, much of the present research into the relationship between chocolate and health concentrates on the presence of polyphenols. Some of these polyphenols are classed as flavonoids, wherein the excitement of the research community lies. A large number of fruits and vegetables contain some level of flavonoids, but cacao has a particularly high concentration of a particular subclass of flavonoids known as flavonols. Ever since 2006, when a group of Kuna Indians from the San Blas islands off the coast of Panama were found to have unusually low incidence of hypertension (high blood pressure, one of the primary contributing factors of cardiovascular disease), heart health has been linked to this property of cacao. The reason for the Kuna's unique characteristic was located in their diet, and in particular in the fact that they tended to consume around five cups of a chocolate beverage every day.[21] Other studies have substantiated the association, with the flavonol epicatechin for instance being found to promote the activity of anti-oxidants, decreasing the incidence of low density lipoprotein cholesterol which can bring on atherosclerosis and arteriosclerosis,[22] while quertetin has likewise been found to help with vasodilation, relaxing the muscles in the walls of our blood vessels and thereby reducing the pressure at which blood is pumped through them. Interestingly enough, the remedy highlighted by this research is an increase to the flow of blood: a function to which cacao was deemed beneficial as early as the fifteenth century. Even outside the study of flavonoids, this is also the key possible benefit associated with theobromine, the alkaloid stimulant that takes its name from the cacao tree. For all the pages spent indulgently mocking the system of the humours, it got this most important nosological assertion spot-on.

In attempting to encourage the consumption of chocolate with the highest levels of flavonols, a problem arises: though dark chocolate, and that with a high percentage of 'cocoa solids' in particular, can be promoted, these characteristics do not ultimately guarantee the presence of flavonols. Rather, this depends, in the end, upon the actions of the industry. The conditions in which processes such as fermentation, 'conching' (the emulsification of the liquor with the butter), 'dutching' (alkali processing) and Ultra-High Temperature (UHT) treatment, are undertaken can be especially harmful to the levels of flavonols remnant in the final product. Quantities in the cacao seed when harvested may be somewhere between five and nine per cent, but, depending on the care taken in these stages (in particular the intensity of heat), may drop as low as 0.7 per cent in the final product, thereby eradicating its nutritional value.[26] What's more, this is no accident; reducing the presence of flavonols is one of the core reasons for which these processes are conducted. Like anthocyanins, flavonols impart astringency on the taste of cacao,[27] thus it is in searching for a chocolate without bitterness that manufacturers create a chocolate lacking value to health.

For Foucault, living life according to a care of the self walks a fine line: it can be the recipe for subjection to power; to expertise, or it can, conversely, provide the platform needed to critique that very same authority.[28] The effects which the chocolate industry can have on the health aspects of their product, long before it reaches the moment of consumer choice, should alert us to the need for critique. But, more so, it is necessary for those concerned with public health to turn responsibility back onto manufacturers. They must account for a fair portion of the damage which they have hitherto externalized onto individual consumers. Regimen is a potentially useful tool here, but only if is applied to all parties. A greater onus should be imposed on chocolate producers to adhere vigilantly to their own regimens so as to preserve the worth of what they produce. Without this double movement, the freedom of choice which the public is claimed to possess is a choice of no choice at all.

CHOCOLATE SORBET, PEPPERMINT SYRUP

Sorbet is often seen as a 'healthy option', with the implication that it does not have the full-bodied flavour of ice-cream. Chocolate sorbet is the opposite. It is more intense than any chocolate ice-cream you could ever make.

On the streets of Ecuador *helados de paila*, fruit-flavoured ice cream is manually churned by way of spinning tin bowls, akin to giant woks, over equally oversized blocks of ice covered in salt. I attempted something like this in my kitchen, and I think it would have worked if only I had had five hours to spare. With a tinge of regret, I have reverted to the cold comfort of the freezer for this recipe, which combines the sorbet with a refreshing peppermint syrup.

For the chocolate sorbet
100 g / 4 oz dark chocolate, chopped
50 g / 2 oz sugar
2 tbsp honey
250 ml / 8½ fluid oz water
2 tbsp cacao nibs
Pinch of salt

Heat the water, sugar and honey together in a pan. Once the liquor is hot, remove and add the chocolate and the salt. Whisk to melt the chocolate and to start getting some air into the mixture, then leave to cool before putting into the fridge, and then the freezer (or an ice cream maker, if you possess one). Every 30 to 45 minutes, take the sorbet from the freezer and whisk it thoroughly to get rid of any forming ice crystals. When the mixture begins to get thicker, whisk or stir in the cacao nibs. Continue to whisk regularly until you can whisk no longer, at which point leave it in the freezer to set completely.

For the peppermint syrup
2 peppermint tea bags

150 ml / 5 fluid oz water
75 ml / 3 oz honey
Juice of half a lemon

In a pan boil the water and add the teabags to brew until the liquid is fragrant but not bitter. Remove the teabags and add the honey and the lemon juice. Now reduce the syrup, tasting, until it has the desired sweetness.

For the chocolate crumble
20 g / 1 oz cocoa powder
30 g / 1½ oz caster sugar
100 g / 4 oz cold butter, cubed
140 g / 5oz plain flour
30 g / 1½ oz milk powder
2 tbsp sunflower seeds

In a bowl, rub the butter into the flour, sugar, milk powder and cocoa powder with your fingertips. Once you have a crumble-like consistence, mix in the sunflower seeds and spread thinly onto a baking tray. Bake in the oven at around 160°C for 15-20 minutes, or until the crumble has attained a good crunch.

Serve the sorbet with the syrup poured around the sides and the crumble dotted over the top.

CHOCOLATE AND SULTANA ROLLS, SPICED MAPLE BUTTER

As well as 'healthy' and 'unhealthy', there is another misleading binary which is habitually resorted to for the description of western food: sweet and savoury. Again, it is often phrased in the terms of competition (sweet versus savoury). This is despite the fact that some of the most appealing foods are those which hint at both categories, but which in the end can be reduced to neither. Croissants and brioche are two of the best examples, joyfully moreish in their indecision, so

I have come up with an enriched chocolate bread which is only just sweet and which, depending on what you spread on it, could easily become savoury.

For the bread
7g / ¼ oz dried active yeast
325 ml / 11 fluid oz milk
600 g / 21 oz strong white bread flour
80 g / 3 oz caster sugar
1 ½ tsp salt
50g good quality natural cocoa powder
3 eggs, plus one for the egg wash
100 g / 4 oz butter
75 g / 3 oz dark chocolate, 70% cocoa solids
150 g / 5 oz sultanas

Pour the milk into a pan over a low heat. While it is heating up, work the butter into the flour with your fingertips in a large bowl. Once this is combined into a crumb, add the cocoa powder, sugar, salt and yeast and mix. Add the chocolate to the hot milk, stirring to melt, then let cool to a lukewarm temperature before whisking in the eggs. Stir the warm chocolate into the yeast mixture, pushing it into a dough. An enriched dough needs a lot of work to develop the gluten that gives bread its texture, so tip it out onto a floured surface and knead vigorously for a good 5 to 10 minutes, until it becomes more elastic.

Work in the sultanas, then return the dough to its bowl, cover, and let rise in a warm part of the kitchen for 2 hours. After this time, the dough should be significantly larger and very soft to the touch.

Knock the dough back, tip it out onto the floured surface once more, and divide into 12 equal-sized rolls. Shape these as neatly as you can and then arrange them on two lined baking trays, giving them as much space as possible into which to expand.

Cover the dough again and let rise for another 45 minutes to an hour, or until, when you push a thumb lightly into the top of a roll, the dough moves back only very slowly.

Preheat the oven to 150°C, delicately brush the rolls with the remaining egg, (mixed with a little water), and then bake for 25 to 35 minutes. Be aware that, because of the chocolate, it will not be possible to tell whether the rolls are baked from their colour; only from tapping their base, or tearing one open.

For the spiced butter
50 g / 2 oz butter, softened
½ tsp salt
1 tbsp maple syrup
1 tsp cinnamon

Whip all the butter ingredients together and serve with the warm bread.

END NOTES

1. *Quoted in* Grant, Mark, *Galen on Food and Diet*, London & New York: Routledge, 2000: 14.
2. Stubbe, Henry, *The Indian Nectar*, London: A. Crook, 1662. *Quoted in* Wilson, Philip, 'Chocolate as Medicine: A Changing Framework of Evidence throughout History', in *Chocolate and Health*, edited by Paoletti, Rodolpho, Poli, Andrea, Conti, Areo & Visioli, Francesco, London: Springer, 2011. pp. 1-16: 7.
3. Lemery, Nicolas, *A treatise of all sorts of foods, both animal and vegetable: also of drinkables*, edited by Innys, W., Longman, T. & Shadwell, T., 3rd edition, London, 1745 (1698): 364. Quoted in Wilson, 'Chocolate as Medicine': 7.
4. Cárdenas, Juan de, *Problemas y Secretos Maravillosos de las Indias*, Madrid: Ediciones Cultura Hispanica, 1591: 117v. *Quoted in* Grivetti, Louis, 'Medicinal Chocolate in New Spain, Western Europe, and North America', *Chocolate: History, Culture, and Heritage*, edited by Grivetti, Louis, & Shapiro, Howard-Yana, John Wiley & Sons, Inc. 2009. pp. 67-88: 70.
5. Foucault, Michel, 'Dietetics', in *The History of Sexuality, Part II: The Use*

of Pleasure, New York: Vintage Books, 1990 (1976): 106.

6. Coe & Coe, *The True History of Chocolate*: 147-8.

7. Susan Mattern relates how in one such demonstration, Galen taught the audience of the functioning of the laryngeal nerves by tying and then untying those of an animal, turning its screams off and on again. (Mattern, Susan, *Galen and the Rhetoric of Healing*. Baltimore, MD: The John Hopkins University Press, 2008: 9).

8. Sugg, Richard, 'Eating the Soul: Forms of Cannibalism from the Aztecs to Charles II', *Mexicolore*, 2007. Available at: http://www.mexicolore. co.uk/aztecs/home/cannibalism-and-corpse-medicine-1 [accessed 16th June, 2015].

9. See Lévi-Strauss, Claude, *Mythologiques, Vol. 1: The Raw and the Cooked*, University of Chicago Press, 1983.

10. Bacon, Francis, *New Atlantis*, 1627, in *Three Early Modern Utopias: Utopia, New Atlantis* and *The Isle of Pines*, edited by Bruce, Susan, Oxford & New York: Oxford University Press, 2008: 168.

11. Bacon, Francis, *New Atlantis*: 177-180.

12. Daston, Lorraine, 'Hard Facts', in *Making Things Public: Atmospheres of Democracy*, edited by Latour, Bruno & Weibel, Peter, Cambridge, MA: MIT Press, 2005. pp. 680-685: 680. *Cited in* Keenan, Thomas & Weizman, Eyal, *Mengele's Skull: The Advent of a Forensic Aesthetics*. Berlin: Sternberg Press/Portikus, 2012: 23-4.

13. Delbourgo, James, 'Sir Hans Sloane's Milk Chocolate and the Whole History of the Cacao', *Social Text 106*, 29(1), 2011. pp. 71-101: 86.

14. Wilson, 'Chocolate as Medicine': 9.

15. Fitzgerald, Robert, *Rowntree and the Marketing Revolution, 1862-1969*, Cambridge University Press, 1995: 129.

16. Wilson, 'Chocolate as Medicine': 11.

17. Wilson, 'Chocolate as Medicine': 11.

18. Swisher, Margaret, 'Commercial Chocolate Posters: Reflections of Cultures, Values, and Times', in in *Chocolate: History, Culture, and Heritage*, edited by Grivetti, Louis & Shapiro, Howard-Yana, John Wiley & Sons, Inc., 2009. pp. 193-198: 194.

19. *See* Foucault, Michel, 'The Politics of Health in the 18th Century', in *Power/Knowledge: Selected Interviews and Other Writings, 1972-1977*, edited by Gordon, Colin, New York: Pantheon Books, 1980. pp. 166-182: 172.

20. Levenstein, Harvey, *Revolution at the Table*, University of California Press, 1988: 152.

21. Latour, Bruno, *The Making of the Law: An Ethnography of the Conseil*

D'etat, Cambridge: Polity, 2009: 208. *Quoted in* Keenan & Weizman, *Mengele's Skull*: 24-5.

22. Keenan & Weizman, *Mengele's Skull*: 24.

23. Bernaert, Herwig, Blondeel, Ieme, Allegaert, Leen & Lohmueller, Tobias, 'Industrial Treatment of Cocoa in Chocolate Production: Health Implications', in Paoletti, Rodolpho, Poli, Andrea, Conti, Areo & Visioli, Francesco (eds), *Chocolate and Health*, pp. 17-32: 17-18.

24. Pucciarelli, Deanna, 'Cocoa and Heart Health: A Historical Review of the Science', *Nutrients*, Iss. 5, 2013, 3854-3870: 3857-8.

25. Wilson, 'Chocolate as Medicine': 13.

26. Bernaert et al., 'Industrial Treatment of Cocoa in Chocolate Production': 24-7; Pucciarelli, 'Cocoa and Heart Health': 3858-9.

27. Pucciarelli, 'Cocoa and Heart Health': 3859.

28. *See* Foucault, Michel, 'The Ethics of the Concern of the Self as a Practice of Freedom', in *Ethics: Subjectivity and Truth*, edited by Ranibow, Paul, New York: The New Press, 1997. pp. 281-301; Foucault, Michel, 'What Is Critique?', in *The Politics of Truth*, edited by Lotringer, Sylvère, Los Angeles, CA: Semiotext(e), 2007. pp. 41-81.

CHAPTER SIX

CHOCOLATE IN THE HOME

In the period between the birth of modernity and the dietetic practises that came about in the late twentieth and twenty-first centuries, the tripartite pact of food, science and health became an uneasy alliance. Particularly uncomfortable was Enlightenment medicine's rejection of ordinary experience and the domestic as the realm of the amateur. In the development of a professional scientific community – envisaged as a beacon of objective truth-discovery – the task of teaching moral virtue was left to others; those unqualified others denounced as hobbyists and housewives. The industrial logic which had deconstructed the cacao bean likewise had its way with Galen's motto: no longer were health and food to be the polymathic realm of the physician. Instead, each should keep strictly to its own quarters. Every good physician should also be a good cook? Ludicrous. The sign of a good physician was that they should be a pure physician; only a physician and nothing else besides. The difference between profession and hobby was not only talent but also devotion, and one cannot be devoted to more than one profession at a time. However, by the process of responsiblisation – that passing down, that internalization of messages – the association of food, and chocolate especially, with moral as well as physical health, took up lodging in private quarters.

The virtue of food was not lost but suppressed, transposed from the public to the private space: from theatres (ceremonial, dramatic and surgical) to homes. The act of cooking, as a practice of healthcare, passed from the remit of the public professional to that of the private individual. But its introverted guise did not mean that its purpose was rendered trivial. On the contrary, domestic health, the health of the family, was indicative of the wellbeing of the nation.

Foucault argues that the nuclear family was important in this respect, providing a well-defined unit which could be medicalised: structured in terms of roles and spaces, as a coherent institution. Fathers were labelled as breadwinners, mothers as housekeepers; together creating the conditions in which their children could socially and biologically mature into healthy, self-sufficient adults.[1] It was hoped in turn that this biological and social institution would be refracted and amplified outwards, or from the bottom up, into the political structure of the nation-state. The intersection of health and food in the private sphere is not new. As mentioned in the previous chapter, before Galen's intervention, home cures were the primary means of medical care. However, what distinguishes modern health food is this connectivity with other spaces, its extension out from the family into the local, regional and national community.

HEALTH, ECONOMY, AND THE FRUGAL HOUSEKEEPER

The cookbook has always been a vital article of material culture. The gastronomical diaries of the ancients have been scoured for clues as to the intricacies of their worlds.[2] Yet these early accounts are problematic as wider representations of society since they tended to be written and read by only that small minority who were privileged with literacy and leisure. They circulated in closed aristocratic circles, and as such their moralizing tone is informed at all times by potentially partisan philosophies. No doubt this problem of representation and circulation persists today. However, the fact that Johannes Gutenberg's printing press, dated to the middle of the fifteenth century, is for many the ignition spark of European modernity, indicates the extent to which knowledge was liberalized by the dissemination of reading materials. The cookbook, which received its first mechanical reproduction in Rome in 1475 with the printing of Bartolomea de Sacchi's *De honesta voluptate et valitudine* (*On Honourable Pleasure and Health*), held matching importance for the place of cooking in society.

At the same time a symptom and a cause of the diffusion of print was the figure of the housewife. This woman was the ideal mother of the medicalized family. She was devoted to the home, and yet, as the author of influential cookbooks, she provided guidance which reached well beyond the simple aim of teaching people how to make meals to the instruction of running whole households, that is, *whole lives* – not only one's own life but also those of familial others, and by extension (via the father) whole nations. The semi-public position which the housewife held is illustrated well enough by the term 'domestic goddess' (private yet omnipresent; mundane yet heavenly). She was, on an individual level, typical of the restrictions placed on female life. Her sphere was the domestic sphere, a space from which it would be promiscuous to stray. But at the same time the foundation of government lay, in fact, in her responsible influence. What was not granted was the social status which might have accompanied such responsibility. In fact, the housewife was supposed to find in responsibility a perfect substitute for liberty. While her responsibility extended to the national scale, her pride – by nature an outwardly-extending, public emotion – was to be felt behind closed doors.

The freedom to experiment with food was, up to this point, the privilege of noble courts. Chefs – predominantly male members of an increasingly respected profession – competed to concoct the most lavish banquets, and it was from these battles of extravagance that many of the earliest cookbooks emanated. These banquets bore the theatrics of Mesoamerican ritual with the added exhibition of material wealth, and the spectacular demonstrative methods of Galen's dissections without their emphasis on health. Like the physician's demonstrations, banquets were contests, and the cookbook was a record of performance, a keeping of the score. Thus the fifteenth century *Du Fait de Cuisine* (*On Cookery*) was written for the court of the Italian Amadeus VIII, Duke of Savoy, in part as a challenge to the Court of Burgundy. The recipes begin only after registering the gigantic scale of the feast by a staggering roll call of ingredients including (but certainly not limited to) 6,000 eggs, 30 loaves of sugar and 130 sheep. And, in the menus that follow, the spectacular ilk of the occasion is made abundantly clear. One plate, for example, is described as 'boars' heads, glazed and emblazoned and spitting fire'. What's more, this is not the table's centrepiece, but an *entremet*, a mere side dish.[3] This extravagant approach remains wherever food is being prepared for aristocratic groups. In eighteenth century Italy for instance, Sophie and Michael Coe inform us that chocolate, as a substance of mystery and exotic taste, was amongst those ingredients that were often experimented with. Besides numerous ice creams, sorbets and meringues, chocolate was a partner to such unlikely compatriots as liver, polenta and pappardelle.[4]

Away from the courts, the technological advances of the nineteenth century, the liberalization of trade, and the financial benefits which the emergent middle classes of industrializing nations accrued from these enterprises together granted the domestic kitchen a far greater variety of ingredients to line its pantry. Yet this period is characterized, in Britain and North America in particular, by a distinct lack of extravagance in the use of chocolate. This is because, though industrial capitalism brought unprecedented wealth for many, it also brought unprecedented turbulence and uncertainty. In the dizziness of a world in which, as Rousseau's protagonist Saint-Preux put it, it is 'only phantoms that strike my eye',[5] there arose an ideology advising restraint in all things, food included.

The North American colonies took a keen interest in the expanding knowledge-base of domestic cookery, importing and reprinting popular English cookbooks. For example in 1742 Eliza Smith's *The Compleat Housewife: Or Accomplished Gentlewomen's Companion*, first published in London in 1727, was reissued in Williamsburg, Virginia.[6] Like the ancient and medieval texts of physicians, many of this cookbook's recipes are aimed at relieving ailments. There are curative meals for coughs and burns, and a tonic for 'a stitch in the side' consists of pounding and sifting rosin before combining it with treacle. The book contains only one chocolate recipe, for 'chocolate almonds' – again, almonds here are used as a descriptive term (there are no almonds in the recipe) – but Smith's work is more notable for the guidance she gives on broader aspects of living. Most interestingly, there is a recipe named 'To Promote Breeding', which advises couples who are trying for a child to follow a strict regime of consumption:

> LET the party take of the syrup of stinking orach, a spoonful, night and morning, for a week or more; then as follows: take three pints of good ale, boil in it the piths of three ox-backs, half a handful of clary, a handful of nepp (or cat-mint) a quarter of a pound of dates, stoned, sliced, and the pith taken out; a handful of raisins of the sun stoned, three whole nutmegs prick'd full of holes; boil all these till half be wasted; strain it out and drink a small wine glass full at your going to bed...[7]

With an ever-wider audience attending to their teachings, cookbooks were increasingly influential and increasingly varied in scope. Smith's 'recipes' are testament to this. By promoting breeding, she involved herself not only in the population's health but also in its demography. It may not have been particularly effective, but, as Patrick Spedding observes, the recipe was deemed sufficiently controversial to be censored from later editions.[8]

After liberating itself from Britain in 1776, the interest held in common between Americans and their former colonial ruler was retained. However, Americans soon began to write their own cookbooks. Most often these came in the form of 'commonplace books', which were not intended for publication, but were scrapbook records of household purchases, recipes, and other instruction to be passed down within the family. As such, they are much more reliable as accounts of the use of food in the average North American home. There are two simultaneous foundations which matter for the development of cooking with chocolate in North America. First, the physical foundation of the country, which took place upon the New World landmass, thus blessing the American housewife with a cheaper supply of cacao than that accessible to the European market: an advantage which allowed them to incorporate cocoa and chocolate as more or less everyday ingredients.[9] Second, the ideological foundation of the nation: formed by defeat of the imperial foe, and with the political structure of a Republic.

In a sense, these foundations – the physical and the ideological – worked in opposition to one another. Despite the relative physical abundance of ingredients, particularly chocolate, the emphasis of the commonplace book carried a heavy note of caution. Republican ideals formed the spine of these books in the same way that they formed the polity's backbone. Their purpose was therefore explicitly humble, based once more on the principle of moderation, but especially in the context of a utilitarian consciousness. Recipes were based not on excess to be resisted but on the active promotion of economy as a positive principle to be applied to all walks of family life.

The first published cookbooks with American authors extended the ideological undertones of the commonplace book. They came to constitute one wall of an echo chamber effect, repeating and reinforcing the message of economic responsibility proclaimed at the national level. The importance of the housewife in this way was acknowledged by the anonymous author of the 1851 cookbook *The American Matron, or Practical and Scientific Cookery*. After stating that the American home is 'the theatre of the highest hopes and proudest pretensions', the book illustrates the connection between the housewife and the wider community:

How worthy a task for American wives and mothers to adapt their households, practically, to those political and social institutions which are intended to afford competence and comfort to all, and overgrown wealth to none! Frugality and order must be the corner-stones of our Republican edifice.[10] Though it remained a colonial force of some considerable power, similar philosophies were echoed across the Atlantic as Britain's golden age subsided and the moral conservatism of the Victorian era came to stand in its place. Thus, as well as recipes for chocolate, the 1861 recipe book of Mrs. Isabella Beeton, *The Book of Household Management*, devotes a whole chapter to the 'arrangement and economy of the kitchen', based upon principles including symmetry, distribution, proportions, lighting, and its position relative to other rooms of the house.

This detailed analysis also demonstrates the way in which, after their separation at the advent of the modern, science, food, and health coalesced once more, both in laboratories – where chocolate was for the first time undergoing chemical analyses – and in kitchens, where economic logic was accruing legitimacy as a measure of responsibility and health.

CAKES, COOKIES AND BROWNIES

The frugal approach to cooking beyond the courts may explain the relative tardiness of the invention of one of our best-loved chocolate delicacies: the chocolate cake. For it appears odd that since chocolate's first appearances in Europe it was served *alongside* flour, eggs, and sugar – in seventeenth century England for instance, it provided a dip for sweet spiced buns known as 'wigs'[11] – and yet it was not until the mid-1800s that these ingredients were amalgamated into a single dough and baked as one. This is especially peculiar given that the original purpose of combining starch with cacao (to absorb its excess fat – practiced from the ancient civilisations of Mesoamerica onwards) was no longer as relevant after the invention of the defatted cocoa product.

Looking upon the early Anglo-American recipe books, we cannot help but be surprised at the number of near-misses between chocolate on the one hand, and cake on the other. In contrast with the culinary adventure of eighteenth century Italy, these books appear to exhibit a lack of imagination. However, for us to draw this conclusion is likely a symptom not of our superior inventiveness but of that narrowness of thought incurred by hindsight. What for us is simply a matter of putting two and two together obscures all the alternative equations of history's murkier reality. For even in these most modest tomes, the use of chocolate was by no means dull. In fact, recipes for chocolate-based desserts were manifold, coming in the form of creams, ice creams and mousses. In the 1718 cookbook of Queen Anne's confectioner, *Mrs. Mary Eales' Receipts*, a basic recipe is given for a particularly popular sweet of the time, chocolate meringues, or what she calls 'chocolate-puffs':

> Take a Pound of fine sifted Sugar, and three Ounces of Chocolate grated, and sifted thro' an Hair Sieve; make it up to a Paste with White of Eggs whip'd to a Froth; then beat it well in a Mortar, and make it up in Loaves, or any Fashion you please. Bake it in a cool Oven, on Papers and Tin-Plates.[12]

The problem then more specifically concerns chocolate cake than chocolate desserts in general. There is one ingredient consistently missing from this and the other chocolate recipes of the era: flour. One of the possible explanations for its perpetual truancy is that, during this period, if starches were imparted into the purchasable chocolate product itself, this was usually without the knowledge of the consumer. Flour belonged, in other words, to that category of dishonest additives known as 'adulterants'. The first food standards agencies were established precisely to combat the unregulated use of these substances by chocolate vendors. Charles Kany's study of late eighteenth century Madrid thus notes that, though it was common to serve hot pots of chocolate with *bizcochos* (sponge cakes or biscuits), the guild of *maestros molenderos de chocolate* (master chocolate grinders) was formed in 1773 with the express purpose of legislating against those grinders whom adulterated their chocolate with ground almonds, acorns, pine nuts, and, most interestingly, cake crumbs![13]

Before it had even been invented, chocolate cake was already a cheat and an outlaw.

As a blend of chocolate, sugar, and eggs with flour, the chocolate cake is a meal that combines luxury and economy, purity and its adulteration. We can speculate from this that another of the reasons for its late arrival on the scene was that such a humble use of a rare and expensive ingredient would not have been considered proper for the Baroque nobility. Even liberal England could not help but inherit the arts which used chocolate as an ingredient – the arts of confectionary and patisserie – from European high society.

The chocolate cake seems elusive. The titles of recipes send the contemporary reader on a wild goose chase. Things named 'chocolate cakes' or 'chocolate biscuits' are merely sugared items to be served with chocolate, in the same way that 'tea biscuits' or 'teacakes' do not contain tea. Similarly, the terms 'cake' and 'biscuit' only sometimes conform to our modern definitions, at others being used only to refer to any item which is rolled and baked. This can give the impression that, like objects set on parallel trajectories, chocolate and its cake seem destined never to encounter one another in spite of their enduring proximity. With hindsight, we wish to find the occurrence of a particular historical event which all of a sudden throws particles off their orbits such that they collide. We desire a chance encounter, like Newton with his apple, by which a piece of chocolate accidentally drops into the cake batter; an unforeseen eureka moment of pure and sudden realization. But for this moment of fortune to occur, the right conditions needed to be present. What needed to change was the way in which chocolate as an ingredient was perceived by Anglo-American society as a delicacy consumed by European aristocrats. While this perception endured, those that revered European culture would have thought the chocolate cake's humility undesirable, whilst those who did not would consequently have been deterred from chocolate's extensive use.

The growing consumption of liquid chocolate in the home was evidenced by the increased ownership of chocolate-making equipment. However, the French origin of one of the predominant pieces of domestic machinery, the *chocolatière* – a jug with a lid and an in-built *molinillo* – points towards the inheritance with which chocolate's culture of consumption in England had to cope. The hereditary European elitism of the ingredient of chocolate in confectionary is clear in early English cookbooks – hence the title of the Regency era London sweet-maker Frederick Nutt's 1789 book *The Complete Confectioner*. In it, he gives instruction for what he calls 'chocolate biscuits', but the recipe contains only the whites of the eggs, and no flour:

> TAKE a quarter of a pound of chocolate, and put it on a tin, over a stove to make it warm, then put a pound of powdered sugar in a bason, and when the chocolate is quite warm and soft, put it in with the sugar, and mix it well with about eight whites of eggs, if you find it too thin, mix more powdered sugar with it just to bring it to a paste, so that you can roll it in lumps as big as walnuts: let your oven be moderate, put three papers under them, let the oven just raise them and make them crisp and firm, and let them be quite cold before you take them off the paper.[14]

These 'biscuits' are more akin to meringues or macaroons, both of which, you will note, are items which we would consider within the bracket of French cuisine.

For many working class Britons, Europhilia had a poor reputation. Europe meant excess and ostentation. It was mocked as a parade of pure bravado, a mask beneath which there lay little real substance. For men, this was manifest in the macaroni and (later) the dandy fashion movements, the first of which was, unsurprisingly, named after the penchant for the Italian pasta of the same name. The perceived effects of the continental lifestyle on these genteel individuals were many, and most were unflattering. For example the anonymously-authored *Women's Petition Against Coffee*, published in London in 1674, bemoans, in impassioned verse, the sexual impotence brought on by the European beverages and the environments – the coffee and chocolate houses – in which they were consumed:

...to our unspeakable Grief, we find of late a very sensible *Decay* of that true *Old English Vigour;* our *Gallants* being every way so *Frenchified*, that they are become meer Cock-sparrows.

Later in the passage, the themes of sexual prowess and economy are tied, and pantaloons summoned as symptomatic of an impotent way of life; the billowing garments filled with nothing but hot air:[15]

... Never did Men wear *greater Breeches*, or carry *less* in them of any *Mettle* whatsoever.

This showiness, this masquerade, was despised, and so chocolate, despite its popularity, was regarded with suspicious glances due to the Baroque mode in which it had been consumed. For chocolate to be modernized, it needed to be given substance, solidity and weight. Things needed to be added to it. In other words, it needed to be adulterated.

In *The American Matron* (1851), the contrast in approach between European (aristocratic) chefs and liberal or republican cooks is made explicit. In her praise of frugality, the author argues that, '[t]he extravagant follies and unmeasured expenditure of European aristocracies are impossible and incompatible here'.[16] Whether expenditure is high or low is not what is on trial, but rather the notion of 'unmeasured expenditure' itself; of not knowing; not calculating. Measure is lauded as the moral principle of responsible consumption. And where this had previously been a mercantilist policy of weighing commodities, totting up glorious trade surpluses, the North American cookbook, following the commonplace book, was a record of daily and minute calculations, bent on minimizing unnecessary cost.

As well as being more cheaply accessible, chocolate gradually shed, for the average North American, that aristocratic symbolism which it possessed for the average Briton. In fact, chocolate's reputation was turned on its head. This was precisely because of the dramatic success of chocolate's rival beverage, tea – increasingly imported from China – in North America's now-rival nation, Britain. Famously, the boycotting of this drink by the Boston Tea Party of 1773 was central to the revolutionary movement. But it is less often noted that this also led, via the logic that 'the enemy of my enemy is my friend', to an official effort to befriend chocolate on a national scale. The beverage was thus endorsed by two successive early Presidents, John Adams and Thomas Jefferson, who expressed wishes for it to become the great American drink.[17]

It is no shock then that the first recorded chocolate cake recipe is often attributed to one of the most prominent North American housewives, Eliza Leslie, in her *The Ladies' Receipt Book*, published in 1847. Many of the recipes still carry a strong French influence, but the book is inspired by the hope of making what were previously considered inaccessible luxuries palatable for the masses. For once 'chocolate cake' really does mean a cake containing chocolate, and the proportions are modest, calling for just 3 ounces (around 85 grams) of chocolate to 14 ounces (400 grams) of flour.

However, there is a rival origin to Leslie's cake: The Sachertorte, named after its Austrian creator Franz Sacher. This cake, distinguished by its twin toppings of apricot jam and chocolate icing, has established itself in the minds of many as the original European chocolate cake. The story goes that it was first created, by a fifteen-year-old Sacher, for a dinner hosted by Prince Klemens Wenzel Nepomuk Lothar von Metternich in 1832. And what's more, the Sachertorte is not without predecessors. Over a century earlier, in 1719, the *Neues Saltzburgisches Koch-Buch* (*New Saltsburg Cookbook*) – penned by another Austrian Conrad Hagger – gives recipes for three chocolate *dorten* (torte's archaic form).

Now, it is interesting that, after all we have said about Europe's ostentation, the first instance of something resembling the chocolate cake emerges from that very continent. However, perhaps the chocolate torte is not the blood relation of the chocolate cake that it appears at first to be. For a start, the torte, like Frederick Nutt's 'biscuit', contains very little flour. The Sachertorte (like the macaroon) contains only ground almonds, and only a minimal quantity – just enough to hold the cake together. It is not chocolate cake as we know it. It is too glamorous; not frugal enough, contrasting dramatically with Leslie's flour-heavy recipe. Furthermore, beyond being a thing of luxury, tortes and other European cakes were concerned with ostentation, with *looking* even more luxurious than they were. Tortes were thus deeply implicated in the European masquerade, the play of appearances which repulsed the Anglo-American working class. Their predominant role was as table decoration, small elements of grand compositions including fire-spitting boars' heads and sugar sculptures. As such, chocolate was appreciated mostly for its strong splash of colour rather than its taste.[18] The use of chocolate as a dye is common also to the early Anglo-American cookbooks. In *Mrs. Mary Eales' Receipts* (1718) for instance, where chocolate is absent from any cake, it is added to decorative sugar paste. This aesthetic tendency highlights a further reason for the noble reluctance towards chocolate cake: when mixed with flour, chocolate is deprived of its shine. That it might make the meal more of a feast for the stomach was unimportant; that it made it less of a feast for the eyes far more crucial. Though all dishes were to some extent part of the show, sweets were especially affected by style over substance, helping to explain why eighteenth century Italian recipes did not include chocolate in cakes, but were less hesitant using it in humble savoury foods such as pasta.

The Sachertorte's ostentation stretches beyond its aesthetics to the story of its invention, which is perhaps even more inventive than it lets on. It seems that Franz Sacher in fact developed his cake in the late 1840s, by which point he had left the kitchen of von Metternich and was instead in the service of a casino in Bratislava. The fact that it was felt necessary to cover up this much less regal origin reveals the Sachertorte to be the edible manifestation of Viennese aristocratic pomp.[19]

BROWNIES AND COOKIES: TECHNOSCIENTIFIC INVENTIONS

Like the Sachertorte, the brownie comes with its obligatory legends. The earliest is the 1893 story of the Palmer House Hotel, whereby the head chef created the brownie at the request of Mrs. Bertha Palmer herself, as a 'ladies' dessert which could be eaten with the hands without dirtying them. And strangely it is not only the legend which bears resemblance to the Sachertorte, but also the recipe itself: the Palmer House brownie also had an apricot glaze, and likewise contained a very large proportion of chocolate relative to flour. It was thus an emphatically luxurious brownie. One might even say it was European.

The recipe for the more modest brownie comes about in a somewhat less romantic fashion, unearthed from within the records of New England's Framingham Normal School – usurper of the influential 155 School – in the first half of the twentieth century.[20] This origin points to a growing trend in the twentieth century: the increasingly systematic and commercially orientated nature of culinary experimentation. The need to invent new products for a growing marketplace led the interests of large-scale industry to coalesce again with those of small-scale producers, bringing with it the eventual recognition of the value of ordinary experience.

Women's rights groups in North American had been fighting for their gender to be represented in professional institutions. Cookery and household management provided one of the stranger vehicles for this progressive movement, playing on the liminal place of the domestic goddess to officially draw out the art of the home into public life. In 1889, a conference of academics was hosted at Lake Placid with the aim of formalizing the discipline of home economics, and their calls were answered in January of 1909 with the formation of the American Home Economics Association (now the American Association of Family and Consumer Sciences).

Ordinary experience was brought in from the cold so that it could be neatly ordered. The test kitchens of cooking schools became centres of experimentation with a growing number of links to, and contracts with, the food industry. Increasingly, this meant that what are today thought of as products in their own right were originally simply the by-products of marketing strategies for other branded goods. Some of the first flavoured cookies, for instance, were devised by peanut butter manufacturers as a form of promotion, while oatmeal cookies were popularized by the Quaker Oats Company.[21]

The ordering and institutionalization of the housewife's talents was a technoscientific rendering, the unusual shaping of *techne* into *episteme*; a skill into a discipline for which there is a codified set of classifications and procedures, and laws.[22] The Boston Cooking School was thus founded in 1879 with the aim to advance the cause of the 'domestic scientist' as opposed to the aforementioned domestic goddess.[23] Since *techne* held more charm, it continued to be employed as the predominant means of advertising even for such systematically invented items. The chocolate cookie most likely emerged from the Boston Cooking School's test laboratories in the early 1900s, with chocolate chips added in 1937 by Ruth Wakefield, a graduate of Framingham.[24] And yet anecdotal Eureka moments and chance encounters – including one which tells of a young housewife accidentally dropping chocolate into cookie dough – remain widely credited.

The early years of the twentieth century were years of parallel development, or perhaps cross-contamination, for the commercial and home kitchens. In both the domestic and laboratory environments, technoscientific methods of creating food became par for the course. This was associated with the aforementioned medicalization of everyday life: a growing concern for hygiene and family health. In *The Book of Household Management*, Mrs. Beeton goes on to warn her readers:

> It must be remembered that [the kitchen] is the great laboratory of every household, and that much of the "weal or woe", as far as regards bodily health, depends upon the nature of the preparations concocted within its walls.[25]

It was in the proceeding decades that the modern method of recipe-writing was born. In contrast to the flowery, almost poetic descriptive passages that adorned the pages of the first cookbooks, a scientific mode of delivery, based upon precisely weighed quantities and pared down, step-by-step instruction, was gradually taken up. 'Proven' recipes were practised experiments, complete with a method, results, and an analysis of the final taste and texture. In 1904, founder of the Boston School of Cookery Fannie Farmer even began mentioning the caloric density of her ingredients, making an important contribution to the meteoric popularization of the calorie as a measurement of health as cultural as it is scientific.[26] The physical space of the kitchen altered dramatically as a result of the scientific movement. In 1919, Christine Frederick, yet another all-American housewife, published her preliminary research. Inspired by scientific engineering techniques, she went about painstakingly counting and recording the number of steps it took her to complete numerous kitchen tasks, and then suggesting arrangements by which a few steps here and there might be shaved off, with a significant accumulative effect over time.

Frederick's theories were swiftly accompanied by a fully-formulated architectural style. 'Functionalism' emerged from Germany, Austria, and the Netherlands to lend the kitchen what June Freeman describes as 'an aesthetic of efficiency'.[27] In what was conceived of as a socialist project, the kitchen developed a standardized model. Like the work of the housewife, the space in which it was conducted was codified, and this code distributed in the form of the fitted kitchen.

The most significant element of this particular development was that it represented the common adoption of the idea to give cooking its own room. A hygienic development then, premised upon the division of the home into demarcated spaces, sealed off from one-another. But also a ritual development, giving the preparation of food its dedicated space, insulated to prevent the violence of its ceremony – the blood; the bacteria; the chocolate – from proliferating throughout the household. The same ritual dedication was applied to the domestic preparation of chocolate. While the beverage was still the most popular form of chocolate, the ceremony of its preparation took place in front of house guests, using the chocolatière as we might a teapot. However, as solid forms of chocolate became more commonplace, there was increasingly less ceremony to be had – chocolate products were usually portable, personal snacks – and where preparation was necessary (in the baking of a cake for instance), it took place within the strict confines of the kitchen.

FOOD ENGINEERING AND THE RETURN OF MASQUERADE

The frugal means of nineteenth century cooking rebelled against aristocratic fashions by declaring substance over ostentation. The direction in which some sections of the chocolate industry have been moving since the entry of commercial technoscience is quite the opposite: in pushing to new frontiers the desire for economic efficiency, it motions towards a peculiar situation in which there could be 'chocolate' almost entirely without cacao, without the very substance which previously defined it. In response to the increasing inefficiency of using cacao butter in the expanding chocolate market – compared to its more profitable prospects in pharmaceuticals – food engineers are investigating possible cacao butter replacements (CBRs). The difficulty of this task is that cacao butter is quite a unique fat. Its most distinctive attribute derives from its melting point. It is relatively high, meaning that, unlike other fats, it is solid at room temperature (25°C), but it is not too high – vitally, it is just below 37°C, the temperature of the human body. This property is deeply embedded in our era's culture of consumption. It is, for instance, for this reason that chocolate is used in association with the word 'fondant', a term which has developed in English usage to mean a certain type of chocolate or chocolate dessert, but which derives from the first French word for the modern chocolate bar: '*fondant*', literally, 'melting' (from '*fondre*', 'to melt'). If the melting point of cacao butter were outside of this range, we would either have a chocolate which needed constant refrigeration to maintain its form, or one which, when eaten, would sit idly on the tongue, silently protesting our taste buds.

The most common substitutes at present are palm and coconut oil, but a great number of others are being studied, including mango seed fat, kokum butter, sal fat, shea butter, and illipé fat. In isolation the results are unsatisfactory. Mango seed fat, for example, melts at between 34°C and 43°C. The upper estimate is far too high. Kokum butter – from the seed of a tree that grows prolifically across India – is even worse: even its lowest melting point is one degree above body temperature. If you want to replicate the experience of eating chocolate containing these replacements, contrast eating a piece of chocolate containing cacao butter before and then immediately after drinking a glass of ice cold water. The water will lower the temperature inside your mouth, and the butter won't melt as it usually does when it hits your tongue, leaving a flavourless, powdery sensation.

Food engineers look for more desirable outcomes by taking the fats apart, splitting them, by fractionation, and then blending the fractions (not only of the same but also of different fats) together in experimental combinations. In spite of the intense technical efforts, it is confessed that CBRs cannot currently replicate the flavours and textures of what they mimic. Like the protagonist in a sci-fi thriller, we can still tell the difference between the real being and its clone. The appearances might be uncanny; the gestures identical, but, when we ask a question of both, the clone gives itself away, there is something not quite right about the way it talks. The admission of this inadequacy lies implicit in the fact that the use of replacements is, for the moment at least, restricted to chocolate products where taste is perceived to be less essential, such as ice creams, cookies, and coatings for certain filled bars. In other words, replacements succeed only where the most essential function of chocolate is to *look like chocolate*.[28] This is strangely reminiscent of the function intended for chocolate in the eighteenth century European torte. The play of appearances, the masquerade, resurfaces.

COOKING WITH CHOCOLATE, COCOA AND CACAO

The majority of the advice given for cooking with cacao centres, understandably, upon its two most familiar and readily available products: cocoa powder and solid chocolate. For putting the chocolate into chocolate cake for instance, a debate is ongoing between those who opt for cocoa powder, given that it is a more intensely chocolatey flavour, and those who swear by solid chocolate. Both sides claim the label of 'purists', raising once more the question of what 'real' chocolate is.

Scientifically speaking, a light chocolate cake is best made with cocoa powder. This is first because it is the simplest cacao product. All of the complications of the original seed have been stripped away – most of its moisture driven off by the drying and roasting processes, and much of its cacao butter extracted by the defatting procedure – and nothing has been mixed back in. This simplicity is especially appreciated for a sponge, where a delicate balance of fat, carbohydrate, sugar, and raising agents is needed for the end result to be airy, evenly risen, and sufficiently strong not to collapse when removed from the oven.

The complications posed by chocolate as opposed to cocoa powder are exacerbated by the uncertainty surrounding its exact contents. If we do not know, for instance, how much of a chocolate bar consists of cocoa solids, then it is hard to know what quantities of fat, flour and sugar to add to it to give a cake the perfect flavour and texture. Further, if the types and proportions of fats which have been used isn't known, – how much is cacao butter and how much is a substitute such as palm oil? – then we cannot be certain what impact there will be on the final product. These arguments in favour of cocoa powder are based upon a strategy of risk reduction.

But cacao butter is not just a 'complication' to the recipe; it also troubles the pocket. It is the presence of this fat which partly accounts for the expensiveness of high quality chocolate. As has been argued, the price is often worth paying for the unique melting point of cacao butter, but this point is less pertinent where cakes are concerned due to the addition of that humble ingredient, flour. On the one hand, flour alters the mouthfeel of chocolate, including the fondant effect for which cacao butter is famed; on the other, its solidity when combined with a raising agent holds the cake's form at room temperature, regardless of whether the fat it contains is in a liquid state. As a result fats with lower melting points – usually dairy butter, which begins to melt at around 32°C, but softens at room temperature, but also many kinds of oil – can be substituted without causing the cake to collapse. Chocolate cakes made with fats that are liquid at room temperature (olive oil, for instance) are therefore moister than that made only with chocolate.

This only applies presuming that the cake is being served at room temperature. As for a chocolate pudding, anything warmer than 36°C containing solely chocolate would give the same, extremely moist, result.

Another approach is to add substances to the mixture, such as milk, cream, or syrup, which will be liquid rather than solid at room temperature. This is similar to the method used to make a chocolate ganache or truffle, but its disadvantage in cakes is that the distinctive bitterness of the chocolate flavour – already diminished by the flour – is diluted still further. The best example is a chocolate fudge cake, which is moist, sweet and intensely rich, but not necessarily especially chocolatey.

CHOCOLATE CAKE WITH *CACHAÇA* BROWN BUTTER ICING AND HONEYCOMB

Cachaça, a spirit which is most famously combined with lime and sugar to make the Brazilian national cocktail, the *Caipirinha*, is here used to give a unique flavour to a chocolate cake made with cocoa and topped with dramatic shards of honeycomb.

For the honeycomb
130 g / 4½ oz caster sugar
50 g / 2 oz golden syrup
1½ tsp bicarbonate of soda

Line a baking sheet with parchment.

Heat the sugar and syrup together in a pan on a medium heat. Once the sugars begin to bubble, watch carefully for a few minutes until they begin to turn a darker shade of caramel. At this point add the bicarbonate of soda, briskly stir with a wooden spoon, and then immediately pour out onto the baking sheet. Once this is cool, store in a dry place or, if it's a warm day, in the fridge until ready to use.

For the chocolate cake
165 g / 6 oz caster sugar
155 g / just under 6 oz soft brown sugar
200 g / 7 oz plain flour
60 g / 2 oz good quality, natural cocoa powder
180 g / 6 oz butter, softened
3 eggs, lightly beaten
1 ½ tsp of bicarbonate of soda
1 ½ tsp baking powder
2 tbsp cachaça

Grease and line a large cake tin and preheat your oven to 180°C.

Beat together the butter and the sugars until light and fluffy, then gradually add in the eggs, combining with care so as to avoid curdling the mixture. Add the cachaça and combine.

In a separate bowl, sift the flour and the cocoa powder and combine with the raising agents, then fold the dry ingredients into the wet ingredients and pour into the prepared cake tin.

Bake for 35-45 minutes, or until well risen and bouncing back when poked.

For the cachaça and brown butter icing
80 g / 3 oz unsalted butter
80 g / 3 oz icing sugar
100 g / 4 oz dark chocolate
50 ml / 1 ½ fluid oz double cream
1-2 tbsp cachaça

Heat the cream on the hob until steaming and pour over the chocolate to melt.

Now, to turn plain old butter into brown butter, place it into a small frying pan over a medium flame. After it melts, the butter will boil for a short time but, once the milk solids separate from the fat, will fall still. In all, the process should take around six or seven minutes, but simply continue to heat until the residue on the sides of the pan begins to darken appealingly, then transfer the contents to a bowl.

Add the icing sugar to the butter, and then pour in the chocolate and measure out the *cachaça* to taste. Don't be concerned by the specks of brown – they are, in fact, the most flavoursome morsels.

Once the cake has cooled, pour over the icing and then break up the honeycomb with your hands (or bash with a rolling pin inside a sealable bag) and liberally sprinkle.

SALTED TREACLE, LIME AND CHOCOLATE TART

If there is an even more blatant way of bringing humility to the torte, it is the treacle tart. It economises on not one but two fronts. Like the chocolate cake, it extends expensive ingredients by adding carbohydrate. But, because in its case the carbohydrate is breadcrumbs, and often specifically stale breadcrumbs, it also uses up leftovers which would otherwise go to waste.

Of all the novel chocolate flavours I have tasted over the last few years – from cardamom to marmite – salt and lime probably heads the list. Combined with the humble glory of treacle and breadcrumbs, it is lively and classical at the same time. If you don't want to bother with the cocoa powder – which will make the cooking of the pastry a little harder to judge, but will also lend it a hint of bitterness to offset the filling – then add a spoonful more flour.

For the shortcrust pastry
100 g / 4 oz cold butter, diced
220 g / 8 oz plain flour
1 tbsp cocoa powder
1 egg
Very cold water

Sift the flour and cocoa powder into a bowl and then work very lightly into the butter with your fingertips. Once the two are just combined add the egg and just enough water so that you are able to form a roughly coherent dough. Push and prod the dough as little as possible. Cover the bowl and place in the fridge to rest for 5 minutes or so, then remove and roll out on a floured surface with a floured rolling pin. Again, try to do this with just a few firm, confident strokes, and you will be rewarded with a perfectly crumbling pastry.

Roll the pastry up and around the pin, and then off into the lined tart tin. Top with a layer of baking parchment and some baking beans or rice, and blind bake in a hot oven for 15 to 20 minutes, or until it is golden brown and firm to the touch.

For the treacle filling
400 g / 14 oz golden syrup
1 tbsp treacle
2 large eggs
50 ml / 1½ fluid oz double cream
Juice of 2 unwaxed limes
1 tsp salt
100 g / 4 oz good quality dark chocolate, 75% cocoa solids, chopped into small chunks
140 g / 5 oz multi-seeded bread

In a pan over a low heat combine the golden syrup and treacle, heating until they are less viscous and then removing from the flame and adding the cream and salt.

Put the bread into a food processor, pulsing until you get fine breadcrumbs, and then mix these into the treacle. Whisk the eggs briefly and then add, followed by the chunks of chocolate and the lime juice.

Spoon the filling into the pastry case and bake for a further 25-30 minutes until any breadcrumbs protruding from the syrup have crisped up, and the treacle is set. Remove from the oven and let cool slightly.

To serve
Zest of 2 unwaxed limes
Soured cream or crème fraiche

Grate the lime zest over the tart, slice, and plate up with a dollop of crème fraiche.

MOLASSES BROWNIES

Because brownies aim at less of a rise than a sponge – their origins lying in the bar cookie rather than the cake – they can afford to have a higher fat content and require a less precise approach. These properties have made them a firm favourite when time or energy is in short supply.

The heavy batter also means that large pieces – chunks as opposed to chips – of chocolate, nuts, or fruit can be added without sinking to the bottom of the brownie as they might do in a cake mix. With brownies then, we can (at least proverbially speaking) have our cake and eat it too, using cocoa powder to get the most intense flavour possible through the batter, while also adding sizeable lumps of chocolate to create molten pockets.

Though the recipe below does not contain any cocoa powder, it takes advantage of the brownie's sturdiness, dotting a buttery molasses-flavoured batter with the unadulterated fruity bitterness of cacao-rich chocolate.

The idea to combine molasses and chocolate in a brownie comes from two quite different origins. On the one hand, under the colonial rule of the French, English and Dutch powers, sugarcane was often grown alongside cacao throughout the Caribbean before being exported to Europe, and molasses (known in the UK as treacle), as well as other brown sugars, remain essential to Caribbean cooking. On the other, the chocolate brownie was first concocted at Framingham by taking a pre-existing recipe for a dark, sticky, tray-baked cookie and replacing some of the molasses used with chocolate.[29] The molasses version is, in this sense, the original brownie.

150 g / 5 oz dark and 100 g / 4 oz white chocolate, broken into chunks
3 large eggs, at room temperature
2 tbsp black treacle
250 g / 9 oz caster sugar

200 g / 8 oz butter, melted
50 g / 2 oz rolled oats
130 g / 5 oz plain flour
1 tsp salt

Line a brownie tray with baking paper and set your oven to 170°C.

Beat the sugar and the eggs together with the back of a wooden spoon for a few minutes until light, and then gradually add the melted butter, continuing to beat as you do. Exactly as if you were making a mayonnaise, you want the mixture to emulsify. Once all the butter has been combined, spoon the treacle into the bowl and then mix in the oats and a large pinch of salt. Sift in the flour and stir until you get a smooth, sticky batter, add the chocolate, and pour into the baking tray, lightly prodding the mixture into the corners.

Bake for 20 to 25 minutes, or until just firm but still slightly 'undercooked'.

CHOCOLATE AND MALT *ALFAJORES*

Quick on the heels of the first chocolate cookie at the outset of the twentieth century was the 'sandwich cookie', a tasty edifice of two small biscuits encasing a soft filling. This concoction is now irresistibly linked to the Oreo cookie, and is yet another victory for the persuasive power of advertising. The first chocolate sandwich cookies held a less familiar name: the Hydrox, released in 1908 by the Kansas company Sunshine Biscuits. It was not until four years later that the more established National Biscuit trademarked the suspiciously similar Oreo, and it is only by using superior marketing clout that the Oreo – now, like Cadbury, a Mondelēz brand – has managed to convince the vast majority of its primacy.[30]

A favourite dessert all over South America, *Alfajores* are a variety of sandwich cookie consisting of bittersweet biscuits – not dissimilar in texture to biscotti – either side of a thick smothering of *dulce de leche*. The tangy sweetness of caramelised condensed milk is no easy thing to 'offset', but the cocoa, malt and brown sugar go a little way towards it.

Makes about 16 *Alfajores*

For the *dulce de leche*
1 tin sweetened condensed milk
½ tsp salt

For the chocolate malt cookies
100 g / 4 oz butter, softened
2 large egg yolks
70 g / 3 oz soft brown sugar
150 g / 6 oz self-raising flour
45 g / 2 oz cocoa powder
65 g / 3 oz malt powder
Pinch of salt
2 tbsp milk

If the condensed milk has a paper label, remove it, then place the tin into a large pan. This has to be big enough to contain enough water to completely submerge the tin. Bring the water to a minimal simmer and leave on the heat for roughly two hours. If the water evaporates to a level where the tin is exposed, top it up.

Before you begin making the cookies, line two baking trays with parchment.

Sift the flour, the cocoa powder, and the malt extract into a large bowl with the salt, and mix together thoroughly. Whisk the sugar into the egg yolks and add the butter to form a smooth golden batter. Don't go so far as to risk dislocating your shoulder, but whisk lightly for five minutes or so to lighten the mixture.

Add the brown butter mixture to the dry ingredients and bring them together into a stiff, dry dough. This is not as delicate as a pastry, so there is no need to be anxious about over-working, but it is still the case that the less you handle the dough, the shorter (snappier and more crumbly) it will be. As the mixture begins to resemble a solid mass, add the milk gradually until you can form a smooth ball. Cover and rest the dough in the fridge for around half an hour, and turn the oven to 200°C to preheat.

Roll out, between two pieces of baking parchment, to a thickness of about half a centimetre, then cut into disks roughly the diameter of a golf ball. Bake the cookies for approximately seven minutes until firm and slightly risen, though the time they take will depend on the thickness and the individual oven. In any case, watch carefully and remove if the edges begin to darken.

Once the two hours have elapsed, take the pan off the hob and place it in the sink under cold running water, as you might do with boiled eggs, until the hot water has been displaced by the cold. Leave the tin to cool to a manageable temperature, then open the can and you should be greeted by the reward for your patience: a luxurious, sunny-coloured *dulce de leche* smiling out at you.

Divide the cookies into matching pairs, and spread – or perhaps, shamelessly smother – the flat surface of one with a dollop of *dulce de leche*, placing the other on top to form a sandwich, and pressing down lightly to force the filling to peak from the edges.

ON BAKING WITH 'DUTCHED' COCOA AND DRINKING CHOCOLATE

Coenraad Johannes van Houten's 'dutch process' of removing the natural acidity of cocoa by washing it in an alkaline bath leaves us with a product – 'dutched' cocoa powder – which has a neutral, or sometimes even an alkaline PH. For this reason dutched cocoa will not react with alkaline leaveners such as bicarbonate of soda in the way that natural cocoa powder does. It will not, therefore, produce the carbon dioxide necessary for a cake or brownie to rise. If we use dutched cocoa powder in a cake, we should therefore use baking powder as the leavening agent.

Though we use them in roughly the same way when making hot chocolate, drinking chocolate is not a direct substitute for cocoa powder when baking. Drinking chocolate often contains added sugar. This means that it is the end flavour that is the predominant issue when using it in baking. This can be compensated for by using less sugar in the recipe itself, but this will in turn alter the proportion of dry to wet ingredients; fats to non-fats, returning us to the problem of texture.

ON MELTING CHOCOLATE

There is no doubt that the microwave was a key revolutionary agent for the scientific kitchen. Never mind the number of steps it took to walk from one side of the room to the other, the microwave brought efficiency well and truly into the heart of cooking. From being an art of perception and judgement, cooking became almost entirely a matter of measurement, not only in weight but also in time, a matter not of hours, nor even minutes, but a matter of seconds. It is now common to see an instruction for microwave melting on the reverse of bars of 'cooking chocolate'. And that table of inputs – x Watts required for y number of seconds – is enough to demonstrate how much chocolate and its ceremony has been altered from the extravagant rituals of the past. The preparation of chocolate now takes place behind not one but two closed doors: the kitchen contains the cook, who in turn peers through the door of the microwave at their ingredients.

The issue with melting chocolate in the microwave is that substances absorb microwaves at different speeds. Fats, for example, will heat up at a faster rate than carbohydrates.

The strength of the microwave – the speed at which its radiation penetrates – is therefore also its weakness when it comes to chocolate. The unevenness of heating is condensed into a smaller time, leaving a tighter margin for error. Cooking and chocolate both would not be nearly as exciting without this margin, without a liminal space in which to stray from the 'right' (that is, the normal) way of doing things without necessarily getting things 'wrong'. Because it has no door, the pan is an open space into which it is constantly tempting to drop things. This is why, where the chocolate in this book's recipes has needed melting, I have chosen to do so by using the heat of other ingredients.

COOKING WITH CACAO NIBS

While cocoa powder (and, in the following chapter, cacao tableau) is preferred for some uses because of its concentration, and chocolate for its melting smoothness, there are equally uses for which cacao nibs are the ideal chocolate ingredient. For instance, unlike other forms of cacao, the nibs, because they have not been powdered, can be added to things without dissolving or melting into them. They can be used like cinnamon sticks, star anise, or vanilla pods, dropped into a liquid, left to infuse, and then filtered out at a later time.

I have used this technique to make crème de cacao, but it could easily be applied to create a cacao-infused custard for a tart or an ice cream.

Lastly, roasted cacao nibs have a brilliant crunch. They can add texture to many plates, from sorbet (the previous chapter) and brownies, to smoked fish and grilled red meat.

In sum, it is the relatively unprocessed, unrefined nature of the nibs which gives them these unique properties. Their rough edges have not been sanded down, and it is this roughness which can be put to good use by the cook.

END NOTES

1. Foucault, 'The Politics of Health in the Eighteenth Century': 172-4.
2. Pucciarelli, Deanna, 'Chocolate as Medicine: Imparting Dietary Advice and Moral Values Through 19th Century North American Cookbooks', in Grivetti, Louis, & Shapiro, Howard-Yana (eds), *Chocolate: History, Culture, and Heritage*, pp. 115-126: 115.
3. Chiquart, Maistre, *Chiquart's On Cookery: A Fifteenth-century Savoyard Culinary Treatise*, translated and edited by Scully, Terrence, Bern: Peter Lang, 1986: 23.
4. Coe & Coe, *The True History of Chocolate*: 215-6.
5. Rousseau, Jean-Jacques, *Julie, or the New Héloïse*, Amsterdam: Marc-Michel Rey, 1761: part 2, letter 17.
6. Spedding, Patrick, 'To (Not) Promote Breeding: Censoring Eliza Smith's

Compleat Housewife, Script & Print, Vol. 31, Iss. 4, 2007. 233-242: 233.

7. Smith, Eliza, *The Compleat Housewife: Or Accomplished Gentlewoman's Companion*, London: J. Pemberton, 1727: 246-7.

8. Spedding, 'To (Not) Promote Breeding: 234.

9. Pucciarelli, 'Chocolate as Medicine': 116.

10. Anon., *The American Matron; or Practical and Scientific Cookery*, Boston & Cambridge, MA: James Munroe and Company, 1851: 6-7.

11. Moss, Sarah & Badenoch, Alexander, *Chocolate: A Global History*, London: Reaktion Books, 2009: 16.

12. Eales, Mary, *Mrs. Mary Eales' Receipts*, 2nd edition, London: J. Brindley, 1733 (1718): 74.

13. Kany, Charles, *Life and Manners in Madrid, 1750-1800*, University of California Press, 1932: 152.

14. Nutt, Frederick, *The Complete Confectioner: or, The Whole Art of Confectionary Made Easy*, 4th edition, London: R. Scott, 1807 (1789): 20.

15. The word 'pantaloon' itself originates in the Italian *Pantalone*, a character of the commedia dell'arte, the masked comic theatre of the early modern. He is obsessed with riches, deeply selfish and immoral, and usually ends up as a figure of mockery.

16. Anon., *The American Matron*: 7.

17. Clarence-Smith, 'The Global Consumption of Hot Beverages, c.1500 to c.1900': 48.

18. Krondl, Michael, *Sweet Invention: A History of Dessert*, Chicago, IL: Chicago Review Press, 2011: 282-3.

19. Krondl, *Sweet Invention*: 289; 286.

20. Krondl, *Sweet Invention*: 356.

21. Krondl, *Sweet Invention*: 356.

22. On technoscience, see for example Latour, Bruno, *Science in Action*, Cambridge, MA: Harvard University Press, 1987.

23. Krondl, *Sweet Invention*: 355.

24. Krondl, *Sweet Invention*: 356.

25. Beeton, Isabella, *The Book of Household Management*, London: S.O. Beton Publishing, 1861: 62.

26. Pucciarelli, 'Chocolate as Medicine': 122.

27. Freeman, June, *The Making of the Modern Kitchen: A Cultural History*, Oxford & New York: Berg, 2004: 33.

28. Hameed, Abdel, & Arshad, F.M., 'Future Trends of the Export Demand for Selected Malaysian Cocoa Products', *Trends in Applied Science Research*, 2013: 5.

29. Krondl, *Sweet Invention*: 356.

30. In 2003 Kellogg, makers of the Hydrox (by then renamed the Droxie) stopped manufacturing the cookie, thus surrending once and for all to the Oreo (*see* Rhoads, Christopher, 'The Hydrox Cookie is Dead, and Fans Won't Get Over It', *Wall Street Journal*, 19th January, 2008. Available at: http://www.wsj.com/articles/SB120069573721101481).

CHAPTER SEVEN

A FUTURE WITHOUT
A PAST

CHOCOLATE, TRADE AND THE MAKING OF
TRADITION IN ASIA

Asia is predicted by many commentators to hold the future of the cocoa industry in its hands. Both cacao's production and chocolate's consumption is said to depend on the future of the region. More than being just about chocolate, these predictions are based upon the more general trends of spectacular economic growth, together with the sheer scale of Asia's population, a growing proportion of which are considered as belonging to the middle class.

But for all the soothsaying, the Asian chocolate market is hesitant to fulfil its twin destinies. The destiny of consumption depends upon chocolate's cultural presence, a presence which is deeply uncertain as a result of its historical absence. And the destiny of production depends, on the other hand, upon which part of chocolate's value chain the

developing economies prioritize.

The History of Chocolate Consumption in Asia

In turning potential consumers into consumers that really consume, chocolate faces a long-standing issue. It is not, as is sometimes presumed, simply that chocolate has no history in Asia, but that it has not, in the terms laid out in this book, benefited from a coherent culture of consumption. It has hopefully been shown how chocolate's success in Europe owed so much to this kind of culture. In this way, a body of knowledge which often goes ahead of the commodity itself makes the way passable, and at the same time renders the substance desirable to the people in its path. Like an icebreaker, it slices a route for the ship in its wake, but, in making a single, crisp incision, it also makes the ship a palatable visitor for the ice. As Marx would say, without perception of the object, consumers felt no urge towards it. Chocolate's visits to Asia have as a result been fleeting and without any lasting significance; so many lonely boats prone on frozen seas. Chocolate's experience of Asia has been only a more extreme case of its experience elsewhere. It does not follow the natural laws of the historical tradition – birth; expansion; stagnation; death. It is a non-linear history; a history of discontinuities, moments marked by their lack of clear consequences.

Mercantilism and Confucianism – An Unknown Divide

When Cortes marched into Tenochtitlan, his men marvelled at a city of 200,000 residents: twice as large as Seville, the most populous city of Spain at that time. But had Columbus corrected his miscalculations and realised his ultimate ambition, he may have marched instead into China, and eyed sprawling metropolises of an even more astounding magnitude. The eastern city of Hangzhou, which even in the thirteenth century was estimated to shelter a population of more than a million, was a reflection of the prosperity of the Asian world during this period. Inter-Asian trade networks, notably of spices, textiles, and porcelain, had been in place for hundreds of years. As far back as 2000 BC there is evidence of trade with Egypt, and by around 100 BC the Han Dynasty's Emperor Wu had constructed the 'silk road' to transfer that and other precious matter between China, Persia, India, and the Roman Empire. By the tenth century AD China had even established a unified system of governance – run by a meritocracy of scholars and regulated by a strong Confucian ideology – something no European state would achieve until nearly one thousand years later.[1] This governance structure was based upon a strong agricultural economy, and was initially not shy to encourage the inclusion of new and foreign crops such as potatoes, peanuts, tobacco, and even the Mesoamerican sacred sustenance crop maize.[2]

China's capacity for foreign trade was expanded further by the Song dynasty (960-1279 AD), who developed the coastal town of Quanzhou into one of the world's largest ports. The maritime trade which this facilitated was most beneficial to the Chinese porcelain industry, which took as its global centre the city of Jingdezhen. It is this city which provides the most compelling piece of evidence for the presence of chocolate in China at this early stage: the manufacture of vessels resembling chocolate pots in the 1690s, probably produced for export to Europe.[3] However, evidence for the Chinese consuming chocolate is extremely hard to come by. While Franciscan missionaries visiting China from the Spanish Philippines in the seventeenth and eighteenth centuries had chocolate supplied to them for both culinary and medicinal purposes, consumption of the beverage does not seem to have made it beyond the mouths of those Chinese with whom they directly associated.[4] It is also written in the 1817 encyclopaedia of J-J Machet, a French confectioner, that the Chinese stored their chocolate as a thick paste, taking it from a small sealed container before making it up with the desired spices.[5] However, these were again likely to be a very select group of European elites, and the habit did not spread more widely.

Part of the explanation for the stalling advance of an Asian culture of chocolate consumption lies again in the early establishment of other stimulating beverages and soft drugs. For centuries, tea had been the preference of east and central Asia, and was joined in the 1500s by the flow of coffee from the Islamic west of the continent.[6] In Asia as in Europe then, chocolate suffered by being a late arrival from a foreign land, but here political and philosophical factors meant that its tardiness was more permanently damaging.

The European colonial trading companies were lured to the east in the sixteenth century by the riches of the inter-Asian trade. At first glance this would be a far easier market to plunder than that of the New World precisely because a market was already in place. There was no natural bounty that needed extracting. Asia was already commodified, thus fostering a space for the exchange of Asian and European goods seemed a mere matter of expanding the existing infrastructure into a larger area. However, this would prove much more difficult than had been anticipated due to the incompatibility of the Chinese and European attitudes towards commerce. Though the region's trading system was extremely well-developed, China did not think of it as a network of commodity exchange. Rather, they thought, not dissimilarly from the Aztecs, that this was a system of tribute at the centre of which sat China itself. Whilst goods were exchanged in both directions, this was only a by-product of the most pressing effect; a symbolic effect which dictated the hierarchy of the participating states.

This form of exchange proved even more perplexing to the Europeans than that of the Mesoamerican civilizations. For, faced with the Aztecs, the conquistadors – after their brief attempt at recognition – perceived a culture that was brutally unfamiliar: what Donald Rumsfeld, were he alive at the time, would have called a 'known unknown'. They reacted violently, causing the destruction of what they did not understand. Faced with Asia, on the other hand, the colonial trading companies saw enough evidence of a trade economy to jump to the conclusion that it was exercised for the same Mercantilist purposes as their own. They stuck, in other words, with what they thought they knew, and in doing so abandoned everything else to the unfathomable terrain of the 'unknown unknown'. The core of this enigma – the truth from which the Europeans were twice-removed –

was that trade was a signifier of wealth, not a means to achieving it.

The ethic of Confucianism, transposed onto the sphere of governance, meant a burning pride in self-sufficiency. China's economy thus possessed a similar end to Mercantilism, that is, the accumulation of wealth and power, but the value of its actions was dictated to a far greater extent by its means. The wealth and power which Confucianism desired could be accumulated only from within one's own borders. The idea of profiting from the productivity of others – the very premise of colonialism and the slave trade, as well as today's global capitalism – was considered a sign of dependence and thus inferiority. Interactions with other states were seen therefore as the proof of the pudding. A country demonstrated its hegemony by the running of trade surpluses. That is, if it exported more of its domestic goods to another territory than it imported of theirs, it demonstrated its greater power.

Akin to the system of symbolic exchange outlined earlier in the context of the Mesoamericans, and the Pacific societies studied by Marcel Mauss, the Chinese tributary network was also founded upon an initial exchange of gifts. This was the act by which any state acknowledged their submission to China's hegemony. But, because power resided in self-sufficiency, the exchange of gifts could not be escalatory. The idea was not to impose (by giving) a social debt as a challenge to the recipient, inciting them to give, at some point in the future, an even greater gift. Instead the two parts of the exchange (gift and counter-gift) were enacted almost instantaneously, and whoever was deemed the junior participant was permitted to reciprocate only with gifts of a *lower value* than that given by the Chinese.[7] The very purpose of the ceremony was therefore to suffocate the development of a mutual exchange, rendering the indebtedness of one party to the other (China) perpetual. This indebted status was not to be resolved, and certainly never inverted onto the Chinese. Rather, it was set to be reinforced by the repetition of the asymmetrical exchange on a regular basis: a renewal of vows pledging a slave's continued servitude to his master.

Where the Chinese conducted trade, they did so at arm's length.

Particularly after the fall of the Ming loyalists in the late seventeenth century, commerce always took place at a distance from the mainland, as if the viral dishonour of commerce might infect the pride of the self-sufficient nation. The merchants who acted as the intermediaries to this trade were consequently regarded as sullied individuals, carriers of the mercantilist disease. As in Aztec society, merchants constituted their own class, but in this case their practices were not to be aspired to but looked down upon with disapproval. The merchants were the only one out of the four Chinese classes – the others being the artisans, the peasants and, at the summit, the scholars – seen as being unproductive. The Confucian system of exchange engendered a contradiction at its base: as opposed to the Aztecs who traded in blood and its symbols, and the merchant capitalists who traded in money and its commodities, the Confucian system traded in self-sufficiency. It was a form of trade, in other words, that set out to acquire as little as possible from the other.

It was for this reason that the merchant class occupied the bottom rung of Chinese society. Far from being warriors paying their way in society with their bravery, Chinese merchants were accused of a cowardly practice: making profits from the labour of others. Hence they did not earn, like the *pochteca*, the right to abstain from the average citizen's duty to the state. On the contrary, extra tributes were demanded of the Chinese merchants – a significant cut of their profits – to compensate for their undeserving riches.

The policy of distancing applied to foreign as well as Chinese traders. Hence the Portuguese, first of the Europeans to reach China, were forced to work out of Macao, establishing a trading post there in 1557, and later out of Ningpo, Amoy and Foochow. By accepting these peripheral spots, the Portuguese took up the self-same role as the Chinese merchant class, essentially doing what was, from the perspective of the Chinese elite, the 'dirty work'. Similarly, when the British East India Company broke into the Chinese market a century or so later, their dealings were contained not only to the coastal city of Canton (now Ghangzhou), but to Whampoa, a small island twelve miles off its shores. From this point, the terms of the dealings were negotiated with the mainland by the *Cohong*, a dedicated guild of Hong Chinese merchants.

As well as putting a moat between themselves and the mercantile men, the Chinese made it a political point to shun the flow of goods from Europe altogether. They might receive tributes, but when they were invited to exchange their wares for those of the Europeans, they consistently refused. A convoy of the British East India Company sent to establish trade agreements in 1793 for instance, was met with a phrase which must have been discordant noise to the ears of a trader. Responding to the grand offerings of the colonialists, the Chinese officials noted, with an indifferent shrug: 'there is nothing we lack', and turned the bemused Britons back west.[8] This meant that, if one wanted Chinese goods, they would need to give '*specie*' (currency in the form of metal coin) in exchange, and so were forced to run continuous fiscal deficits. Such an economic policy, which has these days become the status quo of the largest world economies (not least China itself), was for the mercantilist empires, with all their territorial possessions, a disheartening prospect. For the North Americans it meant mounting debts owed to the very power from whom they had just managed to liberate themselves: with no local supply of either silver or gold, they turned to British banks for the requisite finance.[9] In accordance with this political stance, it would have been a controversial thing in China to admit having a liking for non-Chinese commodities. It was thought an insult upon one's own nation to imply that everything necessary for a good and happy life could not be found upon native soils. Perhaps the Chinese friends of the Franciscans did not like the taste of chocolate, but perhaps, even if they did, they did not dare recommend the foreign delicacy to their fellow countrymen.

Francis Bacon was clearly of the opinion that China's kingdom suffered from its refusal of foreign knowledge, for in *New Atlantis* (1627) he sets forth his ideal world in contrast to what he sees as the epistemological deficit of the time. Bacon adopts the voice of his characters to criticize the Europeans, on the one hand, for travelling the world only to compete violently for its material riches, and China, on the other, for isolating itself from global flows. The utopia of Bensalem is, like China, wary of strangers. The Europeans are taken ashore only after some hesitation, and even then are contained within the 'House of Strangers'. But where the kingdom of China is said to shy away from the world out of fear, Bensalem does so because of its Christian beliefs in peace and humility. It is not greedy for ever-expanding territorial and material possessions, but it does value trade, if only for the knowledge which it acquires and spreads.[10]

Bacon here alludes to an alliance of religious and scientific knowledge which was adopted by the Jesuits in their Chinese missions: the strategy of working the local elite 'with both hands', as the Italian Jesuit Sabatino de Ursis put it: with the right promoting matters of God; with the left, matters of science.[11] Bacon's view was shared by another Jesuit, the Frenchman Louis-Daniel Le Comte, who, though he did not believe Confucianism to be incompatible with Christianity, thought it a shame that the Chinese 'looked upon themselves as a chosen elect people'.[12] Though it had some minor successes, the two-pronged approach ultimately failed. Persecution of Christians escalated over the following century, with de Ursis himself being exiled to Macao in 1616. Bacon therefore expresses the European frustrations of the time: the perceived foolishness of the Chinese in rejecting not only foreign goods but also foreign knowledge, particularly the Christian faith.

In the case of Japan though, it was precisely the foreign insistence on God's 'light' which reinforced the philosophical reluctance to partake in the global game. Prior to the seventeenth century, Japan had been a relatively open society. Unsurprisingly, Japan's first colonial experiences were characterized by the presence of Catholic missionaries. In a culture that was already religiously diverse, there was initially no problem with this presence, but what the Japanese soon came to realize was that the Jesuits were not happy to coexist alongside other creeds. Though there was not even an issue with conversion *per se*, the bullish approach of the Christians was unwelcome. The lack of respect they showed towards Buddhism in particular – eating the beef of the sacred cow; ransacking shrines – led to unease among the ruling Shogunate.

Christianity became the subject of increasingly institutionalized religious persecution in Japan, leading eventually to the 1637-8 Shimabara uprising, a Christian revolt that was brutally crushed by the authorities.[13] As a consequence of this wounding experience, Japan became even more guarded against European influence than China. From 1603 to 1854 it operated a foreign policy of strict isolationism. During this long period of *sakoku*, ('locked country'), Japan's only access to the world beyond its sovereign territory was via a single island, *Dejima*, located in the bay of Nagasaki.

Though isolationism is usually considered an economic policy, its roots were in this case cultural. The Japanese showed, in the construction of *Dejima*, their recognition of the need to trade, together with their determination not to let this necessity contaminate wider society. Much as there is concern today at the prospect of cultural homogeneity as a result of Americanization or 'McDonaldization', the Japanese feared the universalizing attitudes of the Jesuit enterprise. The fate of the native American population shows that their fears were not unfounded, but the tragic irony – a paradox with which we are today so familiar – was that in order to maintain tolerance and diversity, they closed themselves off, thus enacting themselves the very intolerance which they had striven to prevent.

Japan may have been a 'locked country' from the perspective of its people, but from the perspective of the commodity it was more akin to an air-lock. As Whampoa did for China, Dejima acted as a neutral zone with valves that opened out into both Japan and the rest of the world, only never simultaneously. It did not permit a continuous flow between the two. Following the violent exorcism of its Christian population, only a select group of foreigners were permitted to trade from Dejima. The Dutch earned their access by showing allegiance to the cultural lock: when the Christian rebellion was looming, the Dutch decided to side with the Japanese forces rather than their European counterparts, providing them with military and financial support to quash the unrest.[14]

As in China, there are signs that chocolate was not entirely unknown. Japanese chocolate pots were, for instance, given to Louis

XIV by King Narai of Siam (Thailand) in 1686.[15] However, diplomatic interactions like this one do not seem to represent the wider situation.

In spite of the Japanese reaction to it, knowledge of god's 'light' does seem elsewhere to be intertwined with knowledge of chocolate. For it was in the sparse pockets of Asia where Christianity was not rebuked that a taste for chocolate often developed. In the Philippines for example, where Catholicism was effectively promoted by the Spanish – hence its name, in honour of Prince Phillip II – chocolate became a popular breakfast beverage. The capital, Manila, became the focal point of the galleon trade that linked Asia and the Americas across the Pacific. Moreover, there is no better metaphor for the frailty of chocolate's influence in Asia than the fact that, before it travelled to the West Indies or West Africa, the earliest recorded transfer of *T. Cacao* from the New World was on one of these galleons: the arrival, in 1666, of a single plant from Acapulco.[16] It was the cultural melting pot of the Philippines which singled it out as a region in which people of many origins became familiar with chocolate. The galleon trade, for instance, was mainly operated by Hokkien Chinese migrants and Chinese-Filipino *Mestizos*, some of whom, come the industrialisation of the early twentieth century, took possession of small chocolate factories in the islands.[17]

Additionally, this was the one place in Asia where chocolate came to be favoured by those of faiths other than Catholicism. The exchange was not a friendly one, instead coming about in the midst of the long period of Moro-Spanish wars from the sixteenth to the twentieth centuries. The Catholic prisoners of these conflicts were often taken as slaves by the nobility in the Islamic Sultanate of Sulu, and it was possibly from these unfortunate individuals that the habit of drinking chocolate – customarily as a breakfast beverage, served alongside macaroons – was learned.[18] Today, the influence of chocolate on Filipino culture is still evident. As well as being consumed on an everyday basis, *tsokolate*, a thick hot chocolate drink, is often served as part of the large Christian community's Christmas and New Year's Eve festivities.

MILK CHOCOLATE: DAIRY AND COCOA IN UNION

For China, it was the fallout from the first Opium War that provided the first small crack in the region's self-sufficient façade. The 1842 Treaty of Nanjing, which famously ceded Hong Kong to the British on a 150-year lease, also negotiated for the opening of a number of Chinese ports, including Canton and Shanghai.

Although the fortress wall had been toppled, chocolate still struggled to gain any considerable foothold. This was in part because the very modernization which had opened China to the possibilities of chocolate consumption had simultaneously altered chocolate itself, making it inaccessible in another way. Around 1883, in Vevey, Switzerland – the same town where Henry Nestlé was developing powdered milk – the confectioner Daniel Peter combined condensed milk with the butter and liquor of cacao to produce the world's first milk chocolate. The invention was so popular that, by the late 1930s, it accounted for 85 per cent of the chocolate consumed in Britain.[19]

But the creaminess which milk imparts into chocolate was previously performed by another substance: ambergris. Brillat-Savarin names chocolate laced with amber the 'chocolate of the unhappy', describing at length the states which it is able to remedy:

> if any man has drunk a little too deeply from the cup of physical pleasure; if he has spent too much time at his desk that should have been spent asleep; if his fine spirits have temporarily become dulled; if he finds the air too damp, the minutes too slow, and the atmosphere too heavy to withstand; if he is obsessed by a fixed idea which bars him from any freedom of thought: if he is any of these poor creatures, we say, let him be given a good pint of amber-flavored chocolate…and marvels will be performed.[20]

We can see here the comparability of amber and milk in chocolate: the soothing impact of its especially silky texture; its ability to lift one's mood.

Ambergris is, like milk, an animal product, an excretion which originates in the intestines of the sperm whale. Capturing ambergris does not require any direct interaction with the animal – it can be collected from the ocean's surface, or from the beaches upon which it washes up – but as a trade it is irrevocably tied to the whaling industry, and has suffered as a result. In addition, ambergris, like cacao butter, has more profitable uses than chocolate. Since the development of the perfume industry in particular, the rarity of ambergris has acquired even greater value. In September 2015, a 1.1kg block of the substance, happened upon by an Anglesey dog-walker, sold for £11,000 at auction.[21] In view of such expense, there is not much ambergris left for culinary purposes.

Milk proved a more than adequate substitute, but in doing so it tied the fate of chocolate to that of the European dairy industry. Milk and cream had been added to the chocolate beverage in Spain and England since the seventeenth century, but now milk was integrated as part of the manufacturing process, and helped greatly to increase the widespread popularity of chocolate bars. As the early advertisements of Cadbury's show, milk content formed the basis for the narrative pertaining to the medicinal and moral purity of solid chocolate. The mutual interest of these two industries in a single product also sparked some of the earliest mergers, Nestlé combining with the Condensed Milk Co. in 1904.[22]

Ambergris was familiar to China, where it was known as *lung sien hiang*, or 'dragon's spittle perfume'.[23] Milk, on the other hand, had been largely absent from Chinese culinary society since the fourteenth century, when it was exiled by Ming nationalists as a symbol of the defeated Mongol dynasty.[24]

The low exposure of Asian populations to dairy has left a lasting impression on their ability to consume it. Rare encounters with lactose – the sugar in milk – renders the function of the enzyme lactase obsolete, and so over time the body stops producing it. This causes lactose intolerance, a condition which remains far more common among Asian ethnic groups. Considering this intolerance it is no surprise that China has in the past seen no need for a dairy industry.

Thus, though European and North American companies have

attempted to export their obsession, China's inclination to chocolate has been cut off in advance, severed by cultural, physical and economic aversions to both the product itself and its key secondary ingredient.

The lack of domestic dairy production was likewise one of the teething problems for Cadbury as it tried to expand into the continent in the mid-twentieth century. In India, through lack of a local alternative, the company was forced to set up its own dairy farm outside Mumbai, a venture which was found to be inefficient owing not just to the heat and the imposition of strict regulations on foreign companies, but also to the fact that cows, being sacred animals in the Hindu faith, were not permitted to go to slaughter after they had stopped producing milk.[25]

The dairy industries of Asian nations have however shown impressive growth in recent years. In China, for instance, there has been talk of a 'white gold rush' as dairy-centred food companies – often of foreign origin – have raced in to cater for growing demand for dairy products, and farmers have imported large quantities of heifers (milk cows) from more traditional dairy economies.[26] In fact, according to estimates from the UN's Food and Agriculture Organization (FAO), in 2013 China was the third largest producer of cow's milk in the world.

Though China's production growth has been dramatic, its consumption boom has been even more so. Whilst production multiplied by a factor of more than six in the forty years to 2004, consumption's expansion was over fifteen-fold, an imbalance which continues to widen to the benefit of US dairy exporters. It is clear from this and other examples that China has sacrificed its traditional commitment to self-sufficiency in its pursuit of western-style modernization. As Andrea Wiley explains, milk itself has been a prominent object in the official discourse of the Chinese administration in recent years, with the nation's most successful and, notably, tallest athletes employed to advertise the white stuff (once more according to a quasi-scientific notion of strength and growth).[27] Given the centrality of dairy production to the chocolate industry, these statistics facilitate the production and marketing of chocolate in

China, but they cannot guarantee demand for it. The second largest producers of milk in 2013 were India, and yet there chocolate remains rare, with consumption limited to 110-120g (a little more than one large bar) per person per year on average.[28] The consumption of dairy, in other words, does not necessarily equate to the consumption of chocolate. In China, it is currently yoghurt which is most popular among the fresh dairy sector, possibly owing to the fact that it is – like tofu and soy milk – a fermented product.[29] Since economic reforms begun under Deng Xiaoping in 1978, China's trade with the rest of the world has grown from $20 billion to $500 billion in 2001, and to over $4 trillion in 2014. Chocolate has certainly benefited from this boom: sales of cocoa products in China grew by almost 60 per cent from 2009 to 2013. While the quantity consumed remains pitifully low in comparison to that of the West, it is the very potential which this lack seems to indicate that fills the oracles with hope. For instance, in a 2014 KPMG report, a positive outlook for the industry is justified by the very fact that the Chinese do not currently eat much chocolate:

> The potential long-term growth in emerging economies – many of which have growing middle classes – is vast. To give just one example: the per capita consumption of chocolate in China is only a tenth of that in Switzerland.[30]

There is a certain inevitability about the situation. To all of us that love chocolate it seems implausible that a single person, let alone an entire nation, would not. A taste for chocolate is, in this sense, part of the inevitable path of (western) development itself. And China, as a rapidly developing nation, must surely be on the verge of falling uncontrollably for chocolate.

FROM PRODUCTION TO PROCESSING: THE FUTURE SUPPLY OF CACAO

Elsewhere in Asia, it is Indonesia and Malaysia who produce the most cacao. However, the trend of the industries in these nations is, unsurprisingly, towards the more valuable links in the chain. As of last year, Indonesia overtook Malaysia to become the largest cocoa processor in the region. As cocoa grindings for 2013/14 grew 21 per cent on the previous year, the country's production of cacao itself dropped.[31] This shift has been incentivized by government grants for land purchases, cacao imports, and equipment brought in from Malaysia, but it has also been accelerated by the involvement of global commodities traders such as Cargill Inc. In December of 2014, Cargill opened its first processing plant in Gresik, Indonesia, and the Minnesota-based TNC is also involved, alongside the World Bank, in the rapid development of the Vietnamese cocoa industry. These projects will increase cocoa grindings, but the movement towards processing means they are unlikely to significantly boost the supply of cacao beans themselves in the future.

Likewise, Malaysian bean production peaked in 1990, when it stood at an impressive 247,000 tons. As of 2012 it constituted just a small fraction of the previous total, 3,600 tons, while grinding on the other hand had reached 299,000 tons.[32]

Whether or not China does follow the path expected of it in terms of consumption, it is possible that the eastern giant will exercise a significant effect on the cocoa industry over the next half a century. This will not necessarily be intentional, but rather an indirect consequence of China's wider plans for the African continent. Since the turn of the century, China's designs on the global stage have devoted great attention to the developing world, and to Africa especially. As Pádraig Carmody outlines, there are two main reasons for this focus. First, it is a geopolitical strategy which frames Africa as an 'ideological battleground' upon which global hegemony is to be contested between China and the West; second, it is part of China's economic modernization: the ambition to gain access to a huge source of relatively untapped natural resources. Crucially for the cocoa and chocolate industries, these resources include agricultural land upon which Chinese companies, baited by their government's tax incentives, are looking to base export industries.[33] China is, for example, Ghana's second largest trading partner after Europe, and the vast majority of Ghanaian goods exported to the Asian giant are primary commodities such as cocoa. In July of 2015, the state-run Ghana News Agency reported that the government's Minister for Trade and Industry Ekwow Spio Garbrah, had reached out to Chinese investors to request further investment in the country's agro-processing sector.[34] We should not forget here what we have already said regarding scarcity: that 'access' to resources is a matter of the control and restriction of production. On the international scale this control is a geopolitical consideration: if one nation or alliance monopolizes the production of a particular resource, they hold not only the capacity to profit from the sale of the resource at a high price, but additionally an advantageous balance of power over any other nation that demands it.

JAPANESE CHOCOLATE: COMMERCIAL HOLIDAYS AND RITUAL CONSUMPTION

It was not until the middle of the nineteenth century that the Japanese bubble was punctured by the forces of free trade. The liberalizing intervention came, somewhat unsurprisingly, in the form of a North American: the Commodore Matthew Calbraith Perry, whose men, on the orders of President Filmore, landed on the shores of Tokyo in 1858 to demand that the country open up its ports to foreign merchants. Drastic reforms were implemented, transforming Japan from an inward to an outward-looking nation in the space of two decades. In 1867, the last Tokugawa Shogun was overthrown and replaced by Emperor Meiji, a revolutionary leader who abolished the samurai in favour of a conscript army and rid Japan of the shogunate system, setting up a merchant-backed financial elite in their place.[35]

Japan is now the largest Asian consumer of chocolate. Though annual per capita consumption is still relatively small, 1.67 kilos as of 2011, it is growing. Owing to a strong health culture and a considerable ageing population, dark, cacao- and flavonoid-rich chocolates (often flavoured with spices, fruits and nuts) are proving most popular. Furthermore though, chocolate is developing a ritual presence in Japanese culture. Chocolate has entered Japanese society through the concept of gift-giving. As in Western cultures, the giving of chocolate is tied to the ceremonial institution of the holiday. On Valentine's Day in particular, Japanese men are traditionally given chocolates by members of the opposite sex. Whether it was intentional or not, this is an interesting inversion of the European tendency to give chocolate *to* women.

Japanese confectionary firms conduct a significant proportion of their trade around this holiday. Interestingly though, this cannot simply be attributed to the commercialization of religious tradition; 'the secularisation of the sacred', as Belk refers to it. Valentine's Day is not a remotely Japanese holiday: its origins are in the various Christian festivities celebrating Saint Valentinus, and even in Christian communities Valentine's has for a long time been a heavily commercial date largely disassociated from its religious significance. Unlike Christmas then, which is also popular in Japan as well as China, Japanese Valentine's has never been a sacred occasion. Nonetheless, the ritual has been imported. This was in actuality a commercial enterprise all along. The Kobe-based confectionary company Morzoff Limited started promoting the holiday in 1936, and by 1980 Japan's chocolate makers had established another festival: 'reply day' or 'White Day' (the 14th of March), upon which men are supposed to reciprocate, a month after the original exchange, the gift of chocolate.

The use or invention of holidays to promote commercial activity is by no means unusual. It is even argued that, having been secularized long ago, festivals such as Christmas are now being sacralized once more in a commercial sense, with the obligatory shopping trips as rituals, the adverts and films as scripture, and the carrots and sherry left for Santa Claus and his reindeer as forms of sacrifice.[36] However, in these twists and turns between the sacred and the secular and back again, chocolate has always featured as an object particularly well-adapted to symbolic rituals of gift and counter-gift.

INDO-VIETNAMESE GOAT CURRY (*CÀ RI DE*)

Goat is another of those underused meats, and 2015 was supposed to be 'The Year of the Goat'. All the major supermarkets were going to start stocking it, and we were going to be eating it three meals a day, seven days a week. I haven't seen much evidence of this prolific surge, but it is always available from halal butchers, and, with just a little patience, is just as tender and arguably bolder than lamb shoulder.

This curry, which uniquely blends fresh and zesty Vietnamese spicing with the darker, more aromatic base flavours of garam masala, originates out of the colonial trade between two French colonial ports: Hanoi in Vietnam and Pondicherry in India.

As a result of the European influence and the presence of Indian dairy farmers, the curry is made with cow's as well as coconut milk. I have replaced the cow's milk with goat's in keeping with the meat, and because it has a wonderful aftertaste which, like the cheese, is very slightly sour and, in the words of my dad, 'chalky'.

For the marinade paste
800 g / 1¾ pounds goat shoulder, cubed on the bone
4 cloves of garlic, peeled
2 stalks of lemongrass
1 large piece of root ginger, peeled
1 red chilli
1 tbsp garam masala
½ tsp fennel seeds
1 tsp fish sauce
½ a preserved lemon
1 tsp salt
1 tsp sugar

Remove the tough ends of the lemongrass, chop, and then add to a pestle and mortar with all the remaining ingredients (apart from the goat) and pound to a paste. Smother the goat in the mixture, cover with cling film, and leave in the fridge for at least an hour, ideally two.

For the curry
1 large onion, chopped
1 large bunch of Thai basil (or a smaller bunch of regular basil)
300 ml / 10 fluid oz goat's (or cow's) milk
400 ml / 12 fluid oz coconut milk
250 ml/ 8 fluid oz water
50 g / 2 oz dark chocolate, 80% cocoa solids
400 g / 14 oz large leaf spinach

Add the onion to a hot pan and fry for a couple of minutes before adding the basil and the goat. Brown the meat, then lower the heat and add the water and the coconut and goat's milk. Cover this and leave to simmer. Don't be concerned if you find that, when you next return to the pot, the milk has curdled. Simply leave to reduce for 3½ to 4 hours.

To serve
Olive oil
Handful of Thai basil
Coriander
Mini baguettes

15 minutes before the goat is due to be ready, melt the chocolate into the curry and taste for seasoning.

Slice the baguettes and brush with olive oil, rub in half the Thai basil and coriander, and bake for 5-10 minutes in a hot oven.

Check that the goat is tender, and then add the spinach, wilt, and apportion the curry onto the baguettes, topping with the remaining herbs.

MALAYSIAN CHICKEN

Because this curry predominantly uses cocoa powder it remains light and fresh, with a good chilli kick and the crunch of freshly toasted peanuts. The small amount of chocolate is added near the end just to give the sauce a lovely sheen and a bit of depth.

For the chicken
4 chicken legs
1 tsp ground turmeric
1 tsp cocoa powder
¼ tsp ground cinnamon
½ tsp salt
1 clove garlic, crushed
Juice of half a lime
1 tbsp rapeseed oil
Small handful of coriander, roughly torn or chopped

For the curry paste
4 cloves garlic, crushed
3 red chillies, chopped
Generous thumb of root ginger, finely chopped
2 stalks lemongrass, tough outer shell removed and chopped
Juice of half a lime
2 tbsp rapeseed or vegetable oil

For the curry
3 small red onions, finely chopped
1½ tsp ground turmeric
1 tbsp tamarind paste
20 g / 1 oz dark chocolate
A few kaffir lime leaves
2 cinnamon sticks
2 star anise
400 ml / 14 fluid oz coconut milk
500 ml / 1 pint chicken stock
150 g / 5 oz mange tout
To serve 200 g / 7 oz rice
100 g / 4 oz peanuts
Coriander
Red chilli, finely chopped

Mix all the ingredients for the chicken and rub them thoroughly into the legs. Cover these and leave them in the fridge for as long as you can, so that the flavours infuse into the meat.

When ready to cook, place the curry paste ingredients into a pestle and mortar and grind (or mash with a fork) until the juices run together.

Preheat your oven to 200°C (180°C if using a fan oven) and line a large oven tray with foil or baking parchment. Remove the chicken legs from the fridge to come up to room temperature.

Add the curry paste, along with the onions and the turmeric, to a large pan on a low to medium heat, and cook for five to ten minutes, stirring occasionally. Once the onions have begun to soften, add all the remaining ingredients apart from the chocolate and the mange tout. Leave the curry to simmer until reduced by about two thirds, tasting to see whether it needs more seasoning.

Meanwhile, place the chicken legs into the prepared tray (skin side up) and into the oven, roasting until the skin is golden and crisp and the juices run clear – between 35 and 45 minutes, depending on the size of the leg.

When the curry is almost finished reducing, add the mange tout and the chocolate, boil the rice, and toast the peanuts in a frying pan on a medium to high heat, until they are a golden brown.

Before serving, remove the star anise (if you can find it), cinnamon sticks and lime leaves from the curry. Spoon the curry over each portion of rice and top with the chicken leg, followed by a sprinkling of peanuts, coriander, and extra chilli if desired.

FILIPINO *TSOKOLATE*

Two things differentiate this Filipino breakfast beverage from its European 'hot chocolate' and American 'cocoa' brethren. First of all, it is made with cacao 'tableau', giving it more body, and, secondly, it is frothed, giving a light finish to its otherwise thick and intense quality. The frothing is traditionally done using a *molinillo* – a wooden whisk adopted by the Spanish from the Mesoamericans in the seventeenth century – but if you don't happen to have one of these ancient tools lying about in your cutlery drawer a metal whisk works just as well.

Serves 4-6
300 ml / 10 fluid oz whole milk
100 ml / 3 fluid oz whipping cream
75 g / 3 oz cacao
100 g / 4 oz dark chocolate
Pinch of salt
Sugar, to taste
Mini marshmallows (optional)

Heat the milk and cream in a pan, whisking for a few minutes as it begins to steam to give it a light, frothy texture. When it is close to boiling, pour the frothed milk onto the chocolate and cacao and continue to whisk until the mixture is thick but bubbling. Add a pinch of salt and taste the *tsokolate*, adding a little sugar if you feel it needs it, then serve in small mugs or expresso cups.

SESAME-GRILLED BANANAS WITH CHOCOLATE AND ANISE CUSTARD

It has always been a tradition in my family – a tradition which I think we have stolen from the girl guides – to end every barbecue with a debauched banana split, cramming whatever chocolate we can find in the recesses of our cupboards into a banana, wrapping it tightly in tin foil and burying it, to bake in its skin, within the hot coals.

This recipe is essentially that tradition in a more reputable disguise, with anise giving an effect quite similar to the combination of mint and chocolate, only with less heat, and more aromatics.

For the chocolate and anise custard
120 g / 4 oz dark chocolate, 70% cocoa solids
30 g / 1 oz milk chocolate, 35% cocoa solids
200 ml / 6½ fluid oz double cream
250 ml / 7 fluid ozwhole milk
3 star anise
½ tsp vanilla bean paste

75 g / 3 oz caster sugar
3 large egg yolks
1 tbsp flour
Knob of butter

First of all, beat together the egg yolks and caster sugar in a bowl until they are light in colour.

Gradually heat the milk and the cream with the star anise and vanilla to infuse. Once almost boiling, take the pan from the heat and let it cool slightly before removing the star anise, putting it to one side. Now slowly pour the hot milk mixture onto the egg yolks and sugar, whisking as you do so. Put the mixture back into the pan with the flour, a pinch of salt, and return the star anise to infuse further while you cook the custard down. Once it is steaming and has thickened slightly, add the chocolate and stir until it has melted into the cream, and then melt in a knob of butter. Pour the mixture back into the bowl and leave until it is cool enough to go into the fridge to set.

For the bananas
4 ripe bananas
50 g / 2 oz salted butter
50 g / 2 oz caster sugar, plus more for the pan
2 tbsp caster sugar
100 g / 4 oz sesame seeds

Slice each banana lengthways, and then halve. Gently melt the butter with the sugar and then brush onto the flat face of the bananas. Sprinkle liberally with the sesame seeds and then fry, face down, in a very hot pan containing the sugar. You want the sugar to be a nice dark brown by the end, without being burnt – so watch carefully and think oak rather than mahogany.

Remove the bananas from the pan and leave to cool slightly before serving with a generous spoonful of chocolate.

END NOTES

1. Maddison, Angus, *Contours of the World Economy, 1-2030 ad*, Oxford University Press, 2007: 159.

2. Maddison, *Contours of the World Economy, 1-2030 ad*: 159.

3. Gordon, Bertram, 'Chinese Chocolate: Ambergris, Emperors, and Export Ware', in Grivetti, Louis, & Shapiro, Howard-Yana (eds), *Chocolate: History, Culture, and Heritage*, John Wiley & Sons, Inc. 2009: 597.

4. Gordon, 'Chinese Chocolate': 595-6.

5. *Cited in* Gordon, 'Chinese Chocolate': 598.

6. Clarence-Smith, *Cocoa and Chocolate, 1765-1914*: 9.

7. Maddison, *Contours of the World Economy, 1-2030 ad*: 161.

8. Quoted in Maddison, *Contours of the World Economy, 1-2030 ad*: 164.

9. 'Hao, Yen P'ing, 'Chinese Teas to America – A Synopsis', in *America's China Trade in Historical Perspective: The Chinese and American Performance*, edited by May, Ernest & Fairbank, John, Cambridge, MA: Harvard University Asia Center Press, 1986: 24.

10. Bacon, *New Atlantis*: 166-8.

11. *Quoted in* Wright, Jonathon, *The Jesuits: Missions, Myths and Histories*, London: HarperCollins, 2004: 86.

12. Quoted in Wright, *The Jesuits*: 83.

13. Davies, *A Primer of Dutch Seventeenth Century Overseas Trade*: 73.

14. Davies, *A Primer of Dutch Seventeenth Century Overseas Trade*: 73.

15. Gordon, 'Chinese Chocolate': 597.

16. Bartley, *The Genetic Diversity of Cacao and its Utilisation*: 10.

17. Hall, C.J.J. van, *Cacao*, London: Macmillan, 1932: 493. *Cited in* Clarence-Smith, *Cocoa and Chocolate, 1765-1914*: 86.

18. Clarence-Smith, *Cocoa and Chocolate, 1765-1914*: 13

19. Chiapparino, Francesco, 'Milk and Fondant Chocolate and the Emergence of the Swiss Chocolate Industry at the Turn of the Twentieth Century', in *Food and Material Culture*, edited by Schärer, Martin & Fenton, Alexander, East Lothian: Tuckwell Press, 1998. pp. 330-344: 334; 338.

20. Brillat-Savarin, *The Physiology of Taste*. 121.

21. Paterson, Colin, 'Lump of Rare Whale Vomit Sells for £11k at Auction', *BBC News*, 26th September, 2015. Available at: http://www.bbc.com/news/uk-34368198.

22. Chiapparino, 'Milk and Fondant Chocolate and the Emergence of the Swiss Chocolate Industry at the Turn of the Twentieth Century': 339.

23. Gordon, 'Chinese Chocolate': 598-9.

24. Huang, H.T., 'Hypolactasia and the Chinese Diet', *Current Anthropology*, Vol. 43, Iss. 5, 809-819, 2002. *Cited in* Wiley, Andrea, 'Transforming Milk in a Global Economy', *American Anthropologist*, Vol.109, Iss. 4, 2007. pp. 666-677: 670.

25. Cadbury, *Chocolate Wars*: 273.

26. Balch, Oliver, 'China's Growing Hunger for Dairy Raises Fears over Sustainable Production', *The Guardian*, 30.05.2014.

27. Wiley, 'Transforming Milk in a Global Economy': 671-3.

28. Chandramouli Venkatesan (Cadbury India), *cited in* Singh, Namrata, 'Chocolate Consumption Trebles Since 2005', *The Times of India*, 30th June, 2012, available at: http://timesofindia.indiatimes.com/city/mumbai/Chocolate-consumption-trebles-since-2005/articleshow/14518084.cms?referral=PM [accessed 20th June, 2015].

29. Wiley, 'Transforming Milk in a Global Economy': 673.

30. *KPMG*, 'A Taste of the Future: The Trends that could Transform the Chocolate Industry', 2014: 2. Available from: https://www.kpmg.com/Global/en/IssuesAndInsights/ArticlesPublications/Documents/taste-of-the-future.pdf.

31. Nieburg, Oliver, 'Cargill Opens $100m Indonesian Cocoa Plant, *Confectionary News*, 10th December, 2014. Available at: http://www.confectionerynews.com/Ingredients/Cargill-Indonesia-plant-opens [accessed 14th June, 2015].

32. Hameed & Arshad, 'Future Trends of the Export Demand for Selected Malaysian Cocoa Products': 1-2.

33. Carmody, Pádraig, *The New Scramble for Africa*, Cambridge: Polity, 2011: 65-8.

34. *China Daily*, 'Ghanaian official calls for more Chinese investment in manufacturing', 9th July, 2015. Available at: http://www.chinadaily.com.cn/business/2015-07/09/content_21229333.htm.

35. Maddison, *Contours of the World Economy,1-2030 ad*: 148-9.

36. Belk, 'The Sacred in Consumer Culture': 73-4.

'BLESSED MONEY'

CACAO, CHOCOLATE AND THE HOARDING OF VALUE

Any system invents for itself a principle of equilibrium, exchange
and value, causality and purpose, which plays on fixed oppositions:
good and evil, true and false, sign and referent, subject and object.

Jean Baudrillard, *Impossible Exchange*, 2011: 6[1]

Because the world has no equivalent, Baudrillard says, there is
nothing to which we can compare it; nothing we can measure
it against. Value, then, starts from nothing, *ex nihilo*. All
measures of value must therefore be created. I began with the idea that
every culture of cacao consumption (and production) was inextricably
linked to the systems of value and measure in and with which it had
developed. These systems have all brought with them – as their own
creators – mediators of various sorts; priests and physicians; adverts
and sacrificial ceremonies, whose agenda it has been to communicate

certain aspects of cacao and chocolate's value.

Some have mediated cacao more effectively than others. For the Maya and the Aztecs, the mediation of cacao was imbued in the mediation of sacred objects. As a prominent substance in the symbolic exchange of ritual sacrifice and ceremonies of social debt, cacao was a passive object, *mediated by* – prepared elaborately into chocolate, or mixed with blood – but it was in addition a *mediator* in its own right, an object with spirit and the power to create intimate bonds among gods and men.

Upon encountering this spirited object, the first European mediators found themselves lost for words, unable to communicate anything of the crop except for their misconception of it as something known to them, followed by their disgusted rejection of it as something barbaric. The lack of impact chocolate made when introduced to Japan and China makes us wonder for how long, had it not been for Bernardino de Sahagún and the other more curious missionaries, the Europeans might have gone on burning boats full of valueless 'almonds'.[2]

The use of knowledge to communicate the value of cacao has from the outset involved a selective mediation, emphasizing certain things while neglecting, or even denying, others. Cacao was conceived of as valuable by the European nobility, for example, as a way to sample; to get a taste of the New World. And yet it was a mediation that relied upon the idealized images of the fruit's exotic and mystical origins whilst detaching itself from the origins themselves, from the violence that they attributed to the natives but that was in actuality perpetrated by the forces of the civilized.

Advertising refined the art of selectivity and presentation, promoting chocolate first of all as a medicine, under the pretence of scientific expertize – particularly the physician's recommendation – before throwing off these specific attributes in favour of a generalized proclamation of the healthy and the virtuous.

This is where the mediation between production and consumption, cacao and chocolate, comes into question. Considering that the characteristics of chocolate deemed valuable have fluctuated to such an extent, and that the 'experts' charged with making such judgements proceed to be dubious and selective in their use of knowledge, we should ask, first, where the current value of chocolate lies, and, second, how this affects the value of cacao.

Over the course of chocolate's history, there have been only a small number of permanent structural changes to the relationship between consumption and production.

These alterations are rooted in the physical transformation of cacao by technoscientific agents: the inventors of tools and technologies of various kinds. For most of cacao's history, tools have been designed to make its seed into a digestible beverage by grinding it, allowing it to be mixed first with water and maize, and then with sugar and milk. As late as the eighteenth century, *chocolatières* or chocolate mills were popular tools of the fashionable kitchen.[3] Along with the method that produced the drink of chocolate, this equipment differed only slightly from the original Spanish *molinillo*, and performed roughly the same function – both mixing and frothing – as the Aztec pouring of chocolate between vessels.

It was another Mesoamerican tool that inspired one of the most significant chocolate contraptions of the second industrial revolution – the technological revolution – from which solid chocolate emerged, the Bozelli machine. This piece of technology, a copy of which was purchased by the Swiss chocolate maker Rudolph Lindt in 1879, consisted of a mechanical roller set over a stone table, closely replicating the *metatl* and *metapilli* used by the Aztecs to grind their cacao. Lindt used the machine to refine the process of 'conching', laying the path for Daniel Peter's condensed milk 'Gala' chocolate four years later.[4] However, the industrialization of chocolate production; the birth of a cocoa industry which these innovations enabled removed the tools of production from the consumer's hands. Soon after van Houten had devised his machine, for example, the *chocolatière* became obsolete.[5] This dispossession has in turn changed the consumer's perception of the object to be consumed. It is often commented that the vast majority of West African cacao farmers have never tasted chocolate, but the fact that the vast majority of chocoholics have never wielded a machete against the thick husk of a cacao pod is just as relevant. As a result of this distance, we risk following the exploitative/exotic gaze of the colonialist with an all-consuming, all-consumed gaze that is radically detached from cacao's production.

Projects such as Fairtrade are important in that they have demonstrated that it is possible to offer alternative mediators of value with motivations different to, if not outside the influence of both the state and the market. The original ambition of fairer trade, before the existence of Fairtrade™, was to develop a new, producer-centred way to 'add value' to products so that consumers would be willing to pay a few extra pence for them. In this basic respect, the movement has been successful. However, what is not certain is where precisely in the value chain that extra value has been added. Julie Cidell and Heike Alberts observe along these lines that:

> For a highly processed food such as chocolate, it is not surprising that it is the manufacturing process, not the raw materials, that primarily determines quality.[6]

This statement has become ever more applicable to chocolate since the time of Fry, van Houten, Lindt and Peter's industrial innovations. Even where modern advertisers evoke the geographical origins of products, Cidell and Alberts continue, they do so in terms of the traditions or styles of the places where the chocolate was processed, rather than where the cacao was grown. This is how we can speak of Swiss or Belgian milk chocolate despite the fact that neither of these countries grow any cacao. The Swiss origin is located in the long duration for which the chocolate is conched: a legal minimum of 72 hours;[7] the Belgian in the total absence of vegetable fats and the minimum of 35% cocoa solids. The so-called 'European chocolate wars' of the late twentieth century, during which EU member states and their respective chocolate companies argued over how the region's law should regulate the product's manufacture, were contested on a similarly processing-focused basis. Cadbury, for example, argued with eventual success (against more traditional manufacturers in Italy and Spain) for the right to use higher quantities of milk, as well as substituting cacao butter for vegetable fats.[8] There are signs, though, that this obsession with determining chocolate according to its processing might be subsiding. We are more likely now to see on the packaging of our chocolate (often, but not always, alongside the Fairtrade mark) the names of cacao varieties and/or their geographical origins. This is usually confined to the outlets of specialist chocolate merchants, where the names are tied to 'fine flavour' cacao varieties, *Chuao* from Venezuela, or *Nacional* from Peru. But some supermarket retailers have also begun stocking less prestigious products labelled as being grown in Ghana and the Ivory Coast.

But the fact that the wrapper remains the first point of reference for heavily processed goods will always pose a problem to the perception of value. It is the most immediate platform for that mediator, the advertiser; the final reminder that an unmediated experience is impossible. Wrappers that proclaim the genuine and ethical origins and tastes of what lies inside are more inconspicuous than, but similar in function and risk to the figure of the humanitarian celebrity: both hold an exotic sparkle that attracts and detracts the eye simultaneously. The idea is that we are drawn to it, and yet once we are it is found that the surface is reflective. We see only the glint, the mesmeric beauty of our ethical intentions looking back at us, and in this way it facilitates a narcissistic consumption, the acting partner of what Chouliaraki calls narcissistic spectatorship; a consumption which believes it is looking at something real, under the surface of the water – at production – but which is in fact lost in the ideal of its own reflection.

In the case of Fairtrade, this reflectivity can lead us astray from an examination of what the movement actually does and does not accomplish in view of the wider ethical aim. Fairtrade provides a minimum level of economic security. It does so by reverting back to a basic form of the forward contract. This guarantees to every farmer who is a member of a cooperative belonging to its scheme a minimum price for their cacao crop where government prices and the global market price fall below this level. This is a safety net price, intended to meet a minimum level of sustainable production for a particular region (for Ghana this is currently $1600 per tonne). It thus offers a protective mechanism which, though not always relevant, guards against volatility whilst still allowing farmers to participate in price discovery. Above this, Fairtrade also hopes to encourage local investment by supplying a small premium of $200 per tonne, and requires all member groups to decide democratically how this should be spent. Fairtrade does not however extend far beyond this simple mandate. It does not, for example, claim to guarantee the absence of forced labour from its farms[9], nor does it have a mechanism in place to progressively increase the prices paid by buyers beyond the current price floor, or, better still, to increase the proportion of the cocoa industry profits that go to cacao producers.

These minimum standards are best viewed as a temporary safeguard. By their own admission they cannot make fundamental changes to the system itself; they can only protect against that system's worst abuses. The limits of Fairtrade's potential remind us of the movement of functionalism, and the pioneering work of the first domestic scientists, Christine Frederick's in particular. For though these movements might have started with socialist and feminist ideals, their ideas were appropriated and subverted by patriarchal revisionists who supported improvements to the conditions and repute of women's work in the home as a way of preventing them from leaving it; preventing them from threatening male occupations in public life.[10] Like the promotion of Household Engineering as a profession, there is a need to give pause when influencing the course of development taken by West African cacao smallholders. The misconception that minimum standards and sustainability, as crucial as they are, are the sole aim should be avoided, for the result of such a misconception would be to take the prisoner further from liberation by making their incarceration more tolerable.

We have just seen how the Chinese tributary system contrasted with that of the Maya and the Aztecs, rendering the gift as a method of enforcing (and reinforcing) hegemony rather than allowing for any reciprocal bond to develop. Though one was isolationist and the other expansionist, this form of the gift was also employed under mercantilism. For though the resources of the colonies were acquired in order to be cultivated for export, it was part of the role of the administrators to ensure that these goods never competed with those produced by the domestic economy. Consequently colonial outpost economies were structured so that what they produced would only ever be low value-added goods; raw materials and basic commodities (such as cacao beans) which could be transformed into much more valuable products (such as chocolate) once imported into the domestic economy.[11]

It was European liberal capitalists who eventually broke down both this mercantilist approach and China's isolationism, and yet it is questionable whether neoliberalism has managed to escape the logic of these two systems. Though the cacao-producing nations of West Africa are independent, they remain sadly restricted to a low value-added economy, receiving only a tiny fraction of the huge profits of chocolate for their provision of its fundamental ingredient – just 3.5 to 6.4 per cent of each bar[12]. This gives the exchange the impression of the ceremonial act of Chinese tribute. The chocolate industry gives to the developing world the gift of investment, but the direction of it is such that it permits only lesser gifts in return. It will invest in West African cacao farmers (in their sustainability) but not in West African chocolate makers; in suppliers but not competitors, because the latter of these pairs would mean an economy that produced value rather than just cacao.[13]

What some are interested in rendering sustainable in other words is the transient status of the Global South's development: always 'developing'; never quite like us, those who have achieved development. This makes the process itself into an incurable condition, and is clearly incompatible with the view of those who would like to see developing countries develop into wealthy (ie. neoliberal, democratic) states. And has this not been the confusion from the very beginning, from Columbus, Benzoni, and the failed Conquistadors of East Asia? All were lodged between sameness and inferiority; between language and non-language; economy and non-economy; *between an almond and a drink for pigs*. Where is the radical third apart from these two false assessments; the thankful deviation from the perpetually painful trajectory between rocks and hard places?

What is needed is a reallocation of a significant proportion of chocolate's value to cacao; or rather a reallocation of the capacity to mediate value itself. For the consumer, this would involve a novel assessment of what they consume, re-orientating it, despite its heavily-processed appearance, as a product whose value is fundamentally indebted to cacao, and thus whose existence relies upon a reciprocal exchange with its raw material.

THE GIFT OF CHOCOLATE (AGAIN): HOARDING AND RECIPROCITY

In *Given Time*, Jacques Derrida takes Mauss's conception of the gift to pieces. As well as accusing Mauss (perhaps justifiably) of nostalgic idealism in his wish to return to gift exchange as opposed to capitalism as a system of social life, he argues that gifts, if they are to be genuine, must be exactly the opposite to what Mauss observes in his studies. 'For there to be gift', Derrida argues, 'there must be no reciprocity, return, exchange, countergift, or debt'.[14]

Derrida believes that whatever is given by one (a donor) to another (a recipient) cannot be a gift in the true sense because it automatically demands recognition and an equivalent return. When something is given it cannot help but invoke the recipient to calculate the nature of the return; the level of thanks they are required to give, and this, for Derrida, is no different from the logic of capitalistic exchange.

If there is an element of Mauss's theory which Derrida does not adequately address, it is the difference between a reciprocity which demands repayment, and a reciprocity premised upon escalation. The first is a form of revenge; *of getting even*. It is the law of retaliation: an eye for an eye; a tooth for a tooth, and so on. The second always gives more in return. It is both a response to the previous gift and the call, the incitation to another. It repays debt by way of imposing debt, obliging an ongoing cycle of indebtedness passed from one to the other, all the time raising the stakes on which the relationship is premised. Derrida is right in pointing out that the exchange is always based upon an imbalance of power, but it is also vital to note, as Deleuze does, the difference between a 'finite' and an 'infinite' system of debt. When debt is finite, the imbalance of power can be turned on its head; when it is infinite, indebtedness is set in stone.[15] In pre-hispanic Mesoamerica, cacao had a role in both systems. The relationships of social debt which it helped establish between men were finite, but the relationship between the Aztecs and their gods was one of permanent indebtedness, the sacrificial tribute constituting a mere interest payment on a loan that could never truly be paid off.

For a time, cacao resisted being an accomplice in the creation of infinite debt. At the outset of the sixteenth century, the Italian historian Peter Martyr, talking of the Aztec use of cacao and other items as currency, described it as 'Blessed Money' which:

> ...exempts its possessor from avarice, since it cannot be long hoarded, or hidden underground![16]

These properties set cacao in opposition not only to other forms of currency – the majority of which (precious metals like silver and gold) are chosen for their durability – but also to the relationship between West Africa and the West. This relationship exhibits a third form of reciprocity, a discriminatory reciprocity which is asymmetrical and accumulative.

What Martyr is so captivated by – the reason for his exclamation mark – is the sight of a currency which cannot be hoarded. Historically, the perishable nature of chocolate punished those that tried to keep it for themselves. It is rumoured, for example, that Napoleon I took chocolate wafers to war with Russia in 1812, but stashed them away for himself and his high-ranking officers. Napoleon, a man nicknamed '*le petit caporal*' owing to his reputation for camaraderie, paid for the failure to honour his own standards. Upon retreat from Moscow, hundreds of thousands of his *grande armée*, fatigued and malnourished as a result of the Russians' scorched earth tactics, fell victim to the Siberian winter, leaving his dreams of expansion in tatters.

But the industrialisation of cocoa production has to a certain extent negated this characteristic. Technological advances (including the invention of solid chocolate) have decreased the perishability of cacao, allowing it to be warehoused; its supply controlled by the market's middlemen. The temptation to hoard cacao, that temptation punished by the Aztec Hero Twins, has been repeated and amplified by the hoarding of value in the processing of chocolate, and in the increasingly centralised global cocoa marketplace.

But as soon as we hoard instead of exchanging, or as soon as the exchange, being asymmetrical, contributes to accumulation – accumulation on two counts: mounting wealth on the one side; mounting debt on the other – we enter what Baudrillard refers to as 'an exponential phase, a phase of speculative disorder'[17]. Having been relieved of the responsibilities of producing chocolate, we busy ourselves with consumption. Without much thought or imagination, we indulge in the conspicuous habit of speculative consumption. In this sense there is a speculative aspect to gadgetry. Gadgetry as opposed to the tool because it deals in elaboration of the finished product rather than in production itself. Because of this speculative nature, we can never say in relation to gadgetry that we have 'enough'. Gadgets are the things we buy for those who already 'have everything'; those who have no use for tools. The effect of this speculative consumption is not a split between a 'fake' and a 'real' chocolate economy. Rather, it exacerbates the imbalance of power between consumers and producers, creating a debt which is not only infinite but also growing.

We have seen how chocolate has continuously, cross-culturally and trans-historically, been associated with exchange, and in particular with ritual gifting. The religious festival is one of the few social events by which the notion of the gift, in the sense of a reciprocal exchange, continues to exist in the modern world. However, we need only look to the intensely commercial nature of holidays like Christmas to see that the spirit of the festival has been dramatically eroded. Gifts are encased within the logic of capital. Increasingly, we give not for the sake of giving, but for the sake of supplying something that others want or need. With regards to the Christmas period, there are two dominant analyses exterior to the religious sphere. Most commonly, it is welcomed as a boost to the economy, as the time of the year during which local high streets rake in much-needed revenue. However in 1993 the economist Joel Waldfogel published an article in the December issue of the American Economic Review titled 'The Deadweight Loss of Christmas', which came to the conclusion that 'between a tenth and a third of the value of holiday gifts is destroyed by gift-giving'.[18] Some years later Waldfogel authored a book on the same topic (titled *Scroogenomics: Why You Shouldn't Buy Presents for the Holidays*[19]), and the derision of Christmas and other gift-giving festivals as 'inefficient' is becoming more popular. By way of compromise we give money, or gift vouchers, or we give nothing at all. From the perspective of symbolic exchange, these gifts are gifts-without-spirit. They remove the onus of honour by making the value of each interaction calculable.

The fact that symbolism is officially regarded with cynicism, as an irrational deceit, is finding ways to coexist with symbolism itself: so that we can cling to it and disregard it at the same time. It is for example only the 'posh chocolate' – that which wears its monetary value on its ribboned sleeve – which is deemed worth giving. The symbolic notion of the gift as being outside valuation is substituted for the Veblen good: something for which we intentionally pay 'over the odds' for reasons of socio-economic status. This 'rational' fetishism replaces the old, 'irrational' ones.

But despite the inefficiency of giving, we still give chocolates. Chocolates are unnecessary and fleeting. They are often presented to us as 'complimentary', gifted in strange juxtaposition to something – a restaurant bill; a hotel room – for which we are paying a great deal. The cultural signification of the box of chocolates in particular holds that it must contain a few unfavourable flavours, making it wasteful by nature. This does not mean that chocolate is subversive – its portrayal as gift and as excess have been two of the most seductive elements of its advertised image – but it has always been rebellious. Its symbolic values have always sat awkwardly with measure and monetisation.

In their search for the etymological root of the word 'chocolate', Coe and Coe point out that the closest Quiché Mayan word, '*chokolaj*', is a verb referring to the act of drinking chocolate together.[20] In spite of the differences between the cultures examined here, the ways in which each of them has consumed chocolate have been premised on communal experience. As well as the creation of social debt, giving chocolate was an act of hospitality. By exclusively eating our chocolate in bar-form, we forfeit this social function. From drinking chocolate together, it has become more common to eat chocolate apart. And if the meal is a festival in miniature, then snacking; eating 'between meals' or 'on the go' – the main way in which chocolate bars are consumed – is a way of eating entirely without ceremony.[21] In contrast, using chocolate in recipes implies a social ritual. The cake, for example, is accompanied by the witnessed ceremony of its cutting, and it needs to be shared, to be handed out. To eat a whole cake is seen as an act of gluttony, while to cut oneself a piece (or even thieve a finger of icing from the top) before it has been distributed among the whole party, is rude and selfish. The same goes for cookies and brownies which, even if they are individual servings, are always prepared in batches. By increasing the diversity of our chocolate recipes to include savoury dishes, we may develop more ceremonies of this hospitable variety.

While chocolate can be exalted or condemned; divided into 'good' chocolate and 'bad' chocolate; expensive chocolate or cheap chocolate; its myths separated from its realities, it is ultimately far more interesting to examine chocolate for the way in which it evades definition on such terms. We have never been quite sure of where chocolate's value truly lies. At the same time as it seems to have been robbed of its morality and its spirit by the narrow economic motives of the industry, it meanwhile facilitates festivals, rituals of consumption and exchange which appear, though not in themselves sacred, then as the continuation of the sacred by other means. Since the value of chocolate is our own uncertain creation, we have the ability to create more of it, to create it differently and in different locations, and vitally to create it mutually, in exchange with the producers of the crop which lends it its existence.

END NOTES

1. Baudrillard, Jean, *Impossible Exchange*, London & New York: Verso, 2011 [2001]: 6.
2. There were multiple instances of shiploads of cacao being burned by oblivious Europeans, who mistook the beans for almonds and even sheep's droppings (*see* Coe & Coe, *The True History of Chocolate*: 161).
3. Walvin, *Fruits of Empire*: 96-7.
4. Chiapparino, 'Milk and Fondant Chocolate and the Emergence of the Swiss Chocolate Industry at the Turn of the Twentieth Century': 338.
5. Coe & Coe, *The True History of Chocolate*: 158.
6. Cidell & Alberts, 'Constructing Quality': 1004.
7. Cidell & Alberts, 'Constructing Quality': 1002.
8. The Wars, which began in the 1970s, came to an end in 2003 when the EU ruled that Italy and Spain must lift their bans on imports of British chocolate (*see* Cidell & Alberts, 'Constructing Quality'; Osborn, Andrew, 'Chocolate War over after 30 years', *The Guardian*, 17th January, 2003, available at: http://www.theguardian.com/uk/2003/jan/17/foodanddrink [accessed 25th July, 2015].
9. *See* Ryan, *Chocolate Nations*.
10. Bullock, *cited in* Freeman, *The Making of the Modern Kitchen*: 34.
11. Carrington & Noel, 'Slaves and Tropical Commodities: The Caribbean in the South Atlantic System': 232.
12. Goodyear, 'The Future of Chocolate'.
13. In this respect it is encouraging that 2015 saw the first industrial-scale chocolate factory opening in the Côte D'Ivoire (*see for example* Smith, David, 'Ivory Coast president tours country's first chocolate company', *The Guardian*, 20th May, 2015, available at: http://www.theguardian.com/world/2015/may/20/ivory-coast-president-tours-countrys-first-chocolate-factory).
14. Derrida, Jacques, *Given Time*, translated by Peggy Kamuf, Chicago & London: University of Chicago Press, 1992: 12.
15. Deleuze locates the transition from 'finite' to 'infinite' debt as the predominant form of the creditor-debtor relation at the coming of the great empires and the monotheistic religions (*see* Deleuze, Gilles, Course of 7th March, 1972, available at: http://www.webdeleuze.com/php/texte.php?cle=161&groupe=Anti%20Oedipe%20et%20Mille%20Plateaux&langue=3 (in Italian). Cited in Lazzarato, Maurizio, *The Making*

of the Indebted Man: An Essay on the Neoliberal Condition, Los Angeles, CA: semiotext(e), 2012: 77-8.

16. *Quoted in* Knapp, *Cocoa and Chocolate: The History*: 8.

17. Baudrillard, *Impossible Exchange*: 6.

18. Waldfogel, Joel, 'The Deadweight Loss of Christmas', *The American Economic Review*, Vol. 83, Iss. 5, 1993. pp. 1328-1336.: 1336.

19. Waldfogel, Joel, *Scroogenomics: Why You Shouldn't Give Gifts for the Holidays*, Princeton University Press, 2009.

20. Coe & Coe, *The True History of Chocolate*: 118.

21. For Derrida however, the meal itself is also ambiguous. Because it requires the existence of a host – an individual who, by welcoming guests, automatically holds a degree of control over them – the act of feeding someone who cannot feed themselves is balanced on a knife's edge between hospitality and hostility; kindness and cruelty.

BIBLIOGRAPHY

Agnew, John, 'The Territorial Trap: The Geographical Assumptions of International Relations Theory', *Review of International Political Economy*, Vol.1, Iss.1, 1994.

Ajana, Btihaj, 'Surveillance and Biopolitics', *Electronic Journal of Sociology*, 2005. Available from: http://www.sociology.org/content/2005/tier1/ajana_biopolitics.pdf. [Accessed: 18th April, 2015].

Anon., *The Women's Petition Against Coffee Representing to Publick Consideration the Grand Inconveniencies accruing to their Sex from the Excessive Use of that Drying, Enfeebling Liquor*. London. 1674.

Anti-Slavery International, 'The Cocoa Industry in West Africa: A History of Exploitation', 2004. Available from: http://www.antislavery.org/english/who_we_are/resources/reports/english/who_we_are/resources/reports/child_labour_reports.aspx [Accessed: 10th April, 2015].

Aristotle, *Physics*, Oxford University Press, 1999.

Association of UK Dietitians, 'Dietitian, Nutritionist, Nutritional Therapist or Diet Expert? A Comprehensive Guide to Roles and Functions', Birmingham: The British Dietetic Association, 2015.

Bacon, Francis, *New Atlantis*, 1627, in S. Bruce (ed.), *Three Early Modern Utopias: Utopia, New Atlantis* and *The Isle of Pines*, Oxford University Press, 2008.

Balch, Oliver, 'China's Growing Hunger for Dairy Raises Fears over Sustainable Production', *The Guardian*, 30.05.2014.

Balibar, Étienne, 'Racism and Nationalism', in *Race, Nation, Class: Ambiguous Identities*, edited by Balibar, Étienne & Wallerstein, Immanuel, London & New York: Verso, 1991. pp. 37-68.

Bartley, Basil, *The Genetic Diversity of Cacao and Its Utilization*, CABI Publishing, 2005.

Baudrillard, Jean, *Passwords*, London & New York: Verso, 2003.

———, *Impossible Exchange*, London & New York: Verso, 2011 [2001].

Beeton, Isabella, *The Book of Household Management*, London: S.O. Beeton Publishing, 1861.

Belk, Russell, 'The Sacred in Consumer Culture', in *Consumption and Spirituality*, edited by Rinallo, Diego, Scott, Linda & Maclaran, Pauline, London & New York: Routledge, 2013. pp. 71-80.

Benzoni, Girolamo, *History of the New World*, Hayluyt Society, 1857 (1575).

Bernaert, Herwig, Blondeel, Ieme, Allegaert, Leen & Lohmueller, Tobias,

'Industrial Treatment of Cocoa in Chocolate Production: Health Implications', in *Chocolate and Health*, R. Paoletti, A. Poli, A. Conti & F. Visioli (eds), London: Springer, 2011. pp. 17-32.

Bertram, Gordon, 'Chocolate in France: Evolution of a Luxury Product', in *Chocolate: History, Culture, and Heritage*, edited by Grivetti, Louis, & Shapiro, Howard-Yana, John Wiley & Sons, Inc. 2009.

Boucher, Philip, 'The French and Dutch Caribbean, 1600-1800', in *The Caribbean: A History of the Region and Its Peoples*, edited by Palmié, Stephan & Scarano, Francisco, Chicago & London: University of Chicago Press, 2011. pp. 217-230.

Brillat-Savarin, Jean Anthelme, *The Physiology of Taste: Or Meditations on Transcendental Gastronomy*, Everyman's Library, 2009 (1825).

Cadbury, Deborah, *Chocolate Wars: From Cadbury to Kraft: 200 Years of Sweet Success and Bitter Rivalry*, HarperPress, 2010.

Carlsen, Robert & Prechtel, Martin, 'The Flowering of the Dead: An Interpretation of Highland Maya Culture', *Man*, Vol. 26, Iss. 1, 1991. pp. 23-42.

Carmody, Pádraig, *The New Scramble for Africa*, Cambridge: Polity, 2011.

Chouliaraki, Lilie, *The Ironic Spectator: Solidarity in the Age of Post-Humanitarianism*, Cambridge: Polity, 2013.

Cidell, Julie & Alberts, Heike, 'Constructing Quality: The Multinational Histories of Chocolate', *Geoforum*, Vol. 37, 2006. 999-1007.

Clarence-Smith, William, *Cocoa and Chocolate, 1765-1914*, London & New York: Routledge, 2000.

———, 'The Global Consumption of Hot Beverages, c.1500 to c.1900', in *Food and Globalisation: Consumption, Markets and Politics in the Modern World*, Alexander Nutzenadel & Frank Trentmann (eds), Oxford & New York: Berg, 2008.

Coe, Sophie & Coe, Michael, *The True History of Chocolate*, 3rd Edition, London: Thames & Hudson, 2013.

Columbus, Ferdinand, *The Life of the Admiral Christopher Columbus: by his Son Ferdinand*, translated and edited by Keen, Benjamin, Rutgers University Press, 1992.

Coote, Belinda, *The Trade Trap: Poverty and the Commodity Markets*, Oxford: Oxfam Publishing, 1992.

Crosby, Alfred, *Ecological Imperialism: The Biological Expansion of Europe, 900-1900*, Cambridge University Press, 2004 (1986).

Crosland, Maurice, 'The Officiers de Santé of the French Revolution: A Case Study in the Changing Language of Medicine', *Medical History*, Vol. 48,

Iss. 1, 2004. pp. 229-244.

Daston, Lorraine, 'Hard Facts', in B. Latour & B. Weibel (eds), *Making Things Public: Atmospheres of Democracy*, Cambridge, MA: MIT Press, 2005. pp. 680-685.

Davies, David, *A Primer of Dutch Seventeenth Century Overseas Trade*, Springer, 1961.

Delbourgo, James, 'Sir Hans Sloane's Milk Chocolate and the Whole History of the Cacao', *Social Text 106*, 29(1), 2011. pp. 71-101.

Deleuze, Gilles & Guattari, Félix, *A Thousand Plateaus: Capitalism and Schizophrenia*, Trans. B. Massumi, London & New York: Continuum, 2012 (1987).

Derrida, Jacques, *Given Time*, translated by Peggy Kamuf, Chicago & London: University of Chicago Press, 1992.

Durán, Fray Diego, *The History of the Indies of New Spain*, translated by Doris Heyden, University of Oklahoma Press, 1994.

Eales, Mary, *Mrs. Mary Eales' Receipts*, London, 1718.

Economist, 'Cold Cocoa: Berkshire Plays a Vital Role in the World Cocoa Economy', 2015. Available at: http://www.economist.com/news/ britain/21638169-berkshire-plays-vital-role-world-chocolate-industry- cold-cocoa [accessed May 3rd, 2015]

Fabricant, Florence, 'Rare Cacao Beans Discovered in Peru', *New York Times*, 11.01.2011.

Farmer, Fannie, *Food and Cookery for the Sick and Convalescent*, Boston, MA, 1905.

Fitzgerald, Robert, *Rowntree and the Marketing Revolution, 1862-1969*, Cambridge University Press, 1995.

Ford, Henry, *My Life and Work*, New York: Page & Co., 1922.

Foucault, Michel, 'The Politics of Health in the 18th Century', in *Power/ Knowledge: Selected Interviews and Other Writings, 1972-1977*, C. Gordon (ed), C. Gordon, L. Marshall, J. Mepham & K. Soper (trans), New York: Pantheon Books, 1980. pp. 166-182.

———, 'The Subject and Power', in *Michel Foucault: Beyond Structuralism and Hermeneutics*, edited by Drefus, Hubert, & Ranibow, Paul, Hemel Hempsted: Harvester Wheatsheaf, 1982.

———, 'Dietetics', in *The History of Sexuality, Part II: The Use of Pleasure*, New York: Vintage Books, 1990. pp. 96-139.

———, 'Governmentality', in *The Foucault Effect: Studies in Governmentality*, edited by Burchell, Graham, Gordon, Colin & Miller, Peter, London: Harvester Wheatsheaf, 1991. pp. 87-104.

————, 'The Ethics of the Concern of the Self as a Practice of Freedom', in *Ethics: Subjectivity and Truth*, edited by Ranibow, Paul, New York: The New Press, 1997. pp. 281-301.

————, 'What Is Critique?', in S. Lotringer (ed), *The Politics of Truth*. Los Angeles, CA: Semiotext(e), 2007. pp. 41-81.

Freeman, June, *The Making of the Modern Kitchen: A Cultural History*, Oxford & New York: Berg, 2004.

Getz, Trevor, 'British Magistrates and Unfree Children in Early Colonial Gold Coast, 1874-1899', in *Child Slaves in the Modern World*, edited by Campbell, Gwyn, Miers, Suzanne & Miller, Joseph, Athens: Ohio University Press. pp. 157-172.

Grant, Mark, *Galen on Food and Diet*, London & New York: Routledge, 2000.

Girard, René, *Violence and the Sacred*, translated by Patrick Gregory, London: Bloomsbury, 2013.

Goodman, Jordan, 'Excitantia: or, how enlightenment Europe took to soft drugs', in *Consuming Habits: Global and Historical Perspectives on How Cultures Define Drugs*, edited by Goodman, Jordan, Lovejoy, Paul & Sherratt, Andrew, Routledge, 1995.

Goodyear, Dave, 'The Future of Chocolate: Why Cocoa Production is at Risk', *The Guardian*, 2011. Available at: http://www.theguardian.com/sustainable-business/fairtrade-partner-zone/chocolate-cocoa-production-risk.

Grivetti, Louis Evan, 'From Bean to Beverage: Historical Chocolate Recipes', in *Chocolate: History, Culture, and Heritage*, eds Louis Grivetti & Howard-Yana Shapiro, John Wiley & Sons, Inc., 2009. pp. 99-114.

Grivetti, Louis, 'Medicinal Chocolate in New Spain, Western Europe, and North America', in L. Grivetti & H-Y. Shapiro (eds), *Chocolate: History, Culture, and Heritage*, John Wiley & Sons, Inc. 2009. pp. 67-88.

Grivetti, Louis & Cabezon, Beatriz, 'Ancient Gods and Christian Celebrations: Cacao and Religion', in *Chocolate: History, Culture, and Heritage*, edited by Grivetti, Louis, & Shapiro, Howard-Yana, John Wiley & Sons, Inc. 2009. pp. 27-35.

Griswold, Daniel, 'Trade and the Transformation of China', speech presented at *The James and Margaret Tseng Loe Chinese Studies Center Conference*, St. Vincent College, PA, 6th November, 2002. Available at: http://www.cato.org/publications/speeches/trade-transformation-china [Accessed 24.04.2015].

Hall, Douglas, *In Miserable Slavery: Thomas Thistlewood in Jamaica, 1750-1786*,

Kingston, Jamaica: The University of the West Indies Press, 1998.

Hameed, Abdel, & Arshad, F.M., 'Future Trends of the Export Demand for Selected Malaysian Cocoa Products', *Trends in Applied Science Research*, 2013.

Hao, Yen P'ing, 'Chinese Teas to America – A Synopsis', in *America's China Trade in Historical Perspective: The Chinese and American Performance*, edited by May, Ernest & Fairbank, John, Cambridge, MA: Harvard University Asia Center Press, 1986: 24.

Henderson, John, Joyce, Rosemary, Hall, Gretchen, Hurst, Jeffrey & McGovern, Patrick, 'Chemical and Archeological Evidence for the Earliest Cacao Beverages', *PNAS*, Vol. 104, Iss. 48, 2007. pp. 18937-18940.

Henderson, John & Joyce, Rosemary, 'Brewing Distinction: The Development of Cacao Beverages in Formative Mesoamerica', in *Chocolate in Mesoamerica: A Cultural History of Cacao*, edited by McNeil, Cameron, University of Florida Press, 2006. pp. 140-153.

Hooke, Robert, *Micrographia*, London, 1665.

Huber, Matthew, 'Enforcing Scarcity: Oil, Violence, and the Making of the Market', *Annals of the Association of American Geographers*, Vol. 101, Iss. 4, 2011. 816-826.

International Cocoa Organisation (ICCO) website: http://www.icco.org/.

International Labour Organization (ILO), 'A partnership to combat child labour in the chocolate and cocoa industry', *Partnerships and Field Support Department*, Geneva, 2014.

Kany, Charles, *Life and Manners in Madrid, 1750-1800*, University of California Press, 1932.

Keenan, Thomas & Weizman, Eyal, *Mengele's Skull: The Advent of a Forensic Aesthetics*. Berlin: Sternberg Press/Portikus, 2012.

Knapp, Arthur, *Cocoa and Chocolate: The History*, London: Chapman & Hall, 1920.

Krondl, Michael, *Sweet Invention: A History of Dessert*, Chicago, IL: Chicago Review Press, 2011.

Latour, Bruno, *The Making of the Law: An Ethnography of the Conseil D'etat*, A. Pottage & M. Brilman, trans. Cambridge: Polity Press, 2009.

Leslie, Eliza, *The Ladies' Receipt Book: A Useful Companion for Small or Large Families*, Philadelphia, PA: Carey & Hart, 1847.

Levenstein, Harvey, *Revolution at the Table*, University of California Press, 1988.

Linné, Carl von, *Species Plantarum*, 1753.

Maddison, Angus, *Contours of the World Economy, 1-2030 ad*, Oxford

University Press, 2007.

Martin, Simon, 'Cacao in Ancient Maya Religion: First Fruit from the Maize Tree and Other Tales from the Underworld', in McNeil, Cameron (ed.), *Chocolate in Mesoamerica: A Cultural History of Cacao*, University Press of Florida, 2006. pp. 154-183.

Marx, Karl, *Introduction to A Contribution to the Critique of Hegel's Philosophy of Right*, 1844.

————, *Grundisse*, 1857.

Mattern, Susan, *Galen and the Rhetoric of Healing*. Baltimore, MD: The John Hopkins University Press, 2008.

Mauss, Marcel, *The Gift: The Form and Reason for Exchange in Archaic Societies*, London: Routledge, 1954.

Meyer, Kathryn, 'Japan and the World Narcotics Traffic', in J. Goodman, P. Lovejoy & A. Sherratt, *Consuming Habits: Global and Historical Perspectives on How Cultures Define Drugs*, London & New York: Routledge, 1995. pp. 194-214.

Monzote, Funes, 'The Columbian Moment: Politics, Ideology, and Biohistory', in *The Caribbean: A History of the Region and Its Peoples*, edited by Palmié, Stephan & Scarano, Francisco, Chicago & London: University of Chicago Press, 2011. pp. 83-95.

Moss, Sarah & Badenoch, Alexander, *Chocolate: A Global History*, London: Reaktion Books, 2009.

Nutt, Frederick, *The Complete Confectioner: or, The Whole Art of Confectionary Made Easy*, London, 1789.

Pennock, Caroline, *Bonds of Blood: Gender, Lifecycle, and Sacrifice in Aztec Culture*, Basingstoke: Palgrave Macmillan, 2008.

Perkins, Suzanne, 'Is it a chocolate pot? Chocolate and its accoutrements in France from cookbook to collectible', in *Chocolate: History, Culture, and Heritage*, edited by Grivetti, Louis, & Shapiro, Howard-Yana, John Wiley & Sons, Inc. 2009.

Pessoa, Fernando, *The Tobacco Shop*, 1928.

Ryan, Órla, *Chocolate Nations: Living and Dying for Cocoa in West Africa*, London & New York: Zed Books, 2011.

Sahagún, Fray Bernadino de, *General History of the Things of New Spain*, translation by Arthur Anderson & Charles Dibble, School of American Research and University of Utah, 1950-1959 (12 Volumes).

Satre, Lowell, *Chocolate on Trial: Slavery, Politics, and the Ethics of Business*, Ohio University Press, 2005.

Simmonds, Peter, *The Popular Beverages of Various Countries*, London, 1888.

Smith, Adam, *The Wealth of Nations*, London, 1776.

Smith, Eliza, *The Compleat Housewife: Or Accomplished Gentlewoman's Companion*, London, 1727.

Spedding, Patrick, 'To (Not) Promote Breeding: Censoring Eliza Smith's *Compleat Housewife*', *Script & Print*, Vol. 31, Iss. 4, 2007. 233-242.

Stubbe, Henry, *The Indian nectar, or a discourse concerning chocolate wherein the nature of the cacao-nut ... is examined ... the ways of compounding and preparing chocolate are enquired into; its effects, as to its alimental and venereal quality, as well as medicinal (specially in hypochondriacal melancholy) are fully debated*. A. Crook, London, 1662.

Swisher, Margaret, 'Commercial Chocolate Posters: Reflections of Cultures, Values, and Times', in in L. Grivetti & H-Y. Shapiro (eds), *Chocolate: History, Culture, and Heritage*, John Wiley & Sons, Inc., 2009. pp. 193-198.

Sugg, Richard, 'Eating the Soul: Forms of Cannibalism from the Aztecs to Charles II', *Mexicolore*, 25.09.2007. Available from: http://www.mexicolore.co.uk/aztecs/home/cannibalism-and-corpse-medicine-1 [accessed 16.06.2015].

Vail, Gabrielle, 'Cacao Use in Yucatán Among the Pre-Hispanic Maya', in *Chocolate: History, Culture, and Heritage*, eds Louis Grivetti & Howard-Yana Shapiro, John Wiley & Sons, Inc., 2009.

The Cocoa and Chocolate Products (England) Regulations 2003, *Statutory Instruments*, HM Stationery Office, 2003.

Todorov, Tzvetan, *The Conquest of America: The Question of the Other*, translated by Howard, Richard, University of Oklahoma Press, 1984.

US Department of Health and Human Services, Ch. 1: Food and Drug Administration, Subchapter B: Food for Human Consumption, Section 163.130: Milk Chocolate, *Code of Federal Regulations*, Title 21, Vol. 2, Revised 2014.

Varoufakis, Yanis, *The Global Minotaur: America, Europe, and the Future of the Global Economy*, London & New York: Zed Books, 2013.

Waldfogel, Joel, 'The Deadweight Loss of Christmas', *The American Economic Review*, Vol. 83, Iss. 5, 1993. pp. 1328-1336.

———, *Scroogenomics: Why You Shouldn't Give Gifts for the Holidays*, Princeton University Press, 2009.

Walker, Timothy, 'Establishing Cacao Plantation Culture in the Atlantic World: Portuguese Cacao Cultivation in Brazil and West Africa, Circa 1580-1912', in *Chocolate: History, Culture, and Heritage*, edited by Grivetti, Louis, & Shapiro, Howard-Yana, John Wiley & Sons, Inc. 2009.

Wall Street Daily, 'Expanding Markets Drive Cocoa Futures', 2015. Available at: http://www.wallstreetdaily.com/2015/02/13/cocoa-market-futures/ [accessed 23rd May, 2015]

WTO/UNCTAD, 'Cocoa: A Guide to Trading Practices', *International Trade Centre*, Geneva, 2001.

Wiley, Andrea, 'Transforming Milk in a Global Economy', *American Anthropologist*, Vol.109, Iss. 4, 2007. pp. 666-677.

Willis, J.C., *Agriculture in the Tropics*, Cambridge University Press, 1922 [1909].

Wilson, Philip, 'Chocolate as Medicine: A Changing Framework of Evidence throughout History', in *Chocolate and Health*, R. Paoletti, A. Poli, A. Conti & F. Visioli (eds), London: Springer, 2011. pp. 1-16.

Wolfe, David & Holdstock, Sharron, *Naked Chocolate: the Astonishing Truth about the World's Greatest Food*, North Atlantic Books, 2005.

Wright, Jonathon, *The Jesuits: Missions, Myths and Histories*, London: HarperCollins, 2004.

Zarillo, Sonia, *Human Adaptation, Food Production and Cultural Interaction during the Formative Period in Highland Ecuador*, Ph.D thesis, University of Calgary, 2012.

INDEX

INDEX OF RECIPES